D1521223

Setting in the East

Setting in the East

Maritime Realist Fiction

DAVID CREELMAN

McGill-Queen's University Press
Montreal & Kingston · London · Ithaca

Legal deposit first quarter 2003
Bibliothèque nationale du Québec

Printed in Canada on acid-free paper that is 100% ancient forest free
(100% post-consumer recycled), processed chlorine free.

This book has been published with the help of a grant from the
Humanities and Social Sciences Federation of Canada, using funds
provided by the Social Sciences and Humanities Research Council
of Canada.

McGill-Queen's University Press acknowledges the support of the
Canada Council for the Arts for our publishing program. We also
acknowledge the financial support of the Government of Canada
through the Book Publishing Industry Development Program (BPIDP) for
our publishing activities.

National Library of Canada Cataloguing in Publication

Creelman, David Craig, 1962–
   Setting in the east: Maritime realist fiction / David Creelman.
   Includes bibliographical references and index.
   ISBN 0-7735-2478-9
   1. Canadian fiction (English) – Maritime Provinces – History and
   criticism. 2. Canadian fiction (English) – 20th century – History and
   criticism. 3. Realism in literature. I. Title.
   PS8131.M3C74 2003   C813'.50912   C2002-903586-4
   PR9192.5.C74 2003

This book was typeset by Typo Litho Composition Inc.
in 10/12 Palatino.

for Gina, Elizabeth, and Ben

Contents

Acknowledgments

I would like to thank John Lennox for his invaluable encouragement and guidance particularly in the early stages of this project. I would also like to thank Ian Sowton, Len Early, Paul Stevens, John Moss, and Darin Barney for their generosity and their many astute suggestions. Joan Harcourt, Roger Martin, the editors of McGill-Queens University Press, and the readers associated with the AASP were tremendously helpful and their insights guided me through the process of revising the text. I am also grateful to Claude Lalumière, who helped me refine and prepare the final version of the book. Andrea Miller and Lori Gale provided valuable assistance in the preparation of the manuscript. I also owe thanks to my family as well as to my friends and colleagues at the University of New Brunswick in Saint John who encouraged me as this project unfolded over the years. Most of all, I want to thank Gina Barton. Without her confident support and her encouragement this book would not have been possible.

I wish to thank the following journals and periodicals in which excerpts of the material found in this book first appeared: *Dalhousie Review*, *Studies in Canadian Literature*, *Atlantis*, *The New Brunswick Reader*, *The Fiddlehead*, and *Children's Voices in Atlantic Literature and Culture* (edited by Hilary Thompson).

Abbreviations

AM	*After the Angel Mill*, Carol Bruneau
BF	*Before the Flood*, Alan Wilson
BLS	*The Bay of Love and Sorrows*, David Adams Richards
BR	*Barometer Rising*, Hugh MacLennan
BT	*Blood Ties*, David Adams Richards
C	*Candyman*, Simone Poirier-Bures
CC	*Cordelia Clark*, Budge Wilson
CM	*The Cruelest Month*, Ernest Buckler
CS	*The Channel Shore*, Charles Bruce
CW	*The Coming of Winter*, David Adams Richards
F	*Flora, Write this Down*, Nancy Bauer
FYK	*Fall On Your Knees*, Ann-Marie MacDonald
HWD	*For Those Who Hunt the Wounded Down*, David Adams Richards
I	*Island*, Alistair MacLeod
L	*The Leaving*, Budge Wilson
LE	*Losing Eddie*, Deborah Joy Corey
LT	*Like This Stories*, Leo McKay
MAC	*Mercy Among the Children*, David Adams Richards
MIR	*Miracle at Indian River*, Alden Nowlan
MM	*The Glace Bay Miners' Museum*, Sheldon Currie
MV	*The Mountain and the Valley*, Ernest Buckler
NGM	*No Great Mischief*, Alistair MacLeod
NL	*The Nymph and the Lamp*, Thomas Raddall
OF	*Oxbells and Fireflies*, Ernest Buckler

PMB   *Play the Monster Blind*, Lynn Coady
Q   *Quilt*, Donna Smyth
R   *Rockbound*, Frank Parker Day
RSH   *Road to the Stilt House*, David Adams Richards
SH   *Strange Heaven*, Lynn Coady
SP   *Summer Point*, Linda McNutt
TC   *The Courtship*, Budge Wilson
TT   *The Township of Time*, Charles Bruce
VP   *Various Persons Named Kevin O'Brien*, Alden Nowlan
WMI   *Will Ye Let the Mummers In?*, Alden Nowlan
WT   *Wanton Troopers*, Alden Nowlan

Setting in the East

Introduction

Until I left the Maritimes, I did not appreciate how deeply immersed I was in the region's rhythms and assumptions. And not until I had lived outside the region for a few years did I realize how little I actually knew about the history and literature of the place I increasingly thought of as my home. As a graduate student, I had read the work of Alden Nowlan and the novels of David Adams Richards, but after a few years of "being away," my reading of Maritime realist fiction increasingly broadened, turning to the works of writers such as Day, Raddall, Buckler, Bruce, Coady, Corey, and others. Little by little this study of the region's fiction began to take shape.

Setting in the East is an extended analysis of the realist fictions produced within the Maritime region in the twentieth Century. From the outset it is important to clearly define the boundaries of this study.

This book only examines fictions that were produced within three of the four provinces often grouped under the heading "The East Coast." The four Atlantic provinces are linked by their common struggle against the economic hardships of underdevelopment and underemployment, yet, for all the political and economic similarities, the culture of Newfoundland has been shaped by historical, social, ethnic, and religious forces very different from those which have moulded the three Maritime provinces. The literatures of the Atlantic may have some thematic and formal similarities, but the texts of Newfoundland embody a very different set of cultural and ideological tensions and must be considered as a regional literature distinct in itself. Accordingly, *Setting in the East* focuses only on the narratives produced in New Brunswick, Nova Scotia, and Prince Edward Island.

Also, I consider only the writers who have worked with realist conventions after the late 1920s. To further narrow this work's scope, only texts written in English are included. The region's founding Acadian culture is a distinct entity, with its own historical and social formations, which function apart from the trends and patterns evident elsewhere in the Maritimes. Although the novels of Acadian writers like Antonine Maillet are of great importance to the identity of the region, this study confines itself to texts written in English and embedded in the particular ideological assumptions of the Anglo communities.

Starting with the early fiction of Frank Parker Day and concluding with an investigation of the short stories of Leo McKay, this book investigates how realism emerged and eventually dominated the literary landscape, to became the tool through which writers articulated and reproduced the cultural tensions of the Maritimes. Realism has become the most important set of literary conventions in the region, and over the decades the genre embodied and articulated a variety of sometimes contradictory ideological visions. Embedded as they are in a series of competing impulses, the stories our writers have told articulate and communicate the complex cultural experiences of the region's inhabitants.

1 Approaching the East: Transformations, Ideology, and Realism

> [It] is one of those little places that don't really exist, except in the minds of their inhabitants. Passing through it as a stranger you might not even notice that it is there. Or if you did notice it, you'd think that it was no different from thousands of other little backwoods communities …
>
> Alden Nowlan, "Miracle at Indian River"

THE MARITIMES IN THE TWENTIETH CENTURY

Realism arrived comparatively late to the Maritime provinces. Though it had governed European narrative codes for much of the nineteenth century, realism emerged as the Maritime region's dominant literary genre only after the First World War. The genre's rise corresponded with a dramatic period of economic and cultural disruption. Since the early 1900s, the Maritimes have been transformed from one of the most developed, prosperous, and promising regions in Canada into one now characterized by chronic underemployment and underdevelopment. As the region negotiated between its memory of an earlier, more traditional social order and its experience as a modern industrial society, the tensions that emerged within Maritime culture were embedded in the character of its inhabitants. Indeed, these transformations have not only affected the lives of the region's people, they have also shaped the imaginations and the texts of its writers. The best-known realist writers of Nova Scotia and New Brunswick – Thomas Raddall, Hugh MacLennan, Charles Bruce, Ernest Buckler, Alden Nowlan, Alistair MacLeod, and David Adams Richards – all matured as artists and produced their best fiction in the midst of the cultural shifts of the last sixty years. These writers share a common regional identity that shapes the subtexts of their fictions as they find their own paths through the tensions of their day.

In the past, many observers of Maritime society have produced overly simplistic representations of the East Coast. Whether they are describing the region's folk or ethnic practices or reviewing the overall "cultural identity," some critics have constructed essentialist definitions that ignore powerful tensions and divisions in the society and that narrow the field of meanings available to the reader. For example, some observers have suggested that the Maritime people are somehow linked together by their mystical bond to the ocean waters, their long-suffering as a "have-not" region, or their persistent resentment of what they still called "Upper Canada." Similarly, although the region has long had a diverse, and in some areas, multicultural population, commentators have more often dwelt on the seeming stability, consistency, and even homogeneity of the region. While the Germans of Lunenburg, the Africadians of the Halifax area, the many East-European communities of Cape Breton, and the Acadians spread throughout the three provinces have all retained their unique cultural identities, commentators have spent more time attending to the groups of British origin that have historically dominated the region. Focusing on the populations that have descended from English, Loyalist, Irish, and Scottish ancestors, observers have argued that the people of the Maritimes have distinct "tribal" differences but share, through their British heritage, a common language, civil code, and Christian faith (Dyck 1986, 106, 140–1).

In her study of Maritime fiction, *Under Eastern Eyes* (1987), Janice Kulyk Keefer displays this critical tendency to reproduce positivist definitions when she asserts that the region displays a common ethos in its "sense of shared community," its fear and distrust of the "monopoly-capitalist" spirit of the big city, and its vision of nature as "humanized, accessible, inexhaustibly rich or resistant, but never annihilating" (13, 17, 15). Undeniably, the different parts of the region exhibit some common characteristics, but too often these particular elements become the centre of attention, to the detriment of a more complex view of the region. If these essentialist perceptions are set aside, discrete cultural patterns gradually become evident as we examine how particular groups experience distinct changes, absences, losses, and fragmentations. The anxieties, tensions, and contradictions that have arisen over the last century must be examined if the cultural borders within which the region's literary texts have been produced are to be traced.

If diversity and change are the most distinctive marks of the Maritimes, then it is important to note, from the beginning, that those changes and transformations have not always brought misfortune or hardship. Maritime history is not a litany of successive disasters.

While economic disruptions and transformations have reshaped the region, even amidst the financial decline some segments of the society have prospered. Groups that had been marginalized in the nineteenth century by language or gender have managed to transform their condition and bring their concerns into the mainstream. For example, in the second half of the twentieth century there has been a renaissance within the Acadian community as the descendants of the original French settlers, concentrated primarily in New Brunswick, have emerged from their marginalized position to assert a new political influence. Beginning with the election of Louis Robichaud in 1960, the Acadians have become an active political force. Having established a clear presence in the two traditional political parties and having founded their own political party, the Parti Acadien, the Acadians have established cultural centres, theatres, presses, and festivals; they have lobbied for improvements in education, health care, and language services in areas with large French populations (Dyck 1986, 159). Although the Maritimes continue to experience considerable linguistic tension as English and French communities struggle towards economic parity and stability, the Acadian community is no longer as distanced from political or social power as it was during the first half of the century.

During the twentieth century, Maritime communities also witnessed a transformation in the roles played by women. In the decades following Confederation, women played an essential part in agricultural, fishery, and business operations, but, as with women across the country, their legal rights were few and their opportunities outside the domestic sphere were limited (Light and Parr 1983, 181–6). At the end of the nineteenth century, women stepped into the social and political arena to push for social reforms and universal suffrage, finally winning the right to vote in New Brunswick and Nova Scotia in 1919, and in Prince Edward Island in 1921. At the turn of the century, the advancement of numerous social reforms depended on the efforts of key women's groups. Before the First World War, women, working through and alongside the Women's Christian Temperance Union, organized local chapters of the Victorian Order of Nurses, campaigned for the anti-tuberculosis league, and canvassed for funds to build hospitals and playgrounds and to support overseas mission fields (Forbes 1989, 77). Maritime society was able to adjust fairly quickly to the first wave of feminism and its call for basic legal and political rights. As in the rest of Canada, however, the Maritime region has taken much longer to address more substantial problems, such as family violence, employment equity, and sexual discrimination in the workplace. If men in the Maritimes have often had difficulty finding work, then the opportunities for women have been especially scarce. During the Depression women were actively discouraged from entering the workforce, so that the few jobs available could be reserved for men. This social practice was based on the erroneous assumption that the women in society would then be supported by the men in their lives. After the Second World War employment opportunities slowly begin to open up, although most women continued to enter the "traditional professions" of sales, teaching, nursing, and clerical and secretarial work, all of which were characterized by relatively low wages and marginal social status (Prentice et al. 1988, 374; Wilson 1986, 90). In the late 1970s large numbers of women began to enter such professions as law, medicine, and business, and the percentage of the workforce made up of women has been steadily rising: 17.9 percent in 1953, 33 percent in 1973, 45 percent in 1997 (Veltmeyer 1979, 30; Statistics Canada 1999). The social changes that have attended these demographic shifts, including the calls for pay-equity and daycare programs, have not always proceeded smoothly. This gradual redistribution of power to the disenfranchised has produced backlashes that are themselves fuelled by a larger culture of nostalgia. However, in the Maritimes, as in the rest of Canada, patriarchal attitudes in both the home and the workplace are fading, albeit slowly.

While some groups in the Maritimes have successfully challenged their marginalized status and improved their position in society, the region as a whole experienced not just a cultural transformation but also an economic decline. The intensity of the disruptions that have swept the Maritimes in the twentieth century can be best appreciated if we glance back to the period before 1915, when New Brunswick, Nova Scotia, and Prince Edward Island enjoyed an era of prosperity as the primary sector expanded and developed. Within the fisheries, the salt cod industry that was founded in the sixteenth century was expanded and the trade with the Caribbean islands employed a fleet of schooners and inshore handline fishermen. Dried cod was exchanged for molasses and sugar, which were then moved to Britain and the "Boston States" and traded for mercantile goods. Agriculture also expanded as land was cleared across the provinces, first in the fertile Annapolis and Saint John River valleys and, later, on less arable lands. Successive waves of immigrants established subsistence and market farms specializing in such products as apples and potatoes. Similarly, the timber trade was the engine that drove the economy of New Brunswick for the first half of the nineteenth century. Before Confederation, Maritime lumber travelled to markets in Britain and the USA on locally built wooden ships. And, while the shipbuilding industry collapsed after the 1870 depression, Maritime timber continued to find a market in Britain until late in the nineteenth century (Forbes 1993, 61, 136).

Secondary manufacturing also flourished before the First World War. In 1885, the Maritimes had a significant share of the nation's heavy industry, boasting eight of the country's twenty-three cotton mills, three of five sugar refineries, two of seven rope mills, one of three glass works, both steel mills, and six of twelve rolling mills (Rawlyk 1979, 20). Local shops produced mining cars, rails, and barbed wire, while factories turned out soap, shoes, textiles, confections, and pianos (Forbes 1989, 118). The Maritimes prospered while the economy was built on coal, iron, and wood, and goods were moved under sail. However, it was not as successful in its transition to a modern economy based on hydroelectricity, steel, diesel transportation, and high-capital mass-production manufacturing.

The disruptions in the economy and culture of the Maritimes are first evident in the steadily declining number of people employed in the primary sector. In 1881, 56.8 percent of the population was dependent on the primary sector, a number that fell to 43.4 percent in 1921, to 27 percent in 1951, and finally to 8.4 percent after 1971 (Veltmeyer 1979, 22). The fishing industry certainly follows this pattern of decline. Early in the twentieth century, the salt cod trade to the Caribbean began to fail, and, soon after, the nature of the fisheries themselves were affected by a series of technical innovations. In 1910, new modes of refrigerated rail transportation and freezer technologies were developed in the United States allowing for the expansion of the fresh-fish market into the western urban centres. These new canning and freezing operations required a large capital expenditure, and since few of the traditional villages of the Maritimes could finance such operations, the fishing industry became centralized around larger communities with superior hydro, rail, and highway facilities, such as Halifax, Digby, Lunenburg, North Sydney, and Port Hawksbury (Barrett 1979, 135). The appearance of large, company-owned steel trawlers, the development of offshore factory fishing operations, and the decision to close or limit the cod, crab, and turbot fisheries in order to preserve threatened fish stocks have all contributed to the dramatic decrease in the number of people employed in the industry. As their numbers have dropped and their unions solidified, some fishermen have seen their wages rise and their general standard of living gradually improve. But the process of modernization has taken its toll on the culture, for the locally based, labour-intensive, inshore fishery – whose folk traditions and social customs are reworked in, for example, Frank Parker Day's *Rockbound* – has all but disappeared.

The timber and lumber industry has also been restructured in the last ninety years. Late in the nineteenth century, East Coast lumber was being produced for markets across the country by numerous small, independent mill operators and a few larger interests controlled by American capital. Winter cutting operations employed large crews to bring the timber out of the forests and the sawmills provided employment for the local communities. Yet despite low wages and accessible rail and shipping lines, the timber trade began to collapse shortly after the First World War. Maritime lumber encountered stiff competition as wood from the newly harvested forests of British Columbia made its way into the markets of eastern North America through the Panama canal (Reid 1987, 162). Between 1920 and 1922, the price of lumber fell 30 percent and employment in the sawmills dropped 50 percent (Forbes 1979, 58–61). Such losses spelled the end of the traditional lumber camps, and the industry as a whole did not recover to its pre-1919 production level until early in the 1960s. Even now the majority of logging operations are oriented towards the pulp and paper industry.

The decline of the primary sector is most notable in the sphere of agriculture. In the first decade of the twentieth century the children of farming families began to move to the cities to find wage jobs and enjoy the material benefits of urbanization. Between 1910 and 1920, "community disintegration" was a public concern as rural culture began to disappear; the icons of the self-sufficient country life – the sacks of locally ground meal and the barrels of salt pork that Joseph and Martha so carefully "put up" in Buckler's *The Mountain and the Valley* – were replaced by flour from the western provinces and fresh beef from the United States (Forbes 1979, 44). The exodus from the farm slowed during the depression – which in the Maritimes lasted from 1920 to 1940 – as people held on to subsistence farms during the hard times, but after the Second World War the decline in the agricultural sector continued.[1] As people were drawn to the urban centres, low-profit farms were increasingly abandoned; between 1941 and 1961, there was a 39 percent reduction in farm acreage (Bickerton 1990, 98). Those farms that continued to function adopted mechanized technology; these technologies improved the overall efficiency of the farm but removed 36,000 jobs from the market during the 1950s (Wynn 1982, 179). The twentieth century continued to see a larger proportion of Maritimers living in a rural setting, compared to the highly urbanized provinces of Ontario and Québec; but enough people abandoned the traditional farm life and moved to the city to "undermine the sense of local community fostered by the settlement of generations in a single locale" (Wynn 1982, 183).

Combined with disruptions in the fishing and lumbering sectors, the demise of the farming culture gave rise to a persistent sense of longing and nostalgia in Maritime society. As the subcultures that had arisen around these industries have disappeared, a large remnant of people have been left whose beliefs in and memories of the older ways remain long after their ability to reconstruct the traditions has vanished. This nostalgia is present in the romantic idylls of such writers as Lucy Maud Montgomery and Margaret Marshall Saunders and also in such memoirs of community life as Buckler's *Ox Bells and Fireflies* and Bruce's *Township of Time*. Indeed, this local sense of nostalgia was apparent not only in the small communities, but as Ian McKay has argued, this genuine sense of loss was subsequently reworked by the provincial tourist industries into a marketing tool. Eager to attract tourist dollars, individual entrepreneurs, government bureaucrats, and folklore historians constructed an image of the Maritimes as an old fashioned land, steeped in a myth of innocence: a quaint little world to be admired and explored by urban visitors. Images of the folksy fisherman and the kilted highland Scot were widely disseminated in the Maritimes, particularly in Nova Scotia, and this manufactured past, this "romantically reimagined ... folk ... answer[ed] at once to [the average person's] sense of class displacement, their local neo-nationalism, and their diffuse modern sense of anxiety and rootlessness" (McKay 1994, 221–2). But if there was a version of nostalgia that was developed for the purposes of the tourist industry, there was also a more diffused and less clearly articulated sense of longing and loss. If there is a common ethos in the Maritimes, it lies not in a "sense of shared community" but in the *memory* of a shared community. The social networks that emerged in the early era of prosperity may have been just as divided by class, religion, and gender as those of subsequent years, but whatever the actual historical experience, the memory – or the reconstructed memory – of an idyllic/lost continuity has become a powerful driving cultural force in the Maritimes of the twentieth century.

The industries based on primary resources were not alone in experiencing a transformation during the twentieth century. As the traditional fields of work were transformed and lost, the bright industrial future so confidently predicted at the beginning of the twentieth century failed to materialize. The manufacturing sector, which had shown such promise immediately after Confederation, began to collapse soon after the First World War. Thus, while Maritimers experienced the general sense of cultural dislocation and fragmentation that swept through western nations after the war, they also experienced the particular anxiety produced by a prolonged economic crisis.

In addition to the "natural" problems of geographic isolation and a small population base, Maritime secondary industries were plagued by financial pressures from more powerful economic centres. Maritime industries were affected by changes in national transportation policies. Just before the First World War began, political pressures generated by western manufacturers began to mount against preferential transportation policies, specifically the 12 percent differential freight rate, which had allowed Maritime businesses to ship goods out of their province at a considerable advantage over their competitors. When the rates were levelled and transportation costs rose, those eastern producers who had been operating on a narrow profit margin approached bankruptcy (Forbes 1979). The crisis that developed into "The Maritimes Rights Movement" has been documented in Ernest Forbes's influential book of the same name, but despite organized protests that lasted into the 1920s, the changes in the transportation policies were never reversed.

In the early decades of the century, the region's manufacturers experienced a need for increased levels of capital in order to modernize their factories. With few resources at hand, many decided to consolidate with American or central-Canadian firms. In 1881, there were 274 branch plants operating in New Brunswick and Nova Scotia, but by 1919 this number had grown to 950 (Reid 1987, 163). When the North American economy went into recession after the war, many head offices closed their branch operations in the Maritimes and moved them to more centralized locations (Acheson 1977, 98; McCann 1990, 241–4). Between 1919 and 1921, total employment in manufacturing dropped 42 percent (Forbes 1989, 124), and by 1925 the manufacturing production rate was only 45 percent of its 1919 level (Bickerton 1990, 43). As the sugar, cotton, glass, and clothing factories closed, few new industries arrived: the brief national recession became an extended Maritime depression.

A growing pulp and paper industry and the centralized fish processing factories replaced some of the jobs lost after the factory closures of the 1920s, but the recovery was only partial. The manufacturing sector as a whole never regained its prewar influence. Even after the booming economy of the 1960s, it accounted for only 37 percent of the net value of the Maritime economy, compared with the national average of 54.7 percent (Bickerton 1990, 175). Successive provincial and federal governments have attempted to promote regional development, but such programs as Robert Stanfield's "Industrial Estates Limited" in the late 1950s and Trudeau's "Department of Regional Economic Expansion" in the 1970s have had little lasting effect. The region has suffered from chronic unemployment, underemployment, and underdevelopment for most of the twentieth century. Like the Maritimes, the other regions of Canada have modernized their primary industries and have experienced a sense of nostalgia for times past, but in Canada the Maritime region is unique in its brief development of and subsequent loss of secondary industries. Québec triumphantly renounced its "myth of the land" during the Quiet revolution, and Ontario's nostalgia for its displaced folk cultures has been mitigated by its sense of confidence in its own future as an economic power. Only the Maritime region's sense of loss has been compounded by its repeated disappointments and frustrations in the industrial sector.

The one segment of the economy that has experienced consistent growth over the last sixty years has been the service sector. In an attempt to soften some of the economic hardships, the federal and provincial governments have become the largest employers in the region. From 1950 to 1970 there was a massive expansion of the civil service, including particularly rapid growth in the fields of health care and education (Bickerton 1990, 175). During this period, federal transfer payments permitted the modernization of the region's services, though they have also made this previously self-sufficient region dependent on Ottawa, which has bred a certain amount of resistance and resentment towards the wealthier provinces (Acheson 1977, 103). The entrance of the Maritimes into the modern age, characterized as it has been by a decline in manufacturing and an increased dependence on social services, has resulted in a growing sense of alienation as the population encounters conditions of labour, relations of productions, and a widening range of products and institutions over which the Maritime provinces have little control.[2]

Facing hard times, many Maritimers have relied on the time-honoured tradition of migration as to solve their economic problems. With startling consistency 80,000 to 100,000 people have left the region in each decade between 1881 and 1981, travelling first to the "Boston States" and later to central and western Canada to seek work (Wynn 1982, 183). The period between 1921 and 1941 is the only exception to this trend when 150,000 people, nearly 18 percent of the population, left each decade in an attempt to escape the Depression (Veltmeyer 1979, 23). Certainly this constant migration has relieved the economic pressures in the region and has helped supply other urban centres with a large pool of both skilled and unskilled labour, but the continual departures have also acted as another source of disruption for the traditional local community.

It would be difficult to overestimate the influence that the failure of the industrial sector and the resulting persistent economic hardships have had on the people of the Atlantic coast. Just as Maritimers share a common *memory* of a lost community, so they share a distinctive fear or hesitation about their tenuous future. These forces of memory and hesitation form the central cultural boundaries of the region. The Maritimes no longer fit the image of a slow, stable, "folksy" society. The region is distinguished by its balance between hesitation about the future and its memory of the past and this fragile equilibrium is at the root of its distinct style of realist fiction.

LITERATURE AND IDEOLOGY

> Ideology is not a dreamlike illusion
> Slavoy Zizek

An appreciation of the transformations that have swept the Maritimes is necessary if the forces shaping the texts of the region are to be understood; the precise way in which a Maritime realist text is related to and anchored in its cultural context should not be glossed over. Theorists have long debated whether texts are produced by the unique and solitary imaginations of individual artists, or whether they are the product of a broad collective or social unconscious. One key that might help us understand how a Maritime fictional text is linked to its economic, political, or regional context can be found in the term "ideology." We accept as a given, in the poststructuralist age, that no individual or group of people has reliable or unmediated contact with the real, concrete world that surrounds them. Individuals may live in one of the Maritime provinces, but their connection to their immediate environment is conditioned by the assumptions of the larger society. The individual subject, who is already constructed by and within language, experiences their "real" world only through a mediating body of assumptions. This body of assumptions does not lie about the "real"; rather, it alludes to the world and then shapes the subject's perceptions of and experiences within their specific context: "Ideology is not a dreamlike illusion that we build to escape an insupportable reality; in its basic dimension it is a construction which serves as a support for our 'reality' itself: an 'illusion' that structures our effective, real social relations and masks some insupportable, real, impossible kernel" (Zizek 1994, 323). The individual subject does not feel any sense of coercion by the ideological, for each individual absorbs and is absorbed into the assumptions of their culture, which teach them to see the "real" in accordance with the interests of the established systems. As Althusser observes, the assumptions or ideologies of the society are the "imaginary relations of the individual to the real relations in which they live" (1969, 165), and no individual escapes the assumptions that seem to naturally structure the community: "Ideologies slide into all human activity [and are] identical with the lived experience of human existence itself" (223).

As an ever-present veil that mediates the subject's experience of the real, "ideology" would initially seem to function as a deterministic force: Maritimers can only experience their region through the set of assumptions they have inherited but do not define. This threat of determinism recedes as we note that the very ideologies that shape our imaginary relation to the real are not homogenous or totalizing forces. The ideologies that structure individuals and their perceptions are "multiple" in their sources, "relatively autonomous" from the direct control of the political state, and manifest themselves in a plurality of concrete material practices, such as the use of language, the teachings of the schools and churches, and the subject matter of the arts and media (Althusser 1969, 149). Because ideological assumptions within any society are only loosely controlled by the institutions of the state, they can rarely be brought into complete harmony or unity with one another. Thus broken and prone to contradiction, ideological fields produce gaps and offer the subject the opportunity to negotiate not complete "freedom" or "independence" but a series of distinctive differences and or self-determined positions. The individual subject is thus aware of and embedded in their main assumptions of time and place, but within that position particular persons, or a particular creative writers, can develop their own particular range of responses to social and economic environments.

Ideologies are multiple, but they are not so amorphous as to be un-identifiable. Ideology is the way in which what people say and believe connects with the power structure and power-relations of the society in which they live. The realm of the ideological can thus be distinguished from the domain of the cultural, which is distanced from the mechanisms of power. Broad patterns of nostalgia and hesitation are the hallmarks of Maritime culture, and these tensions are the arena in which the specific ideological assumptions emerge. Maritimers move within a field of cultural tensions and are then inscribed within the ideological as they reproduce specific assumptions about their place within the community, their role in the work force, and their position within the family unit. To the degree that these more precisely located assumptions are necessary for the maintenance of a particular social, gender, or class system, they can be considered "ideological." Indeed, most of the Maritime novels considered in this study tend to reproduce assumptions that lie somewhere between the ideological positions of conservatism and liberalism.

In the course of the twentieth century, the Maritime region has produced numerous conservative texts. There are many strands of conservatism, and it would be a mistake to suggest that particular novelists are attempting to promote one version of philosophic conservatism instead of another. It would be more useful to note that conservatives, in general, are characterized by "their conviction that liberty is the precious inheritance of an historically-established community, rather than an individual right to assert self-interest against that community" (Barney[3]). Whether they spring from the philosophical Platonism of Leo Strauss or anchor themselves in the more concrete historicism of Edmund Burke, conservatives regard existing, traditional political institutions, cultural practices, and hierarchical social relationships as time-tested repositories of virtue and so defend these against radical alteration. What distinguishes the prudent conservative from the "thoughtless reactionary is that while the reactionary dogmatically opposes change, the conservative's commitment to societal continuity includes a willingness to embrace the moderate changes deemed necessary for the preservation of social order" (Barney). Upon this foundation, conservatives build a number of related ideological commitments to the priority of collective welfare, stability, and order, and they stress the importance of maintaining those traditional social relationships upon which collective order and well-being rest, including established hierarchies of status, class, race, gender, and religion. The notion that community security is dependent on this adherence to a set of collective traditions has been especially appealing to Maritime writers who have observed the economic and cultural disruptions of the twentieth century and recognized that many rich and varied traditions of the past are being cast aside or lost.

In contrast to this conservative impulse, numerous Maritime fictions explore the liberal ideal, as articulated by Grant, that "man's essence [is] his freedom" (1969, 56). Liberals emphasize the independent, self-determining nature of the subject and represent community and social institutions as structures that facilitate the individual's search for freedom. Freedom is not necessarily a good thing in and of itself, but rather it constitutes the condition required to pursue those projects and tasks that are deemed valuable. In its most general form, then, liberalism asserts "that a valuable life has to be a life led from the inside ... in accordance with our beliefs about what gives value to life," and that we must be "free to question those beliefs, to examine them in the light of whatever information and examples and arguments our culture can provide" (Kymlicka 1988, 183–4). This very general version of the liberal position has not been static over the centuries. Of the various permutations of liberalism it will be sufficient, for the purposes of this study of Maritime fiction, to identify the two major streams of liberalism: individualist liberalism, which focuses on the rights and liberties of the single individual, and communitarian liberalism, which attends to the role of the larger community in ensuring the individual's quest for a full and complete identity. This individualistic/communitarian dichotomy implies a contrast between two conceptions of the self in relation to the larger community.

Individualist liberalism finds its roots in the political writings of Locke and Mill and argues that as an individual, each person has a unique identity, which includes the capacity and the inalienable right to form and carry out the projects that gradually unfold as a personal history. As Daly and Barney both note, this form of liberalism stresses the concept of rights and holds that individual freedom takes priority over any other ideal or objective that would be defended or accomplished by rescinding that freedom. Thus, this brand of liberalism directly opposes the conservative notion that objectives such as "collective welfare, cultural integrity, order, stability, or tradition ought to moderate the free exercise of individual will" (Barney). Individualist liberal values are most succinctly expressed by John Stuart Mill's claim that, "The only freedom which deserves the name, is that of pursuing our own good in our own way, so long as we do not attempt to deprive others of theirs, or impede their efforts to obtain it. Each is the proper guardian of his own health, whether bodily, or mental and spiritual. Mankind are greater gainers by suffering each other to live as seems good to themselves, than by compelling each to live as seems good to the rest" (Mill 1994, 17).

Communitarian liberalism recognizes the importance of the individual, but notes that "at the practical level ... each person belongs to a network of family and social relationships and is defined by this membership ... Each person forms an identity through personal attachments with others and finds a life and purpose as a part of an established social practise" (Daly 1994, xiv–xvii). Rooted in the philosophy of Jean-Jacques Rousseau and G.W.F. Hegel, communitarian liberalism locates the individual in a broader historical tradition and notes that the rational, self-aware members of a community are willing to compromise their own agenda in order to address the needs of the collective. Though some communitarian philosophers would view individualist liberalism as being excessively atomistic, for the purposes of this analysis of regional ideologies, the two positions can be viewed as branches of the same larger tree of liberal thought. Just as otherwise distinct conservatisms are united in their commitment to collective order and continuity above dynamic private liberty, so too are liberals united in their commitment to the essential nature and priority of individual freedom – regardless of their different views regarding its relationship to community. The rather general distinctions established here between conservatism, individualist liberalism, and communitarian liberalism will be further refined as each writer's particular ideological stance is examined.

While the ideological perspectives of texts can be identified by such broad labels, it is essential that the critic resist the notion that these texts embody a single uniform position. The very novels that seem most committed to a particular liberal ideology may also contain a subtext that is deeply indebted to conservative assumptions. Just as the subject negotiates the gaps of a contradictory ideological field, so the literary text is produced within the competing versions of the "real" that emerge from the economic, social, sexual, and political conditions. East Coast texts are produced within the matrix of tensions created as the ideals of the declining traditional culture come into conflict with the modernist assumptions and sense of alienation associated with the region's incomplete entrance into the industrial age. Texts are not mirrors of societies. They do not simply reflect a region's concerns, and they cannot be read unproblematically as sociological documents of how a community functions. Literature, as James Kavanaugh points out, is an activity that wrestles in its own particular ways with the necessities and insufficiencies of a given set of ideological assumptions; the "literary event itself enacts, restores, constructs, and disrupts an ideological relation" (1982, 33). The text becomes a site where the ideologies of the larger society, the author's own reactions to that complex set of assumptions, and the ideological assumptions facilitated by the forms themselves all come together. In this model the critic's task is not to evaluate the realist work to determine whether it is an accurate rendering of the "real." The critic works within his or her own set of assumptions and then attempts to trace how the ideologies that are embedded in the society, the author, and the forms combine to produce the text.

In order to explore the various competing assumptions embedded in a text, the reader must attend closely to each aspect of the fiction. The traditional New-Critical practice of "close reading" can be used to study the forces that drive the events and plots of a narrative. Similarly close attention must be paid to the development of the characters, for "whether it is the opposition between feudalism and liberalism, liberalism and socialism, patriarchy and egalitarianism, or more specific oppositions, [characters] must always deal with the ideological oppositions of the world in which they move" (Bal 1985, 37). Just as the actions and words of the characters may reveal various assumptions, so the competing ideologies of the novels may be unveiled as the reader explores the levels of story, text, and narration and examines the differing subject positions of the narrator.

Finally, any investigation into ideological assumptions needs to attend to what the text struggles to avoid saying. The critic must attend to the stylistic disruptions, the unexplained leaps in logic, the uncanny silences, and the moments of repression, for such gaps may point to ideas to which the text adheres, but is hesitant to make explicit (Macherey 1978, 79–94). The ideologies of a novel may be buried like an unconscious, to be read more through its symptoms of anxiety than through its own assertions. For example, Charles Bruce's strange and sudden use of the traditions of romance in his depiction of the antagonist Anse in *The Channel Shore* are symptomatic of his desire to marginalize a representative of industrial modernism from the more conventional, positive, and secure characters of his novel. Each piece of fiction fuses several literary genres and a variety of discourses, and as these sometimes competing forces come together, gaps or fissures inevitably occur. Far from being an aesthetic blemish to be mourned by the critic, such moments are often the most intriguing parts of the narrative; they provide us with the opportunity to search further into the competing impulses at the heart of the fiction.

I will not attempt to organize these different analytic techniques into a system that can then be applied to the fictions. Literary works reproduce the competing ideologies that structure the societies from which they emerge, but there is no template or system that can give us immediate access to the complex impulses that are embedded in a text. These different analytic tools may be combined and mixed according to the demands of the novels, for in every case, the theoretical approach will be at the service of the text; the text will not be reshaped to fit the needs of the critical position.

"PLEASE AGAIN DEFINE EXACTLY WHAT YOU UNDERSTAND BY REALISM."

On the 28 June 1938, Anna Segher asked the renowned Marxist literary critic Georg Lukacs to respond to a "simple" request: "Please again define exactly what you understand by realism." Segher's request echoes beyond the work of Lukacs, for of the many terms circulating through the study of literature, few have proven more difficult to stabilize than the word "realism." Indeed, in Maritime texts, the genre of realism more often functions as "a hybrid, and the definitions we work with, however useful they may be locally, correspond to ideals rather than to works" (Levine 1974, 142). The term realism has always been difficult to define, at least in part because the word itself seems to promise a direct correspondence between the text and the world beyond it. Rene Wellek notes that many critics stress the mimetic function of realist texts and argue that the genre strives to be a "truthful representation of the real world" (1963, 228). The link between the terms "realism" and "verisimilitude" led some critics in the late nineteenth and early twentieth century to celebrate realist fictions as more authentic and admirable than other types of fiction, such as the romance novel or the gothic tale, which were viewed as antiquated or escapist. Such early attempts to connect realism and the real world must be resisted, because realism, of course, is as bound by its own set of artificial conventions and characteristics as any genre of literature. Realist novels are not "real" because they mirror the world itself; the novels seem realistic because the central features of the genre reproduce the assumptions – the preconceptions, expectations, and biases – through which the author, the reader, and their wider society view and recognize their world as real. Realist texts are not accurate portraits of an external world, rather they are productions that embody the widely held assumptions that mediate between the community and its context.

Realism cannot be defined by its faithfulness to its subject matter, but it can still be distinguished from other literary genres by three characteristics. Realist novels presume that there is a split between the subject and the object; they attend to historical context; and they employ a style that is not self-reflexive.

First, realism assumes that there is a stable, permanent split between the viewing subject and the perceived object. As Elizabeth Ermath notes, realism is a movement with the solid faith that "an invariant, identifiable reality is present despite [the] refractions to which our successive angles of viewing subject it" (1981, 514). This faith in the integrity of the Cartesian subject and in the existence of a stable, knowable, and objective world manifests itself in several ways. Realist texts frequently foreground the integrity of the speaking subject by focusing on a single central protagonist and chronicling his or her maturation or development. Lawrence Mathews notes that the Canadian canon is particularly rich in texts that insist upon "the significance of the protagonist's experience is personal ... [there is] no indication that collective action may be as interesting or important as individual action" (1991, 159).

Realism's acceptance of such traditional philosophic positions as the subject/object split carries with it some ideological baggage – for example, realism's intense interest in a unified, integral self has lead some feminists to argue that the genre is inherently patriarchal in character (this tendency within realism will be examined in more detail in chapter 7) – but even this conventional philosophic ground has historically supported a variety of ideological projects, both conservative and revolutionary. The formal conventions adopted in a Maritime text do not necessarily determine its ideological stance, though the way a text adapts and shifts between genres is symptomatic of its ideological or metaphysical propositions and tensions.

Just as realism attempts to focus on the individual subject, so it is also intensely interested in chronicling the particular, concrete details of the character's objective world. Many realist writers flesh out their texts with descriptions of furniture, rooms, houses, cityscapes, and landscapes in greater detail than is necessary for the progression of the story. The technique of inundating the text with descriptive signifiers, regardless of their narrative significance, is part of an attempt to convince the reader that the textual world is a real world: "the absence of the signified, to the advantage of the referent alone, becomes the very signifier of realism: the *reality effect* is produced" (Barthes 1968, 148). The belief in a permanent subject/object split is also manifested through techniques of narration that provide the reader with a secure sense of time and place. Often the text is related by an omniscient external narrator or an informed internal (character-based) narrator who knows much of what has happened and lends his or her position of knowledge to the reader. Similarly, realist narratives are frequently set in the past tense, a temporal move that acts as an organizing principle by positioning the reader in the present at a specific moment when all the enigmas and mysteries of the story are resolved. In both cases these techniques afford the reader a stable place from which to view "objectively" the narrative events.

Second, realism attends to historical context, but even more importantly it is deeply embedded in the assumptions of historicism. The rise of realism in the late eighteenth and early nineteenth century is connected with two phenomena. First, by the turn of the nineteenth century many people were intensely aware, through the French and American Revolutions, that individuals are embedded in and affected by the historical events of their times (Lukacs 1962, 204). Second, the emergence of German historicism "laid the aesthetic foundation for modern realism" by demonstrating that all particular events become comprehensible only as they are seen to be partial links in a larger economic and historical chain (Auerbach 1946, 391). The realist novel is created within this awareness of "the subsurface movement and the unfolding of historical forces" and creates a credible portrait of the world by ensuring that the events and characters of the narrative are embedded in specific social and temporal contexts: "the meaning of events cannot be grasped in abstract and general forms of cognition, and the material needed to understand them must not be sought exclusively in the upper strata of society and in major political events but also in art, economy, material and intellectual culture, [and] in the depths of the workaday world and its men and women" (Auerbach 1946, 391). Realism's commitment to the metanarratives and the assumptions of historicism can be seen in its overwhelming concern with tracing lines of cause and effect.

In realist narratives the attempt is made to document how each event has its origins in a previous context – how each character's thoughts and actions are the result of that individual's past. The realist novel links each effect to an earlier cause, whether this manifests itself as the stark determinism that threatens many of Richards's Miramichi characters or the careful documentation of historical events and their repercussions in Raddall's historical adventures. Even those characters who act without coherent motivations or in an arbitrary fashion are often situated within the explanatory context of madness. This desire to ground the characters in a specific social and historical context, and the need to search out logical and probable causes for events, spells an end to such literary devices as the *deus ex machina*, which resolves the complicated plots of many comedy of manners, or the *anagnorsis*, through which the hero of the romance achieves victory. The formulaic happy ending and the idealism characteristic of romance are usually absent from realist fiction. Of course, the realist text is never a "truthful" record of history any more than it is a faithful reflection of reality, but, nonetheless, the assumptions arising from historicism have made a deep impact on the genre.

Finally, realist fictions are characterized by their lack of linguistic self-reflexivity. Styles vary widely among writers, ranging from the sparse minimalism of Richards's *Road to the Stilt House*, to the poetic eloquence of Buckler's *The Mountain and the Valley*, but the realist text ultimately keeps the role of language, and questions about its own fictionality, in the background. Once a style has been established it rarely calls attention to itself. As Roman Jakobson notes in his essay "The Metaphoric and Metonymic Poles," the dominant trope of realism is the metonym, which unobtrusively leads the reader from one signifier to another along an ever extending line; this facilitates an easy movement from accounts of character and plot to detailed portrayals of setting and contexts (Jacobson 1965, 243; Lamont-Stewart 1986, 26). Unlike postmodernist fictions, which are by definition self-referential, realist fictions treat language as a natural medium and a simple tool of communication.

These three characteristics – the subject/object split, the historical positivism, and the absence of self-reflexivity – are the defining features of realist texts produced in the last two hundred years, and they are certainly applicable to the realist novels written in the Maritimes over the last sixty years. The region's realist fictions have been particularly influenced by the assumptions of historicism and have struggled to construct coherent, detailed social and cultural contexts in which the characters are deeply immersed and through which various ideological tensions can be explored. This book will proceed chronologically, investigating how Maritime fictions embody both the various assumptions generated within the writer's specific context and the powerful social tensions created as the Maritimes have made their transition from a rural to an industrial-urban existence.

We will begin by examining a group of writers whose texts fall within the traditions of realism, yet are still influenced by the patterns of romance. Frank Parker Day, Hugh MacLennan, and Thomas Raddall attempt to use romance patterns to impose moments of coherence and stability on their fictional worlds. Their texts bear the marks of the region's cultural disruptions, but often respond to those changes through a return to and celebration of traditional values and ideals. Yet there is a threatening undercurrent of modernism that often undermines the effectiveness of the romance genre and forces the reader to recognize the inevitability of the region's entrance into a difficult industrial age. In these particular ways Day's, MacLennan's and Raddall's texts are the first to encounter and struggle with the economic and social forces of change that affected the Maritimes after the First World War.

Charles Bruce's only novel, *The Channel Shore*, stands out among Maritime fictions for its carefully constructed tension between the conventions of realism and those of nostalgia. The traditions of realism govern the central elements of the text, such as the general style, the development of character and plot, and the placement of the reader, while a strong nostalgic impulse controls the novel's representation of contemporary events, the depiction of women, and the development of the villain. The tensions between the formal conventions are symptomatic of the novel's central ideological conflict between divergent strands of liberal historicism and conservative idealism. Bruce's *The Channel Shore* has shed the utopianism of the historical romance, yet it displays an interesting resistance to any representation of postwar alienation.

Even more than Bruce's *The Channel Shore*, Ernest Buckler's first novel directly confronts the transformations within rural Nova Scotia. More complex than his subsequent texts – *The Cruelest Month* and *Ox Bells and Fireflies* – Buckler's *The Mountain and the Valley*, published in 1952, is the region's finest example of a novel that both balances and fully expresses the divergent cultural experiences of the region. On one hand, Buckler's novel reproduces an elegiac vision of the past: he reproduces the traditionally polarized gender roles, explores the rural/urban binary, and employs a forcefully nostalgic narrative voice – all of which point to a conservative ideology. On the other hand, the central narrative, which traces David's obsession with controlling his world through language, emerges as the vehicle through which Buckler ponders an existential search for meaning, confirming that *The Mountain and the Valley* is one of the first East Coast texts to be self-consciously influenced by the cultural forces of modernism. Buckler's novels are more willing than Bruce's to face the postwar void, yet he does not disconnect himself from his longing for a remembered past.

In the aftermath of Buckler's attempts to address modernist concerns directly, such writers as Alistair MacLeod and Alden Nowlan are interested in exploring the possibility of human agency, but increasingly this seems to be an ideal to contemplate rather than a goal to achieve. Nowlan's early fictions demonstrate that the individual subject is essentially trapped within a deterministic social structure, and even the later writings can only proclaim a multiplicity of the self rather than a complete freedom for the individual. MacLeod also demonstrates, in his short stories, that the individual's sense of self is difficult to maintain in the modern Maritime setting, and his more recent work begins to employ a conservative ideology and the conventions of the romance in order to attain a measure of security.

Of all the texts considered, only those of David Adams Richards deal exclusively with the social and cultural problems of the post-1960 era. In his nine novels, Richards repeatedly uses realism to examine the social disruptions and the economic hardships that have plagued the Miramichi region since its descent into chronic dependency and underdevelopment. Richards consistently explores how individuals are restricted and confined by their familial or socioeconomic contexts, and at times his fiction adopts the determinism typical of naturalist fiction. This shadow of fatalism does not rest easily on Richards, however, and throughout his narratives the characters are driven by a longing for personal independence and freedom. His characters' desire for a self-determined existence sometimes comes into conflict with the interests of state and community structures, and when such tensions arise the texts pursue a position reminiscent of individualist liberalism in order to affirm the rights of the subject. Indeed, Richards's ideological commitment to individual liberty is so strong that his narratives are subject to some sudden and remarkable shifts whenever these assumptions come under attack.

Following a careful analysis of some of the dominant Maritime writers who have emerged in the course of the twentieth century, this study will turn, in the final chapters, to consider a selection of recent writers. In the last two decades women writers finally turned to the conventions of realism and challenged the often patriarchal canon with a series of remarkable short stories and novels. Anchored in the various assumptions of liberalism, these women have articulated a powerful feminist sensibility and have given voice to aspects of the culture that have previously been silent or silenced. Numerous other fiction writers have continued to explore the divergent nostalgic and despairing strands of Maritime culture and the last chapter will examine how their work continues to be shaped by the forces that have defined the region throughout the century.

The Maritimes appears to some as a nostalgic paradise of small, close-knit communities that lead a traditional, slow-paced way of life closely bonded to the rhythms of the land and sea. Others have seen the region through less idealistic, but no less reductive, eyes, dismissing it as "rural without being pastoral, industrious without being profitable, the exporter of brains and the importer of money, everyone's half forgotten past and no-one's future" (New 1976, 3). For Maritimers themselves it can seem a constantly shifting and fragmented region that perpetually promises future stability but experiences a seemingly endless series of transitions and changes. By examining the ways in which the realist texts are embedded in these shifting ideological, cultural, and historical conditions, we can try to reach a deeper understanding, not only of the texts themselves, but also of their role as products of this distinct region.

2 Realism with Reservations: Frank Parker Day, Hugh MacLennan, Thomas Head Raddall

Yet will I stay my steps and not go down to the marshland ...
Lest on too close sight I miss the darling illusion,
Spy at their task even here the hands of chance and change.
                              G.D. Roberts, "Tantramar Revisited"

When compared to other parts of the world, the Maritimes' encounter with the realist aesthetic has been relatively brief. Techniques of realism emerged in the region at the same time as they were being partially displaced in Europe, England, and the USA by avant-garde movements such as expressionism, dadaism, and surrealism. At the beginning of the twentieth century – with the exception of a few writers (C.G.D. Roberts, for example, who played a role in the creation of the realist animal story) – almost all the region's writers were engaged in the production of romance fictions. The reputations of some of these writers have survived and flourished through the years. Lucy Maud Montgomery and Margaret Marshall Saunders are now household names, as are the titles of their most popular novels *Anne of Green Gables* and *Beautiful Joe*. Other eastern romance writers such as Carrie Jenkins Harris, Alice Jones and her cousin Susan Carleton Jones, Frederick William Wallace, Basil King, Hiram Cody, and James MacDonald Oxley all produced popular fictions, but their novels are not well known today (MacMillan 1987, 80–1).[1] In the decades following the First World War, many Maritime novelists still relied on the romance style and the conservative pastoral and idyllic themes that had characterized prewar fiction. The undiminished popularity of the genre, evident in the international sales of such novels as Mazo De La Roche's *Jalna* and Margaret Mitchell's *Gone with the Wind*, is indicative of a broad-based desire to find temporary escape from the hardships of the depression in the comforting depictions of a once-gallant past. Regional producers of romance in the postwar era certainly found a wide audience as Evelyn Eaton published historical sagas – like *Quietly My Captain* (1940) – and Louis Arthur Cunningham wrote nearly thirty romance fictions, including *Fog over Fundy* (1936), *Tides of the Tantramar* (1936), and *Moon over Acadie* (1937) (Toye, 513).

The enduring appeal of the romance throughout the early twentieth century, for both writers and readers, is not surprising given the sense of confidence and security that is generated by a genre that functions within carefully defined limits. The boundaries between realism and romance are frequently blurred, but the two genres can be distinguished in several ways. Unlike the plot structures of a realist text, which are anchored in the assumptions of historicism and rely on the concept of probability to trace lines of cause and effect, the romance genre is defined by its quest structure. In the romance, a heroic character moves through minor adventures towards a moment of climactic confrontation with an antagonist, before emerging as an exalted figure either in life or in death (Frye 1957, 187). This quest may take the form of an archetypal descent into the demonic or ascent into the idyllic, but, regardless of the direction, the journey articulates and celebrates the assumptions of the hero and the community he or she represents (Frye 1976, 129). While the realist text is guided by the writer's assumptions about what could happen and tends to reproduce a wider range of social experiences, including the "crude and miserable pleasures [of the lower classes, and the] early depravity and rapid wearing out of human material" (Auerbach 1946, 451), the romance is "a form in which pattern dominates over plausibility, in which central figures achieve the fullest possible freedom from [the] limitations of a restrictive context, and in which ideal values are worked out and shown to be viable" (Levine 1974, 238).

As was noted above, realist texts often foreground a single protagonist who functions as an organizing figure for the narrative and subtly reasserts the split between the subject and the object. The characters of realist texts, particularly the later psychological realisms produced at the turn of the twentieth century, are often drawn from the ranks of ordinary humanity and are not easily confined within moral categories or defined by their narrative roles. In the romance, characters perform specific functions and are more carefully tied to their prescribed roles as hero, villain, helper, or opponent: they "exist primarily to symbolize a contrast between two worlds" – light and dark, good and evil – and this facilitates the romance's "simplif[ication] of moral facts" (Frye 1976, 50). The enduring patterns that structure the romance help produce a powerful sense of affirmation that validates the audience's dominant assumptions. While realism's ability to transmute "the real" through its filter of preconceptions, expectations, and biases can be adopted to suit a wide range of positions, some critics have argued that the romance's commitment to the affirmation of the larger community tends to limit its ideological range.

There was no sudden metamorphosis of the Maritime novel, but as the century wore on, writers began adopting new techniques to confront the tensions of their age. Frank Parker Day, Hugh MacLennan, and Thomas Raddall resisted the aesthetics of modernism as they produced their fictions for markets outside Canada; nonetheless, all three were inadvertently in step with a national trend, exemplified by such writers as Martha Ostenso, F.P. Grove, and Philip Child, as they fused the quest motifs, the mythic patterns, and the impulse to create moments of coherence and stability typical of romance with a realist style characterized by the construction of historicized figures and careful attention to concrete detail. Day, MacLennan, and Raddall found in the romance conventions a means of defending the pre-industrial culture of the region, while simultaneously resisting contemporary disruptions. Day's *Rockbound*, MacLennan's *Barometer Rising*, and Raddall's *The Nymph and the Lamp* celebrate a restoration/return to a stable traditional world after a period of crisis and instability. Yet in the midst of these often conservative texts – in the actions of the secondary characters as well as in the silences, tensions, and shifts of these narratives – the reader can recognize a complex struggle with contemporary economic hardships, social pressures, and the alienation of the post-First World War era. The narrative ruptures that emerge as realist discourses disrupt the romance patterns, provide us with a variety of insights into the effects of the region's cultural transformations on both the writers and the ideologies within their texts.

FRANK PARKER DAY:
ROMANCE AND REALISM

Born in 1881, Frank Parker Day led a remarkable life. Fisherman, academic, Rhodes scholar, administrator, boxer, and soldier, Day was also an accomplished author. He produced a reflective memoir of his youth, entitled *The Autobiography of a Fisherman* (1927), several novels, including *River of Strangers* (1926) and *John Paul's Rock* (1932), and six unpublished romances (which remain among his papers).[2] The best-known of Day's texts is undoubtedly *Rockbound*, published by Doubleday, Doran & Company in 1928. Well received by reviewers – who judged it to be starkly realistic with "but a little romance" (Ritchie 1929, 129) – the novel went out of print in the early 1930s. It was "rediscovered" when it was reprinted in 1973 by the University of Toronto Press, and since then it has been viewed as a text in which the realist elements are secondary to the mythic structure; Janice Kulyk Keefer notes that the novel is a romance with "the most fairy-tale of plots – a dispossessed orphan, having gone to seek his fortune and reclaim his possessions from his wicked Uncle-King, ends by winning fair maid and founding his own kingdom" (1987, 72). More than Raddall and MacLennan, Day's novel weaves together a plurality of ideological positions. *Rockbound* creates a fascinating tension as the dominant romance blends a conservative chronicle of a fading way of life with a thoroughly liberal celebration of the potential of the human spirit. These competing ideological positions are both challenged, in turn, by the moments of foreboding realism that depict the hero's increasing sense of sorrow and despair and threaten to undermine the optimism of the larger narrative.

The romance embedded in *Rockbound* strives to perform a double function as it fuses a conservative/conservationist representation of the Nova Scotian fishing culture with an ethical system founded in a liberal humanist vision of the individual. Day's impulse to act as conservator was rooted in personal experience; the author spent his teenage years in Mahone Bay and financed his university education by working on coastal vessels (Davies 1989, 298). Familiar with the communities of the South Shore, Day choose the area as the setting for his novel when the early draft was produced in 1925 or 1926. In a clear attempt to anchor the text in the local folkways, Day visited the island of Ironbound in the summer of 1926, interviewed the local people, collected folktales and gossip, and integrated his research materials into the next draft of the novel. Day perceived in Ironbound an elemental, pre-modernist lifestyle, and, in an attempt to preserve the atmosphere of cultural innocence, he set his novel at the turn of the century, well before the First World War and even before the fisheries had fully incorporated modern innovations like refrigerated rail transportation.

As he spins his tale about David Jung's and Gershom Born's heroic struggles, Day makes a special effort to document and conserve some aspects of the local fishery's culture. The romance plot is fleshed out with descriptions of the shifting seasons, the work environments of the fish houses, the details of the herring runs, and the intricacies of the boats. Rockbound's cultural practices are carefully detailed, and the story is frequently suspended in order to record a south-shore ballad, folktale, song, or legend. When David Jung and Gershom spend their holiday on Barren Island following Old Gershom's death, ten pages of the novel (114–23) are devoted to retelling the folktale of how Johnny Publicover captured the "Sanford ghos'."

Day attempts to accurately represent this pre-modernist culture from his postwar perspective, but he is also anxious about the impact of contemporary experience on the Maritimes and engages in the conservative politics of cultural selection; as he depicts the folk, he presents them as a distinct, self-contained, coherent community whose strong sense of self-definition facilitates the reader's tendency to view them as the "Other." The text's tendency to distance the folk is first evident in the voice and style of the narrator; for example, the narrator of *Rockbound* rarely uses free indirect discourse to echo the speech patterns of the local people. Though not condescending, the narrator adopts a polished and grammatically correct style that tends to mediate and even interpret the experience of the less educated local population. The narrator is more knowledgeable than the characters in the text, and the speaker goes off occasionally on tangents that would be beyond the experience of the island-bound characters like David Jung. One such moment occurs when David is learning the alphabet, and the narrator reflects on how the shapes of the letters were influenced in turn by "some smiling Greek … some pompous Roman … and by some mincing clerk of Britain" (R, 157).

Similarly, each of the chapters in the novel opens with a quotations from Chaucer, which suggests that in their struggle against the elements the characters are as attuned to the rhythms and experiences of the medieval society as to those of the modern world. The quotes emphasize the romantic "Otherness" of the Rockbounders at the same time as they legitimize Day's claim that they are worthy of literary attention. Even the speech of the Rockbounders itself was carefully revised to accentuate their regional and folk origins. In the early drafts of the novel, Day's characters speak in a standard English dialect, however, after his visit to Ironbound, Day painstakingly revised the dialogue to "capture the distinctive flavour of the 'Lunenburg Dutch' spoken along the South Shore of the province" (Davies 1989, 312). This use of dialect "provides an economical way of 'Othering' the Folk primitive by establishing through language a sense of cultural strangeness and difference"(McKay 1994, 245). Given this tendency not only to conserve but also make distant these folk elements, it is not surprising that the citizens of Ironbound did not endorse Day's recreation of their island as the backdrop for his romance. In a letter to the *Progress and Enterprise* of Lunenburg, they criticized the author for depicting them as "Ignorant, immoral, and superstitious," and claimed that his "ridiculous book … belittl[ed] the inhabitants of his native province and those who befriended him" (Davies 1989, 295).

As Ian MacKay has argued in *The Quest of the Folk*, Day's depiction of the fisherman on the fictional island of Rockbound is closely aligned with the work of such writers as Helen Creighton and Mary Black, who were producing highly romanticized versions of the folk culture, in an attempt to depict these subcultures as innocent and natural. Day's tendency to idealize the folk is evident as he celebrates the heroic actions of particular fisherman and avoids reproducing the economic patterns that governed many of the workers in the salt cod industry. For example, in *Rockbound*, Day presents a gilded version of the financial trials that plagued the average sharesman. Until the late 1920s, the salt cod fisheries and the offshore schooner operations were dominated by the merchant-traders, who bought partly processed fish from the smaller family operations and sold to the fishermen the "flour, lumber, salt, and sugar" that they needed to maintain their operations (Barrett 1979, 128). Some historians now argue that the merchant-traders were a necessary, rather than Machiavellian, part of a system that afforded the fishers a kind of credit and maintained their contacts with the industrial system, but by purchasing the fish at low prices and selling their goods at an inflated cost some merchant-traders were able to keep small operators in a constant state of debt and dependence (Barrett 1979, 129). Day is accurate in his assertion that some fisherman were able to live comfortable lives, but he avoids the full historical narrative about the industry. His versions of the financially secure folk better fit the demands of the romance genre, and reinforce the conservationist agenda that affirms the inherent value of the traditional systems and minimizes the economic hardships of the workers and presents as quaint their distinct cultural practices. Certainly, Day oversimplifies aspects of the cultural experience of Nova Scotia's South Shore, but McKay is mistaken when he claims that Day is "driven by a reductionalist passion" to produce a novel that is "of a piece with the entire Quest of the Folk" and thereby party to the conservative and antimodernist politics of that project. Much of the centre of Day's novel is more closely linked to the ideals and assumptions of liberal humanism.

The core of *Rockbound* is anchored in a clearly defined ethical and ideological agenda. In a lecture entitled "Some Aspects of Modern Fiction," delivered in the 1920s, Day states, "the artist is ... to help us to interpret the beauty of life as it may be, to present to us romance, adventure, idealism, and to reveal the nobility lying latent in every human breast" (Davies 1989, 318). *Rockbound* expresses this deep faith in the essential integrity and inherent goodness of the individual, by applauding heroic figures who are "great-hearted," courageous, steadfast, and compassionate to the weak and condemning those figures who have allowed themselves to be corrupted by their base motives of greed or jealousy (Bevan 1958, 347). The text shifts from the ethical to the ideological as it moves beyond the simple recollection of David and Gershom's heroic struggles against the unforgiving Atlantic waters and the schemes of the Jung dynasty. It develops specific positions on the social significance of religion and education, the efficacy of capitalism, and the limitations of patriarchy. The romantic elements that culminate in David's return to an edenic state continue to resist the disruptive forces of the modern world, but they are driven by Day's individualist liberal conviction that a person can attain freedom and liberation from corrupt communities and exist as an autonomous enlightened subject.

David Jung, the central character of the novel and the primary focalizer of the first half of the novel, is initially presented within the discourses of romance. He appears as an impoverished, ragged orphan/fisherman when he first goes to Rockbound to reclaim his birthright from his uncle Uriah; his superior skills as a fisherman help him quickly secure his place in the heroic tradition; and, like a charmed prince guided by "destiny," he magically becomes the "fish pilot for the fleet" (R, 84). Struggling to attain physical, emotional, mental, and eventually spiritual maturity, he becomes the very embodiment of Day's moral vision. When he is cheated, despised, and ostracized by the Jung brothers, David bears the hardships "patiently" and "with a lightness of heart" (R, 97). When "Molly Biddle of Big Outport attribute[s] a love child to him," he proves to be generous and "ungrudgingly pays her a monthly dole," though he is "none too sure of the parentage" (R, 86). The reader is aligned with the hero's value system and admires not only his tremendous ability for hard work but also his sympathy for others and his desire for communal peace on Rockbound: "O God, if dey is a God what cares fur men at all, give me some peace an quiet in my life afore I dies" (R, 148).

The text's reproduction of an individualist liberalism is clear as David's integrity emerges "naturally" from his personality and not as the product of an external religious or educational system. The text echoes Day's own skepticism about the basic tenets of Christianity: while David has heard that there is an "omnipotent God who created the world and punished those who disobeyed His laws," he has serious doubts that such an all-powerful figure is still in control: "the devil seemed stronger than God!" (R, 71–2). The education system fares only slightly better. After Tamar dies in childbirth, David is spurred by his paternal instincts to campaign for a school on Rockbound and then he proceeds to further his own education by becoming a pupil of the new teacher, Mary Dauphiny. The narrative celebrates the literary arts, but after David survives the wreck of the *Sylvia Westner* and returns home, even Mary agrees that the insights offered through education prove to be less valuable than direct, individual experience: "Over and over she made him tell her the story of the storm and the loss of the *Sylvia Westner*. Her imagination exalted the tale into an epic. Their former relations were reversed: she was no longer the teacher but the learner" (R, 207). For the first part of the text, Day's vision of individual integrity and broad humanitarianism remains at the core of David's heroic stature.

Two thirds of the way through the novel, the focal point moves away from an increasingly isolated David, but the liberal veneration of the individual continues as the narrative shifts to examine the secondary hero, Gershom Born. Born emerges as the second representative of Day's ideals, a romantic maverick who defends the standards of justice. Except for the occasional reference to Old Gershom, the narrative carefully avoids any mention of young Born's formative years. He surfaces fully formed and is described as a kind of local folk hero, a carnivalesque figure who operates outside the normal social structures of Rockbound. "Merely biding his time with Uriah ... till he could inherit Barren Island Light," Born is not subject to the tyranny of the Jung fishhouse, which he undermines with his "gay boisterous laugh and booming voice" (R, 81, 57). When his relationship with Mary is sabotaged by Uriah, young Gershom is willing to move beyond the moral codes of the community to secure his revenge, though the narrator seems to sense that his decision to replace an ethical with a personal code will be difficult. In order to ensure that justice prevails in an unlikely situation, the text suspends narrative probability and shifts between the discourses of romance and folklore, bringing forth the devil "clad in sea boots, blue dungaree pants, and jacket" to help the independent hero with his plans (R, 255). Nelly Broddy, Day's editor at Doubleday, felt that the appearance of the devil was "the only unreal part" of the text and "could be cut," but Day needed the satanic scapegoat to protect the integrity of his hero (MS 2, 288, C60).[3] While the text does not fully endorse Gershom's murder of Casper and Uriah, responsibility for the crime is conveniently shifted to the metaphysical realm of the demonic, allowing the lightkeeper to maintain his role as a sympathetic and tragic figure. After crashing his boat into the "jagged cliff bottom ... [of the] Bull" Gershom sinks "triumphant," and the reader recognizes that his act constitutes a satisfying if rough justice, which frees the island from malevolent forces of greed. Social and narrative conventions are both sacrificed in the celebration of this valiant deed.

Gershom's death also echoes the text's anxiety that the traditional cultural practices of the fishing communities are in decline. As a representative of the local folk culture, Gershom's demise signals the end of a traditional way of life, in much the same way that Big Alec MacKenzie's heroic death in Hugh MacLennan's *Barometer Rising* signals the end of Cape Breton's folkways.

Through the romance figures of David and Gershom, *Rockbound* "documents" the heroic traditions of the Nova Scotian fishing culture and maintains the ideology of individualist liberalism. The defence of the individual continues – and becomes more complete – as the romance structure is used both to celebrate the stability of the island's economic and sexual codes and to question the island's capitalist and patriarchal structures when they threaten to dehumanize vulnerable characters.

Day does not repudiate the capitalist system itself. David is eager to enter the marketplace and exchange his labour for cash, and he makes careful plans to "paint his house, to get himself some clothes and gear, to buy himself a fast stout boat ... [and] to buy some day a fiddle and learn to play jigs" (R, 74). Nevertheless, the text is troubled by those characters whose acquisition of capital limits the opportunities of other individuals or threatens the health of the larger society. Uriah, the "avaricious," "rich," "king of all the ... Jungs," is drawn as an ahistorical antagonist, characterized by his destructive greed and his tyrannical hold over his family (R, 11, 4). His desire for a dowry lies at the root of his tragic marriage plans for Casper and the young schoolteacher, and his excessive greed leads to his own destruction when Gershom tempts him to the fatal duck-hunting expedition with the promise of a winter's cheap meat. Greed leads to death: the old villain is destroyed like the evil dragon at the end of a fairy tale.

As Day is critical of the economic system when it impinges on the freedom and happiness of the individual, so he is critical of the patriarchal tradition when its controlling impulse is pushed too far. Initially, he represents as "natural" the sexual hierarchy that operates on Rockbound. His liberal humanism lapses into conservatism as he salutes women who fulfill their conventional role as helpmates: "Rockbound women study how to be of use to their husbands. They work, for there is no-one to hire to do the work that somehow is naturally expected of them and which seems right and proper to themselves. They rear their children, tend their houses, milk cows, feed chickens, hoe the gardens, help with the hay, and when necessary give a hand in the fish house ... As in all conditions of life, where men daily face death and danger, the women occupy a secondary position and subordinate themselves to the men" (R, 95–6). Similarly, Mary – who is "the acme of wisdom and beauty" (R, 164) – happily accepts a masculinist definition of her role and believes that "perhaps nothing in life was finer than to bear children to some of these great-limbed fishermen" (R, 207). Yet if the text constructs a narrow, subservient role for women, it does not condone those times when repressive systems of patriarchy are revealed to be openly tyrannical.

The clearest indictment of patriarchal power occurs when Mary must suppress her own desire and judgement and marry Casper Jung, whom she rightly believes to be "artificial," "hollow and insincere" (R, 207). Mary is overwhelmed by the commands that issue not only from her father, but also from the women of Rockbound who have been interpellated into the hierarchical system. Anapest Kraus is the powerful "empress of the Krauses" who resists Uriah's power and would seem to be a natural ally for Mary. She is willing to suspend clan rivalries to show compassion for David and Ralph, and she fights for the right to vote in favour of the school; but she is unwilling to subvert some island traditions. When faced with Mary's desire to defy her father, Anapest recognizes her own investment in the hierarchical system and advises submission: "Anapest gave this advice thinking of the necessity of retaining a guiding hand in the affairs of her own empire. Like the absolute monarch, she was fearful of the establishment of a republic on the fringe of her kingdom" (R, 236). The narrator clearly links Anapest's warning not to "go agin yur fader's will" with her desire to preserve the patriarchal power structure that supports her own position (R, 236). As the Day criticizes Anapest for her shortsighted advice, he also implicitly critiques those aspects of the patriarchal system that generate the matron's reply.

When Mary's "resistance [is] broken and under cumulative pressure she consent[s] to marry Casper," the novel's dissatisfaction with the distorted aspects of patriarchy becomes apparent. However, Day's faith in the figure of the individual as it is constructed within a masculine power structure is not seriously challenged. Mary might not have married Casper if David – her source of strength and guidance – had not been trapped on Barren Island. Moreover, Mary does not liberate herself; rather she must surrender to her father and passively wait to be rescued by Gershom, who is driven by a primal desire to avenge the trick that robbed him of his bride. The power of the masculine subject is reaffirmed even when the aspects of the patriarchy are questioned.

Day fuses his desire to conserve with his celebration of the individual – he weaves together his conservative defence of tradition and his vision of the lone, heroic figure – and thus he maintains a confident and optimistic tone so long as the text remains within the discourse of the romance. The symmetry of this idealistic romance is threatened for a time, however, by a troubling, realist undercurrent of despair and isolation that surrounds David in the second half of the novel.

While Gershom, Mary, and Uriah are created to fulfill their functions as romantic champion, heroine, and villain, David is constructed within the conventions of both romance and realism. The text, which strives to depict the traditional Nova Scotian folkways, distils many of the cultural disruptions associated with modernism in the complex character of David. Though Day attempts to contain the influence of modernism by setting the text in the prewar era, his postwar experiences and anxieties cannot be silenced.

David Jung is the text's only historicized figure. The opening chapter records the hardships of his youth and provides a historical context for his behaviours – a specific matrix of cause and effect through which his character can be understood. Beaten by his stepfather and abandoned after his mother dies of consumption, David is taken in by Jennie, the "unofficial harlot" of Outpost, and spends five years learning a "great deal about drunkenness and lust" (R, 18–9). Associated with the forces of change and transformation, David shifts the age-old customs of Rockbound. He rejects old ritual superstitions declaring "I ain't skeered o' no haunts" (R, 12), and he is the first Jung to own "a stout fast clipper equipped with a gasoline engine" (R, 82). In the first half of the novel the narrator records David's inner emotions and frequently mentions his "lightness of heart," but following Tamar's death he is increasingly isolated from the local community and becomes "heartily sick of Rockbound" (R, 148). David's sense of alienation deepens as local traditions prevent him from courting Mary, and near-suicidal despair sets in as he looks ahead to see a future void of romantic possibilities: "the tiresome procession of years that stretched before him offered endless labour but no striving for a goal that seemed worthy of attainment. For a moment he stood struggling with the temptation to throw himself over the cliff into the dog hole and let ice and sea batter him to pieces." (R, 170).

As a character embedded in a local time and place, it is logical that David should be the primary focalizer of the wreck of the *Sylvia Westner*, the "high line of all the Liscomb fleet" (R, 174). Relying on articles from *The Halifax Herald*, the *Halifax Morning Chronicle*, and the *Yarmouth Telegram*, Day fashioned his account of the *Sylvia Westner* from the actual destruction of two storm-struck Lunenburg ships that sank off the coast of Sable Island on 9 August 1926 (Davies 1989, 302). In Day's version, Johnny Westner is a "young skipper" who represents the traditional fishing culture, but his traditionalism is part of his downfall. Without a "wireless to warn him of the approaching storms," "Hand-line Johnny" continues to fish through the early warning signals of a hurricane, only to have his vessel and crew destroyed on a hidden reef (R, 192, 196). The loss of the *Sylvia Westner* signals the decline of the conventional fisheries, and the cultural alienation produced by this transformation is related through the figure of David, who is washed ashore with "his right hand black and cruelly swollen" (R, 201).

Following the loss of the *Sylvia Westner*, the text's commitment to the idea that a free and independent individual should be able to exist within a stable community is thrown into question by David's apparently inescapable despair. Threatening and disruptive, David's internal conflicts are contained only through a series of narrative shifts and sudden reversals that move him into the background. In chapter 10, Day removes David from his role as a central focalizer and places him on the margins as a mere observer of Mary and Gershom's relationship; his role in their tragic love story is simply that of "unheeded prompter, [and] mute and disregarded spectator" (R, 209); for sixty pages, David hardly appears in the novel.

Day's discomfort with representations of modernist despair is apparent even in the early drafts of the novel that are lodged at Dalhousie University Archives. In an early version of *Rockbound*, entitled *The Devil in the Sea*, David is not even an observer of Gershom's agony on Barren Island (MS2, 288, E4h, p. 133). When Day sent a copy of the manuscript to Doubleday in 1927, Nella Broddy remarked on the sudden disappearance of the hero and noted that while "all that about Gershom is necessary and fundamental," it is not "closely woven into David's life ... and a little careful rearrangement might, without altering them, make these incidents seem part of David's life" (MS2, 288, C60). Day seems to have accepted Broddy's advice and subsequently placed David on the edge of Gershom's revenge plot, but his discomfort with David's despair did not diminish. Once David has cooled his heels on the sidelines for a period of time, he is reintroduced as a figure whose disruptive qualities have been miraculously purged. He reappears as a purely formulaic romantic hero.

David's late transformation into an ahistorical romantic figure is immediately made evident in chapter thirteen by the narrator's lack of interest in his internal life. The narration, which once regularly reported on David's "heart," suddenly represents him only through external and physical cues. When Gershom is buried the narrator signals David's sorrow only by noting that he "stood bareheaded beside [the] grave" (R, 279). His transformation into an archetypal hero – a new Adam – is complete when he takes the symbolically rich position as the region's lightkeeper, moves to Barren Island, and then transforms the wasteland into an Eden; a paradise with "hayfields, [a] pasture lot, and [a] kitchen garden" (R, 285–9). David is given the task of renaming his land "Gershom's Island," and with his kingdom intact he weds Mary, his other/self. The confident and restored David who reenters the garden at the end of the text is a world apart from the earlier, alienated version of David who had provided Day with the means of exploring some of the implications of the cultural shifts of the early twentieth century. The new David/Adam signals the text's final conservationist retreat from the challenging narratives of history towards the secure narratives of myth.

Day's *Rockbound* is characterized by its multiple ideological perspectives. It blends its conservative and conservationist impulse with its celebration of a liberal ideology, echoes modernist anxieties in the realist portrayal of David, and thus emerges as a complex narrative. The partial integration of the conventions of romance and realism help Day avoid a stereotypical romance plot, while allowing him the opportunity to explore contemporary experiences of instability and disruption, before returning to celebrate the restoration of a stable traditional world. The tensions produced by the introduction of realist elements make *Rockbound* more sophisticated than some of Day's unpublished formulaic novels, and before the novel concludes Day manages to weave together a surprising diverse blend of ideological and cultural assumptions. However, his decision to introduce and then completely silence some of his modernist anxieties produces a novel that does not generate the sustained ideological tensions that characterize the later Maritime texts of such writers as Hugh MacLennan and Thomas H. Raddall.

HUGH MACLENNAN: MYTH AND REALISM

Few writers from the Maritimes have attracted the kind of sustained, national critical attention given to Hugh MacLennan. Born in Glace Bay, Cape Breton, MacLennan once "half facetiously" summed himself up as "a Scotsman, a Presbyterian and a Nova Scotian," but in this brief résumé he neglected to note that he was also a Rhodes scholar, a classicist with a doctorate from Princeton, a Guggenheim fellow, and, in his adopted home of Montreal, a respected teacher at both Lower Canada College and McGill University (Buitenhuis 1969, 9). Acknowledged as a pioneer of the modern Canadian novel, celebrated as an essayist, and remembered by many as a mentor, the numerous awards and honours bestowed on MacLennan attest to his place as one of the most important writers to emerge in the decades following the Second World War. MacLennan's many accolades include the Lorne Pierce Medal for Literature and five Governor-General Awards for fiction and nonfiction. He was elected to the Royal Society of Canada and made a Companion of the Order of

Canada in 1967. Though he is no longer widely read, MacLennan's work has recently been reassessed, and his place in the canon of Canadian literature has been both reevaluated and confirmed. Yet while much has been written about MacLennan's role as the first "literary nationalist" and "spokesperson for Canadian society," less has been said about the ways in which his Maritime novels, and particularly his first novel *Barometer Rising*, reproduce the region's ideological and cultural tensions (MacLulich 1983, 1).

Several of MacLennan's novels are set in the Maritimes, and *Each Man's Son* in particular is often cited as MacLennan's strongest East Coast text. Given the wealth of critical attention already directed towards to *Each Man's Son*, I will only be referring to the later novel on occasion and will devote most of my analysis to the first novel, in which MacLennan sets out his central ideological struggles.

MacLennan's sometimes complex, sometimes uneven fictions resist easy categorization. Certainly in his early novels MacLennan employs a wide variety of literary forms and constructs a number of ideological positions. Roger Hyman argued that "MacLennan is writing basically realistic fictions" (1975, 515), and when *Barometer Rising* was first published it was greeted as a realist tour de force. MacLennan's realist technique is evident in his first novel, as he records the period that both precedes and immediately follows the devastating explosion of the *Mont Blanc* on 6 December 1917 and chronicles the life of the city of Halifax in the almost photographic detail. One of the first novels to be set in an identifiably Canadian urban centre, it employs a style reminiscent of the "literature of protest" that was prominent in the 1930s, as it provides itemized descriptions of the city streets and slums: "He glanced through the dirty window of a cheap restaurant, saw the interior was empty and went in through the double doors. There was a counter and a man in a soiled apron behind it, a few table and chairs, and a smell of mustard" (*BR*, 1). Critics have long noted that in *Barometer Rising* the city of Halifax itself emerges as a central character.

MacLennan's descriptive passages owe much to the traditions of realism, but when he then turns to explore the characters who are caught in the grip of fate and attempts to chronicle their actions, the structural elements begin to replicate the patterns of romance. As George Woodcock noted, MacLennan's narratives reproduce the mythic quest of Odysseus, and thus "the general plot of the novel belongs to the more romantic verge of social realism" as MacLennan traces the efforts of Neil Macrae to return to his home city, his family, and his real identity (1989 54). These assertions are echoed by Helen Hoy, who notes that MacLennan employs a "formulaic plot, though in the service of social realism and modified in significant ways" (Hoy 1990, 170).

MacLennan's multifaceted texts have not always been viewed patiently by readers or critics. Some have argued that MacLennan's uneven incorporation of different formal traditions is a mark of his inexperience as a novelist and a result of his refusal to incorporate the technical innovations of twentieth-century modernism. In this vein, Laurel Boone's critique of *Each Man's Son* could be applied to *Barometer Rising*: it "is too strongly romantic to be what the author intended, a true-to-life account of real [people] in real situations. Yet it contains such vividly realistic episodes and characters that its romance capabilities are undermined" (1980, 155).

If MacLennan ranges freely through a series of narrative forms, his political vision is no less eclectic. George Woodcock has argued that MacLennan defends an ideological territory that moves towards the right: "in some ways MacLennan seems the epitome of the conservative mind" (Woodcock 1969, 29). In contrast, William New examines *Barometer Rising* and maintains that the character of "Angus Murray … exists … as a reservoir of liberal thought" (1967, 303); an observation about MacLennan's moderate political views that is echoed by Cameron's assertion that the writer never wavered "far from the centre" (1994, 31). To round out this picture, a few writers like Robin Mathews have looked back to MacLennan's time as a student in the 1930s – when he was attracted to the politics of the left – and suggested that *Barometer Rising* is his most class-conscious novel. Key characters and elements in MacLennan's first published novel reproduce, in part, each of these political positions.

MacLennan employs a number of different literary forms, and he speaks from a series of different political positions, but there is, nonetheless, a clear pattern in his early fiction. MacLennan's many shifts between realist and romance discourses function as indicators of the ideological and cultural tensions of the text and of his time. When MacLennan is completely confident and clear about the position he is constructing, as is usually the case when he is reproducing a conservative perspective, the romance genre emerges as the dominant mode. This tendency is most evident in MacLennan's almost seamlessly romantic depiction of subordinate women, gigantic helpers, and one-dimensional villains in *Barometer Rising*. In contrast when complicated and uncertain ideological positions are advocated – as when the role of the alienated individual is considered, or when complex concepts, like regional or national identity, are explored – the text disrupts the romance model and adopts a more realist mode. Such is the case when MacLennan constructs such figures as Neil

Macrae, Roddie Wain, and Angus Murray. This analysis will begin with an exploration of MacLennan's use of romance traditions.

Characters in a romance rarely move beyond their prescribed function as hero, helpless damsel, villain, helper, or opponent, and many of MacLennan's characters fulfill these carefully delineated roles. Certainly, characters like Penny Wain remain within the narrow confines of the distressed damsel defined by the assumptions of a patriarchal perspective. Penny initially appears to be a rather nonconformist woman for her time. She is an innovative ship designer who is so much "better than her male colleagues" that her designs are eventually adopted by the British Admiralty (*BR*, 11). Helen Hoy goes so far as to claim that "Penelope is established as a New Woman" who works in a "male profession ... and bears a child outside marriage" (171). But if Penny seems like a proto-feminist in the opening pages her independence is quickly and systematically curtailed. She is adept at calculation and is able to manage the "pedestrian details" of her job (*BR*, 20), but "Penny's apparent role as a feminist rebel is ... undercut, [when] it turns out that the revolutionary design is really based on an idea casually mentioned by Neil" (MacLulich 1983, 35). Though she is well educated and articulate, the most memorable event of her life is her single sexual encounter with Neil: the evening when she silently effaces herself with the phrase, "Into thy hands I commend my spirit" (*BR*, 106). After the explosion lays waste to the urban landscape and the men are called to perform heroic feats, she must be rescued by Neil Macrae, operated on by Angus Murray, and then remains quiet and demure while she wonders whether she "look[s] awful" (*BR*, 172). MacLennan's heroine is modelled after the passive wife of Odysseus, whose defining trait is the ability to wait for her wandering mate: she is "a mirror ... of passive femininity to Neil's active, phallic, rising wind" (Leahy 1994, 159). The unselfconscious quality of these characterizations suggests that MacLennan is not working hard to enforce his patriarchal perspective. Indeed, he simply seems to be replicating the dominant gender assumptions of his society as a matter of course.

Penny is significant ideologically, not simply as a conventional representation of the feminine, but also as an emblem of a conservative vision of the individual's relationship to the world. Conservatives emphasize the importance of social order and stress collectivist models whether they be located in the family unit, the local village, or the nation as a whole (Cantor 1988, 279). The secure identity of the individual is important, but individuality itself is not valued unconditionally within a system that emphasizes the transhistorical and universal "character of humanity." Conservatism is thus more likely to assert that the stability, continuity, and collective welfare of the community itself is the primary goal and that the individual must recognize and submit to their role in the larger social structure. Penny not only reinforces a traditional vision of the feminine, she is also celebrated for her decision to tie herself to the established model of the community and replicate its values. The ending is happy, not simply because she waits to be reunited with her soulmate, but because she already has a daughter and a place in a pastoral setting within which the returning soldier can make a home. After years of steeling herself against her lonely condition to the point that her "want of normal things became … chronic," Penny is hesitant to make herself vulnerable to her newly returned lover, but we are not to have any doubts that she will be happier within her family unit, than she was as a single working woman (BR, 145). By reintegrating Neil into the larger community, she validates one of the dominant political visions of the text.

The text's solidly patriarchal position is reinforced by other minor characters. Mary Fraser is able to live in "moderate defiance" of tradition, but, given her role as a nurturing, sacrificial, and patient mother, it is hard to determine how her defiant identity differs from that of a compliant female (BR, 23). Maria Wain appears as a stereotypical shrew who is cast in a negative light, so long as she is domineering and demanding; she seems softened only in the aftermath of the explosion, when she must submit herself to Murray's commands in order to create an efficient emergency hospital.

"Big Alec" MacKenzie functions as a helper to the main protagonist and is the second significant character who is shaped within the tradition of the romance in order to defend the text's conservative perspective. "Tied both to the sea and the land, governed by the natural rhythms of the earth," and appearing as a giant helper in the traditional quest narrative, MacKenzie – including his memory of Wain's flawed battlefield orders – is the key to Neil Macrae's defence against charges of cowardice and dereliction of duty (Arnason 1972, 69). This towering man "is honest and noble"; he does not hesitate to sacrifice his own interests, as well as the financial security of his family, in order to ensure that the truth is made known to the larger community. Neil knows that he can depend on the worker's "clannishness to compel him to speak" (BR, 131).

Alec MacKenzie reflects a traditional perspective as he upholds the values of his community, but he also embodies a conservative position in a more subtle way. Alec embodies the best of the Gaelic culture of Cape Breton and "effectively defuses Neil's radicalism" (Kulyk Keefer 1987, 141). With this helpful giant, MacLennan constructs an idealized folk character who has much in common with the other cultural productions of the early twentieth century, which viewed the folk as innocent and idyllic. Like Angus Murray's father, and John Macrae before him, Alec represents a powerful tradition that lends to the region a sense of identity conveniently free of obvious political baggage. MacKenzie is celebrated neither as a working-class hero nor a spokesperson for the exploited dockworkers from whose labour Wain extracts a profit. By depicting Alec as a simple man from a quaint culture, MacLennan is able to sidestep political issues of class, which might undermine his conservative assertion that the community is an entity worth restoring and regenerating (McKay, 221). Pious and hard-working, Alec represents the best of the folk while simultaneously reminding the reader that this race is slowly disappearing. Alec clears Neil's name, but he is then extinguished by the explosion: the militaristic and modernist catastrophe overwhelms his "Sampson"-like strength (BR, 162). His extinction functions as a clear moment of ideological closure: MacLennan again reinforces his conservative perspective, warns his fellow citizens about the dangers of rapid change, and stresses the importance of traditional, communal values.

Just as Penny and Alec are modelled after the damsel and helper of the quest romance, so Colonel Geoffrey Wain fits the mold of the stereotypical villain. Wain is not – as Forster would say – a rounded character. Compared to the other major characters, virtually no information about his life as a child or his struggles as a youth is provided, and he is only rarely used as focalizer. MacLennan is not interested in accounting for his evil nature, he simply wants to ensure that we react against him. Wain is uniformly despicable. He is a distant and remote father, a harshly demanding boss, a dangerously incompetent military officer, and a sadistically cruel lover. When Wain asks Angus Murray to join him in his library to sample a port that is "almost an Amontillado," the story nods to Poe's famous short story "The Cask of Amontillado" and the villainous murderer Montressor.

Wain is a flat, one-dimensional character, whose very name signals that he and his values are in decline, but MacLennan is a skillful writer, and he uses his antagonist to convey his ideals at several different levels within the text. Within this moral discourse of the novel Wain's self-centered behaviour amounts to a representation of humanity's sinful tendencies. Wary of excessive individualism, MacLennan warns the reader to turn from Wain's selfish ways.[4] While numerous characters are killed by the explosion, including the idealized Jim and Mary Fraser, only Wain's body is found in an embarrassing and ignoble setting, and thus we leave the novel with the satisfaction that the character's moral lapses were publically recognized after his death, if not during his lifetime. Wain is also a significant figure in the historical discourse of the novel. Attempting to depict the fullness of Nova Scotia's encounters with the modern age, MacLennan details the demise of the traditional industries, including the collapse of the inshore fisheries. Wain and his forefathers, as representatives of the big merchant wholesalers, underpaid the fisherman and are blamed for contributing to the chronic and miserable poverty of the small fisherman: "Few fisherman in Nova Scotia made any money because they could not easily market their catches, and prices paid by wholesalers like himself were infinitesimal" (BR, 69). Wain recognizes his complicity in the suffering of his fellow human beings and his role in prompting social change, but he refuses to modify his behaviour. Wain's excessive selfishness advance's the conservative notion evident in Penny's and Alec's experiences, that the individual should be willing to make some sacrifices for the general good.

But if Wain's actions reinforce conservative ideals, his character also confirms that this perspective must operate within carefully defined limits. MacLennan is not as conservative as Thomas Raddall, for he does not celebrate the notion that communities should structure themselves as economically hierarchical systems.[5] One of Wain's most offensive qualities is his colonialist/imperialist mentality, as exemplified by his promotion of the outmoded British class system. Certain that "everything in this damn country is second rate" (BR, 101), he is confident that the postwar world will be ruled by a military society that he is eager to join. His political agenda borders on fascism and is viewed by the narrator as akin to madness. Similarly, in the first chapter, Wain asserts, "I don't believe the ordinary man is capable of real courage" (BR, 29). Given that the novel was published in the early years of the Second World War, MacLennan could be sure that his readers would resist Wain's elitist remarks with all the energy that could be mustered by a public well-fueled on war propaganda. Wain is condemned for his "anachronistic, colonial attitude to Canada" (New 1967, 309), and thus the character establishes the limits of the conservative elements of the text while promoting a postcolonial, nationalist perspective. Wain's own fate is summarized nicely by the changes that affect his house. Initially described as being "solid British colonial," "neither gracious nor beautiful," it is transformed after the explosion into a makeshift hospital that serves the wounded of all classes, until it is finally abandoned emotionally by Penny who longs to make her new home elsewhere (BR, 214). Though Geoffrey Wain is clearly drawn as a one-dimensional character, he serves a number of different functions within the text.

Neil Macrae, Roddie Wain, and Angus Murray do not fit as easily into the romance patterns and conservative ideology reproduced by the other main characters. MacLennan employed romance motifs to articulate an ideological position with which he was obviously comfortable, but as he turned to explore other more troubling experiences of the twentieth century, particularly the emergence of the alienated individual, he tended to disrupt the romance structure and draw from more realist conventions.

Early critics argued that Neil Macrae, the novel's central protagonist, is essentially a wanderer, a romantic Odyssean figure who is longing to complete his arduous journey, return to his home, and "move towards dignity, love and responsibility" (O'Donnell 1968, 13). While the text certainly echoes aspects of this general pattern, the character of Neil Macrae is more complex than these early explorations suggest. David Arnason develops a more convincing analysis when he argues that Neil is given two distinct personalities and that his behaviours before and after the explosion cannot be connected. This position helps illuminate the ways in which MacLennan has used particular realist elements to develop a less uniformly conservative perspective.

When Neil appears in the novel's opening chapter, he is a figure embedded in realist conventions: an impoverished, nervous man who carries "himself without confidence" (*BR*, 3). Less like Odysseus than Sisyphus, he has been deeply traumatized by his experiences in the war. Forced to lead his men into a disastrous battle, falsely accused of insubordination, and then persecuted, shelled, and wounded, Neil has lived in exile as an anonymous and lost soul on the edge of despair. Bereft of the features typically expected in a romantic lead, he becomes the exhausted embodiment of the modern era and represents MacLennan's anxieties about the impact of the contemporary militarized and industrialized society has on the single individual: "To continue like this indefinitely would turn him into a ghastly, groping automaton who would ultimately accept an invalid psychosis as a substitute for real life. Another two years of it would finish even the courage necessary for suicide" (*BR*, 93). His attempt to reestablish the identity he had been forced to abandon after escaping from military arrest suggests that the text recognizes the liberal assertion that individual freedom and personality are primary concerns. Operating apart from the conservative values developed through Penny, Alec, and Wain, Neil is cast in a positive light as he attempts to disrupt and even destroy aspects of the conventional society in order to reclaim his sense of self. His struggle to resist the oppressive military and class systems and his determination to rediscover his own sense of identity make him sensitive to the plight of other disadvantaged members of his society. He occasionally becomes the mouthpiece for some of MacLennan's lingering leftist ideals, as he wanders through the North End Slums of Halifax and comments at length about the injustice that these "houses like cracker boxes standing in rows on a shelf" should exist is a city that is "backed by millions of acres of space"(BR, 88). His assertion of his independence deepens as he rejects the notion that he is guided by providence, or fate, and with a very unromantic flare, ascribes instead to the notion that "chance and preposterous accident had complete control of a man's life" (BR, 134).

MacLennan admires his protagonist's independence in the first half of the novel, but Neil's isolation becomes a problem when he is unable to reconnect with his former community. As Neil is increasingly haunted by a sense of existential anxiety, MacLennan's interest in Macrae's project to become an independent individual falters, and he becomes uncomfortable with the instability of his hero. Regardless of his interest in liberty, Neil must eventually complete his emotional return to Halifax and MacLennan has little choice but to dramatically rework his personality. His first tactic for dealing with his rogue wanderer is to distance him from the reader, in much the same way as Day moves David to the margins of his text. While we hear much about Neil's activities immediately following the explosion, all of that information comes to us through the observations of other characters. The narrator does not use Macrae as a focalizer for a full quarter of the text, between late Wednesday night and midnight on Friday. When Neil is discussed by other characters or represented by an external narrator who retains a documentary distance, he is, surprisingly, a transformed man who has suddenly overcome his ennui to coordinate rescue operations in the devastated sections of the city. Struggling to find a place for his protagonist, MacLennan turns him first into a rescuer and then into a heroic spokesperson for a hyperbolic form of nationalism. Neil's assertions that Canada would someday emerge as "the central arch which united the new order" would seem appropriate to MacLennan's audience in 1941, but his declarations are not as subtle as Murray's and they are awkwardly pronounced during a romantic encounter with Penny (BR, 218). Neil's nationalism and sudden confidence allow him to step rhetorically into a heroic role, but his celebration of Canada seems artificial and forced, and the novel has clearly had to sacrifice its exploration of his modernist anxiety in order to produce a sense of narrative closure. Neil's nationalist pronouncements are completely untainted by the earlier fears about the modern industrial world; any hesitations that one might expect from a Maritime writer who has watched his province pass through two decades of debilitating poverty are not represented (*BR*, 208). The reader is simply expected to believe that together the Maritimes and the nation will weather the storm. But if MacLennan reshapes his main hero to ensure that ideological anxiety is replaced by nationalism, he intervenes less dramatically with his other "realist" male characters, Roddie Wain and Angus Murray.

At first sight Roddie Wain seems to follow the same pattern of crisis and restoration that characterizes his elders, and he thus functions as a youthful emblem of the country itself. Penny's twelve-year-old brother is energetic, though not wholly innocent, for his naiveté has fallen prey to the corrupting assumptions of British imperialism. Dressed in a "stud and tie ... [and an] Eton collar," the young boy has absorbed and accepted the patriotic jingoism of his war-obsessed society, and his inner life – moral and emotional – has been sadly neglected (*BR*, 21). The explosion abruptly refines Roddie's character and awakens him from his vicarious bloodlust. When he learns that his aunt and uncle have been killed, he fully understands the impact of the explosion on his human community: "Roddie blundered down the steps ... He liked his uncle and was fond of his Aunt Mary" (*BR*, 187). Though he is initially startled to realize that the modern society is disorienting – that there is an "abrupt and ruthless impingement of the unseen and the incalculable into his own life" (*BR*, 187) – this sense of disorientation lessens as he accepts Murray's liberal vision of history's progressive movement:

> "How long before things are going to be like they used to be?"
> Murray smiled gently and shook his head. "We'd better not worry about things like that, do you think? After all who'd like things to stay the same, for ever?"
> "I never thought of that," Roddie said. (*BR*, 191)

Roddie has been tempered but not scarred by his encounters with death, and his last appearance suggests that he, like the youthful nation itself, can look forward to the future with a tentative optimism. The problem, of course, is that this moment of nationalism within Roddie's world rests on a carefully constructed silence within the text itself.

The novel is able to use Roddie to reinforce Neil's affirmative pronouncements only by underrepresenting his relationship with his father. Loved and scolded in turn by his sister, Roddie has almost no direct contact with his father, Geoffrey Wain. In part, the father's absence is a typical feature in any fiction by MacLennan, whose own relationship with his coldly puritanical and rigid father has been well documented by biographers (MacLulich 1983, 15). But Roddie's disconnection from Colonel Wain is also a necessary textual strategy if he is to be constructed as a child capable of reform and redemption. In order for Roddie to fulfill his function in the narrative and echo the novel's recreation of romantic heroes and its larger ideology of national restoration, he must be distanced from the contaminating presence of his corrupt father and then protected from truly horrific or threatening experiences. The text shows this child's encounters with death as instrumental to his development and excludes any account of his discovery that his father has been killed. The moment Roddie accepts Murray's reading of the future – at which point he has only learned about his aunt and uncle's death – he is dropped from the novel. MacLennan is unable or unwilling to represent the child's deepest familial loss and still find a way to maintain his affirmative tone. The romance structure is thus developed only by silencing the issue and turning to Penny and Neil's voyage to reunite with their daughter Jean. *Barometer Rising* closes with the image of a family united by death, rather than disrupted by death. This interesting silence becomes a marker signalling that MacLennan's affirmative tone is not confidently constructed. The celebration of national strength that helped establish MacLennan's reputation as a truly Canadian writer, also carries a distinctly Maritime anxiety about the modern age.

Finally, this distinctly Maritime anxiety is also evident in Angus Murray, the novel's most complex character. Dogged by a tragic past, haunted by his memories of war, longing to reintegrate into his community, but skeptical about his future, Murray's character synthesizes the central and sometimes competing tensions of the text. Though David Staines has argued that MacLennan's first three novels are concerned with nationalist themes, while later fictions such as *Each Man's Son* and *The Watch that Ends the Night* are primarily "character novels," MacLennan demonstrates with Angus Murray that even in the early fiction he is capable of developing ambiguous and effective studies of the human condition (Staines 1978, 138). Murray is clearly fashioned within the realist tradition. In the course of the novel, through a series of flashbacks, his rural childhood, his education, his tragic first marriage, and his service in the military are all reviewed. This carefully constructed background allows the reader to interpret his actions as internally motivated behaviours, rather than actions demanded by a textual formula. While wise older physicians like Murray appear in a number of MacLennan's novels, Murray himself is not a romance character, and his distance from the text's mythic structure gives MacLennan a bit of room in which to work.

In some ways, Angus Murray echoes traits evident in Neil Macrae, though he is a less extreme portrayal of modern man. Like Neil, Murray focuses the reader's attention on the problem of establishing a sense of identity: as an older professional man he brings to this task a higher degree of self-consciousness. In a validation of the liberal search for a stable subject position, Murray awakens on the morning of the explosion to honestly take stock of himself: "he was seeing everything very clearly, seeing himself and his world without benefit of intoxication or self-pity, and for the first time in many years a vision of the truth failed to make him afraid" (BR, 142). While Neil needs the chaos of the explosion to help him transcend his sense of ennui, Murray has centered his life on more private and aesthetic concerns before the ships collide: "the beauty of the world remained and he found himself able to enjoy it" (BR, 143). Yet for all his attention to his self-identity Murray also, eventually, turns outward to address the needs and demands of the community. He overcomes his own self-doubt in order to perform "eleven operations without assistance and do the dressings for nearly fifty more" (BR, 205). In the midst of the destruction and death following the explosion, Murray reflects, in a tone that reproduces the conservative spirit that drives Penny, that the individual can find meaning and security only by connecting him or herself to the larger society: "He was still capable of being moved by the sight of a whole community standing about the grave of someone who had been a part of the lives of them all" (BR, 207). Murray is so carefully crafted a character that he is able to emerge as a centrist figure who blends conservative and liberal values depending on which scene he is in.

Just as MacLennan can use realism to reproduce a complex ideological position, so he uses Murray's fully realized personality to make him a strong representative of the Maritime sensibility itself. "Born in a farmhouse in Cape Breton," Murray has clear memories of his father's subsistence farm, and he pays tribute to his father's efforts to secure a good life for his children (BR, 31, 207). Murray's sense of nostalgia is strengthened by his memory of his own wife, who died when they were just a young couple; this sense of loss shadows him through much of this text. Murray's longing for an idealized past is combined with his sense of hesitation and skepticism about the future. Wounded in the war and unsure that he has the stamina to return to a medical career, Murray is uncertain, but he is not silenced or sidelined like David Yung or Neil Macrae. Instead, MacLennan uses him to explore the general uneasiness of the modern condition. Indeed, Murray does not even achieve a conventionally happy ending. He manages to regain his confidence as a surgeon, but he remains a lonely figure who recognizes that even if Neil had not returned, he would not have been able to sustain a satisfying relationship with

Penny. While Neil's nationalist pronouncements sound forced, Murray makes similarly exaggerated claims that Canada will become "the keystone to hold the world together" only to immediately "dismiss these ideas as too artificial to entertain seriously" (*BR*, 208). Throughout the text, Murray exhibits the traits that can be recognized as characteristically Maritime, and in the closing pages MacLennan makes his regionalist personality explicitly clear. Murray reflects on the various characters and notes that while Alec was a "primitive" "anachronism," and while Penny and Neil are destined to be urbane cosmopolitans, he remains "caught somewhere between the two extremes, intellectually gripped by the new and emotionally held by the old, too restless to remain at peace on the land and too contemptuous of bourgeois values to feel at ease in the city" (*BR*, 208). Murray embodies the central cultural tensions of the Maritimes.

After publishing *Barometer Rising*, MacLennan anchored his next two texts in recognizably Canadian locales and become a teller of national tales set in Québec and Ontario. He consciously chose to look beyond regional boundaries and to examine the larger issues of the country. But the mantle of "national myth maker" did not sit easily on his shoulders, and the absence of a western novel, the recurrence of Gaelic characters, and his constant tendency to reproduce the competing tensions of nostalgia and hesitation suggest that he may have remained a Maritime writer at heart. The most convincing character in MacLennan's *Barometer Rising* is forged within a regional, not a national, sensibility. And while such novels as *Two Solitudes*, *The Precipice*, and *Return of the Sphinx* echo the kind of intense nationalism espoused by Neil, they have been identified as being overly polemical in their politics and underdeveloped in their characterization. MacLennan's fictions might have been more complex and compelling if he had chosen instead to use Murray and his regional perspective as a template to guide his future work.

THOMAS RADDALL: REALISM, CONSERVATISM, AND ANXIETY

On 22 April 1921, at the age of seventeen, Thomas Raddall stepped ashore on Sable Island to begin a year-long assignment as one of three wireless operators. He did not pursue his career as a "brass pounder," but his experiences on the barren island – the sparse accommodations, the long eerie nights on duty, the explorations of the sand dunes, the misadventures while duck hunting and pony riding – were recorded in his diaries and later reshaped into the strikingly detailed island of Marina in *The Nymph and the Lamp*. Published in

1950, Raddall's fourth novel bears certain similarities to Day's *Rockbound*. Both blend the conventions of realism and romance and both focus on the experiences of island communities, which to varying degrees function as idealistic havens of traditionalism. However, Raddall's vision of the twentieth century is more problematic. Whereas Day and MacLennan are confident about the possibilities of familial regeneration, Raddall sometimes questions whether any human relationship can endure. While Day and MacLennan celebrate moments of individual integrity and freedom, Raddall explores the difficulties inherent in any attempt to create a stable self. When Raddall turns his pen to reproduce twentieth-century Nova Scotia, the tensions between the desire to return to traditional communal structures and the unavoidable sense of alienation in the modern world move directly into the foreground.

"Modernism" refers to a variety of literary aesthetic movements, as well as to a broad cultural zeitgeist. Raddall, MacLennan, and Day rejected the narrative innovations and experimental techniques developed by such writers as Joyce, Woolf, Faulkner, and Lawrence. However, all three Maritime writers lived under the shadow of the modernist sensibility as it emerged as a cultural phenomenon, a "spirit of the age." After the terrible destruction of the First World War, a deep sense of anxiety and doubt – which had its roots in the late nineteenth century – undermined men and women's faith in the central ideals of traditional society. Cut adrift from their conventional ideological positions, individuals in the modernist era experienced a powerful sense of loss and alienation as they encountered an increasingly urbanized and technological society (Cantor 1988, 36–40).

Thomas Head Raddall was born in 1903 in Hythe, England, and emigrated with his parents and two sisters to Halifax in 1913, where his father was a militia instructor before enlisting in the First World War. As a teenager, Raddall experienced two traumatic events that deeply affected his philosophic perspective (Young 1983, 1). The first occurred after the Halifax explosion of 6 December 1917, when he guided a "small group of soldiers" to the local school, where he remained for several hours as hundreds of bodies arrived and the building was converted into a temporary morgue. By the light of a lantern, the fourteen-year-old Raddall watched the "soldiers who carried ... the frozen bodies ... down the steps one by one and dropped them with a distinct 'flap' on the cement floor ... Soon another sloven came with a load of ... bodies, each gashed and bloody and there was the same flap on the floor" (Raddall 1976, 38). The second traumatic event occurred eight months later, when his father was killed in the battle of Amiens. In the wake of these two emotional blows, Raddall's childhood sense of security vanished; he recalls feeling the "stirrings of a doubt that grew as the years went by … [that] God remained invisible and aloof" (1976, 44). Raddall's reactions to the traumatic experiences of his youth are reproduced in the competing impulses that structure his novels, particularly *The Nymph and the Lamp*. On the one hand, Raddall's early experiences prompted a lifelong search for stability, which often took shape as a conservative desire to reconstruct and reinhabit the past. This conservatism becomes the strongest ideological force in his third novel. While the novel revives traditional social structures, it also recognizes that the modern condition of alienation and uncertainty is inescapable, and a sense of anxiety winds through the narrative eventually threatening the very stability it strives to attain.

As was noted earlier, conservatism reinforces the notion that the individual's identity must not take precedence over, indeed could never be maintained or stabilized apart from, the broader community and a wider social order. For the human character and our sense of tradition to be maintained, people ultimately must come together to form a hierarchical, patriarchal, cooperative unit for the society to function, and even if communities decay and need to be renewed, reformed, or even restructured, the guiding model is always communal (Horowitz 1966, 144). To ensure the solidity of the collective bond and the hierarchical order, Raddall's texts champion a strong sense of ethnic/national identity and insist upon the celebration of a core of cultural traditions. A strong faith in the practices of the past helps defend against immoderate change that might threaten the established structures. Cultural traditions are particularly effective if they are first naturalized so that they appear to be "common-sense," rather than ideologically constructed behaviours.

The conservative ideology that runs through Raddall's fiction is first evident in the forms and structures of his narratives. Often classified either as historical romances set in the eighteenth century – *His Majesty's Yankees* (1942), *Roger Sudden* (1944), *Pride's Fancy* (1946), *The Governor's Lady* (1960), and *Hangman's Beach* (1966) – or as contemporary realist fictions set after the First World War – *The Nymph and the Lamp* (1950), *Tidefall* (1953), and *The Wings of Night* (1956) – Raddall's novels all share a core romance plot structure that invariably represent the protagonist's return to hierarchical/patriarchal structures or traditional values. That Raddall never wrote a novel set in Nova Scotia's relatively stable and prosperous nineteenth century is not surprising. The more turbulent and disruptive eighteenth and twentieth centuries are more conducive to Raddall's recurring interest in protagonists who confront the chaos of their surroundings and embark on romantic quests for personal security and social stability. While his plots follow the formulaic pattern of "agon," "pathos," and "anagnorisis," Raddall also insists that his narratives operate in a clear linear fashion. His faith in rational, intellectual hierarchies is highlighted in his 1973 interview with John Sorfleet, when he notes four times in the course of two pages that his conclusions are "truly logical"(Sorfleet 1973, 53–4). Raddall does not indulge in the meta-lyptic flights into folklore that characterized Day's *Rockbound*, nor does he risk fragmenting the sequential timeline as Richards does in *Lives of Short Duration*. Instead, he relies on strong authoritative nar-rators to relay the story and constructs carefully defined representa-tions of the past, which he expects the reader to accept as true (Smyth 1991, 62). Kulyk Keefer notes that "objective truth appears to be, for him, an unproblematic concept ... there is not only 'one story', but also one true side to that story" (1987, 105).

The conservatism manifest in the formal elements of *The Nymph and the Lamp* is developed in more detail in the opening chapters through the character of Matthew Carney. Unlike Day, who happily switches to mythic and folkloric discourses to protect his ideological project, Raddall avoids overt nostalgia or simple escapism and coun-sels a return to a "plausible" traditional life. Initially, the narrator sur-rounds Carney with a romantic aura reminiscent of the mythic Gershom Born: he is "a giant with a yellow beard ... a latter day Rob-inson Crusoe ... a Cossack ... [and] a fearless boatman" (*NL*, 12). Car-ney is then quickly recast in a more realist framework, which undercuts these mythic attributions by noting that some were "false, some garbled, and some true" and that the rumours tended to origi-nate from unreliable "young, fresh-water radio operators" (*NL*, 12). By simultaneously invoking and questioning Carney's legendary stature, the narrator creates a focalizer who is admired for his devo-tion to his work as a sable island wireless operator while at the same time being a vulnerable figure who unobtrusively encourages readers to accept as natural his experience of confusion when faced with the chaotic city of Halifax: "they were all fast – going like mad ... was this 'progress'? He was bewildered" (*NL*, 16). From the opening pages, the text is aligned with his reliable conservative perspective, which reads the "traditional" as safe, comfortable, and inherently more valuable than the contemporary.

Throughout Carney's journey to Newfoundland to find his long-lost mother, the narrative continues to advocate for the comforting world of tradition, while downplaying sentimental nostalgia. Indeed, Carney must be purged of his sentimentality before he can recognize his proper role in the society of Marina. His attempt to recreate himself as "a prince out of a fairy tale" ends in failure with the discovery that the maternal icon of his dreams is "dead, thrust away and forgotten in some patch of soil amongst the rocks" (NL, 28). The text does not endorse the idealism inherent in the hope of a successful reunion, but neither is Carney doomed to isolation. Recognizing that he is a true orphan in the outside world, he retreats permanently to the communal and traditional life of Marina, "the only place where I feel at home," where "clothes don't mean much [and] money's nothing" (NL, 32). As Glenn Willmott notes, Carney escapes to his offshore island in the same way an antimodernist, cowboy hero flees from urban corruption by riding out on the range. His rejection of Halifax stands as a symbolic rejection of the "dandified, domesticated and superficial" aspects of the "mechanistic and commercialized mass culture" that threaten the traditional masculine order (Willmott 1998, 61–2). His retreat from postwar society seems eccentric at first, but even the skeptical Captain O'Dell eventually recognizes that when Carney's isolation on the island is linked to his restored marriage, a kind of paradise is created far from the troubled world.

Given Raddall's wide knowledge of Canadian and Maritime history, it would not be an accident that the captain who transports Carney and Isabel to their island paradise is named after the famous Maritime loyalist leader Jonathan O'Dell, nor would be a mere coincidence that they are transported on a ship named after Lord Elgin, the Governor General who implemented Lord Durham's recommendation that Lower and Upper Canada be granted a degree of self-control in the form of limited responsible government. These names, taken together, remind the reader that the two central protagonists are being transported to their haven by figures who embody the Canadian search for a unique, loyal, and stable form of independence.

In the first two chapters, Carney is a quiet and attractive hero who establishes a baseline conservatism, but he is not a figure Raddall can use to develop fully the text's analysis of "traditionalism" and "modernism." If Raddall is to avoid Day's final textual attempt to simply isolate his heroes and ignore the world, he must engage and examine the forces of modernism and then demonstrate the validity of traditional social structures. Not only does Carney not have the deep contact with postwar society that would allow him to produce such a detailed critique of the modern condition, but his role as a focalizer is sharply curtailed by the onset of his blindness. Though Carney discovers his sight is failing immediately after he leaves Newfoundland in chapter 3, this central fact of his inner experience is not revealed until chapter 35, in order to create the conditions of mystery necessary for Isabel's journey from despair to self-knowledge and for the audience's parallel journey from incomprehension to enlightenment. Carney's vacation in urban Canada and his withdrawal to Marina function as a prologue to and synopsis of Isabel's more elaborate quest for a stable, meaningful position in the social order. Isabel's quest produces interesting deviations and contradictions, which make the novel an ideologically sophisticated and aesthetically challenging exploration of conservatism.

In his interview with Sorfleet, Raddall recalls that when he finished *The Nymph and the Lamp* he knew it was "the best novel I've written … I knew I would never write anything as good as that again" (1973, 57). The success of the text is due in no small part to the complexity of the central character Isabel Jardine. While Day and MacLennan avoided dealing with the questions posed by David's despair and Macrae's alienation, Raddall develops a multifaceted character in Jardine as he traces the ways in which she reshapes the very structures of her psyche as she journeys towards her final conservative homeland. In his article "Life and the Way Out in Thomas Raddall's Visions," Bruce F. MacDonald notes that though Raddall claimed "he had no real knowledge of existentialism," he was "in tune with the spirit of the age," and certainly *The Nymph and the Lamp*'s "vision is existential to the extent that one makes one's existence with one's own effort" (1991, 168, 173). Jardine's attempts to define and reshape her subject position exemplifies Sartre's assertion that "man [sic] is nothing else but what he purposes, he exists only in so far as he realizes himself, he is therefore, nothing else but the sum of his actions … he is the sum, the organization, the set of relations that constitute these undertakings" (Sartre 1975, 358). In the beginning, Jardine is a blank space – a floating signifier – constantly attempting to define her self and her place. When Carney attempts to grace her with clothes and jewels she asserts, "I am not 'women' … I'm me. Don't ever forget that" (*NL*, 89). But her declaration "I'm me" has little power until she clarifies exactly what the assertion means. Unlike the stereotypical versions of femininity that populate Raddall's other texts, Isabel Jardine actively struggles against fragmented, and alienating modernist environments. She functions as a self-conscious, historicized, and articulate character who is aware of her attempts to verify her sense of self and able to evaluate her changing environments as she searches for happiness in Marina and Kingsbridge. Her romantic and existential quest for a stable identity becomes the text's central vehicle for its critique of modern society and its celebration of conservative, patriarchal *mythologies*.

Born in the country and left a virtual orphan like Carney, Miss Isabel Jardine is typical of the many rural inhabitants who migrated to urban centres in the hope of finding wealth and the opportunity to accomplish their "ambition." Initially a naive and untested figure, Jardine's isolated position is emphasized in the opening chapters by the persistent use of the title "Miss," which accentuates her status as a single woman. In the midst of her insecurities, Miss Jardine recognizes Halifax's deficiencies and becomes an effective focalizer who is able to unveil the vacuousness of the modern urban environment. Seeking the prosperous "garden of life" her name evokes, Miss Jardine is surprised by the material poverty and isolation of Halifax. She soon discovers she cannot afford the "smart clothes" and "theatres" she desires, but instead wears a "brown skirt ... too long to be fashionable" (NL, 18) and sits alone at her bedroom window longingly watching, across the courtyard, the card-playing sailors, who are "free and utterly sure of everything" (NL, 45). If the urban environment is bewildering for Carney, Miss Jardine finds its predatory capitalism harsh and inhumane. Her landlady, the arachnid Mrs Paradee, is a particularly impersonal, threatening figure who treats her lodgers as "a species of animal, not to be loved or hated but simply preyed upon" (NL, 65). Mrs Paradee's house is the very antithesis of the edenic paradise her name implies. With her "evil ... hard black eyes" (NL, 67), she is emblematic of the dislocation of the city against which Miss Jardine cannot mount an effective defence – from which she must simply flee in the hope of finding a setting more conducive to her search for her self.

Within the harsh urban environment, Jardine intensifies her own sense of alienation when she avoids her responsibility to become an active agent and internalizes superficial narratives of feminine passivity: particularly those that celebrate romantic love and domestic bliss. When she considers Carney's marriage proposal she does not contemplate her real future as the companion of a wireless operator and is captivated instead by a dream of domesticity as she pictures "a bungalow beside the Northwest Arm, and herself clipping flowers in the garden or busy at housewifery, at peace and secure at last" (NL, 74). Raddall critiques such early moments of self-delusion, not because he is skeptical about the patriarchal systems that structure her fantasies, but because her responses to these changes are too passive.

Miss Jardine takes the first step towards the realization of a stable identity only as she actively resists modernist agents of alienation and personally embraces the programs of the traditional patriarchal world. After being falsely accused of an immoral liaison with a fellow boarder, Miss Jardine follows her deep longing for the love Carney offers and takes her first step to a new level of self-awareness. Miss Jardine's attempt to become a more active and authentic individual is textually manifested as the narrative is increasingly focalized through the heroine's perspective and by the sudden use of her first name, Isabel. Raddall's conservative position is also strengthened, for Isabel's moments of self-perception and self-definition continue to be constructed within the text's patriarchal assumptions. Immediately after her first sexual encounter, Isabel is presented as being a more mature and introspective figure when she rereads her body not as an independent entity but rather as a mirror reflecting male desire. She feels the "satisfaction of a woman whose physical properties have passed the supreme test, the gratifying of a man" (NL, 80). Having started on her quest towards a stable existence, Isabel is able to escape from Halifax, to seek her "place" in the communities of Marina and Kingsbridge.

Isabel's move to Marina constitutes her next concrete step towards self-knowledge, but a stable identity is not constructed simply through a change in locale. For Carney and his fellow islanders, Marina provides each person with a secure identity embedded in years of island tradition. The women follow the customary roles of "wife" and "mother," and the men – when plagued by the desire for "something to do" – pursue such "primitive" activities as duck hunting (NL, 126), bone collecting (NL, 137), dangerous swims in the Atlantic (NL, 145), and the annual pony roundup (NL, 159; Matthews, viii). For Isabel, who is unsure of her identity as "wife," life on Marina soon instills a sense of anxiety even more acute than her feelings of dislocation in Halifax. Isabel is not only uncertain about her role as an island wife, her social status is uncertain because she and Carney do not have time to formally and legally marry before they flee to the island. Fearful that she has ruined Carney's sense of contentment, Isabel utters the partly romantic but also existential cry that she "long[s] to do something that matters" (NL, 171). The novel demonstrates that it is not enough simply to escape the trappings of modernist society. Without a complete "text" of her own surroundings – without the knowledge of Carney's impending blindness – she cannot integrate herself into the traditional community and find relief for her ennui.

Isabel adopts a number of different roles in an attempt to integrate and create an active life for herself. Her job as the station's cook and den mother soon loses its appeal, and though her decision to learn the code, "the language of modern technology," occupies her for a period, it does not provide her with a full and satisfying role (NL, 197). In her article "*The Nymph and the Lamp* and the Canadian Heroine of Consciousness," Helen Buss successfully interprets this passage as an instance of "cultural resistance," a moment in which Isabel suspends normal signifying practices to adopt a title that is legally not applicable

(1991, 53); but Isabel's ability to recreate herself within a new medium still ultimately proves unsatisfying. She feels exalted when she communicates with the shipping lanes, but her entrance into the male realm of wireless operators leads her to erase her name as she identifies herself as "C's wife," signalling that her essence is not secure (NL, 197). Eventually, she must move on to other means of rewriting her social position.

The meaninglessness of Isabel's existence on Marina is most apparent when she is trapped in the symbolic grave of "Old Number Two" with Skane and feels "the cold clutch of Marina itself, the evil sea-monster with its belly full of wrecks and dead men's bones and still unsatisfied" (NL, 207). Faced with death, she turns "instinctively" towards Greg Skane, but her passive reaction to him signals that their relationship will be an unfulfilling parody of romance: "She did not move. She lay ... with her face averted and eyes closed, the attitude of one wearied of struggle and submitting herself to the Fates" (NL, 209).

Isabel reaches a kind of dead end on Marina. Carney refuses to provide Isabel with the information that would allow her to fulfill her role as wife and companion, and the alternate narrative provided by Skane is worthless for a young woman attempting to escape the anxieties of modernism. Skane is without the malicious egotism that characterizes Anse Gordon in Bruce's Channel Shore, but he shares a similar perspective of postwar, cynical disillusionment that distances him from both Isabel and the readers. For Raddall, the "great war represents the end of romantic innocence and the beginning of harshly modern reality" (West 1977, 44), and no character whose perceptions are shaped by that period of destruction can succeed within a text that celebrates the importance of traditional structures. Skane is the third most important actant on Marina, yet the narrative is rarely focalized through his eyes. When he relates his wartime experiences as a wireless operator and recounts how he was adrift twelve days on the North Atlantic ocean, the narrator prevents the reader from fully sympathizing with his agony by noting that his history is told with a "sneer" and look of "utter disdain" (NL, 179). Isolated from Carney and unable to bear Greg's intense sense of alienation, Isabel flees from him in one final attempt to find security by returning to her Annapolis Valley hometown of Kingsbridge.

Isabel's recognition that she must refine her identity within a conventional/nonmodern environment sends her to a town that is nestled in the heart of an idyllic rural "green world," untouched by the forces that have transformed other parts of the Maritimes. Isabel feels attracted to the serenity of the countryside and notes with relief that "whatever else had changed, this remained, the massive calm of the land itself" (NL, 248). Except in the texts of Ernest Buckler, such exquisite laudatory hymns as those expressed by Raddall's narrator are rarely found. The elegiac quality of the passage is fuelled by the text's ideological commitment to the "traditional" Maritime community: "The air over the miles of lush farmland quivered and the long ranges of hills to the north and south wavered gently in the sunshine as if stirred by the breath of Glooskap, the ancient Indian God whose habitat they were ... The corn ripened. The oats ripened and were mowed, and flocks of sparrows fed and chattered in the stubble, rising together at every petty alarm and setting down again. The apples ripened and the branches bent under their weight"(NL, 265–6).

Within this familiar community Isabel continues to serve the patriarchal order, but her job increasingly allows her to develop a sense of purpose. She becomes the secretary, bookkeeper, and manager of the local business entrepreneur, Mr Markham, and rises to a position of considerable prestige and power. She is not represented as a feminist, but within the context of both the setting of the text and Raddall's own time period, Isabel's existential project leads to an intriguing level of independence. Her ability to stand on her own is apparent in her negotiation of the Valley's cultural tensions. While appreciative of local traditions, she spurns the most oppressive and conformist aspects of the community, rejecting for example, the "fiery gospel" of the local Baptist preacher. Similarly, she is aware that the disillusionment following the First World War has infected the region's youth and recognizes that "eventually theirs would be the only voices to be heard" (NL, 258). However, she personally rejects the philosophies of cynicism as they are reproduced in the person of Brocklehurst. Just as the reader is distanced from Skane by his forbidding disdain, so the audience endorses Isabel's rejection of the local principal whose name would remind many of Raddall's readers of the corrupt schoolmaster of *Jane Eyre*. Brocklehurst's "cool indifference," "effrontery," and "sneers" signal a forfeited "sense of decency" for which he and the entire "lost generation" he represents are condemned (NL, 275). Balancing the disparate ideologies of the Valley, Isabel discovers a level of self-sufficiency; though, as ever, complete fulfillment apart from a male companion is impossible within the text's patriarchal norms. Even when she sunbathes in her private retreat – a sexually liberating activity that she experiences with "the utmost pleasure ... of utter freedom" – the narrative carefully reinscribes her as an object of male desire. She envisions herself first as a "nymph enjoying the caresses of a sky-god" (NL, 266) and then as one of the apples, which are "made to be enjoyed in their time ... after that they are withered and were spoiled forever" (NL, 271). Isabel continues to define herself as she did after her first night with Carney; she is an object to be validated through the masculine perspective.

Isabel Jardine does not reach the last stage of her romantic quest for a stable identity until Skane finally reveals that Carney is going blind, and thus allows her to reread her life in the light of Matthew's selfless love. Markham's commercial ventures begin to fail, and the Maritimes start to slide into a twenty-year depression; but this does not matter. Isabel recognizes her final destiny as Carney's guide and helpmate, and she overcomes her sense of alienation and ennui: "A lamp for Carney ... I've craved to have someone need me absolutely and completely. To feel that I was doing something that mattered, that nobody else could do. To feel that my life had a purpose" (NL, 310). With her commitment to Matthew solidified, Isabel finds the means to become a full member of the Marina community. The final chapters echo the conclusion of *Rockbound*: Isabel rejects Skane, her business career, and the entire city of Halifax, and retreats to the now-edenic Marina with its "possibilities for human joy, growth, and renewal" (Kulyk Keefer 1987, 78). The romantic quest for a stable identity draws to a satisfying close, with the couple's reunion on Marina and their mutual escape from the forces of modernism. As Isabel and Carney unite, the text celebrates the traditional and patriarchal social structures that lie at the heart of the Raddall's conservative ideology. Yet more than any other of Raddall's fictions, this vision of an ideal Maritime community is threaded through with a host of overdeterminations and contradictions that subvert this dominant vision.

The final chapter of *The Nymph and the Lamp* salutes Carney and Jardine's unchanging love and their return to a stable communal world. Raddall's novel, however, is not a homogenous text. Throughout the final sections of the novel, a strong vein of uncertainty surfaces and in its closing passages this romance verges on self-deconstruction. At the same time as the novel's conservatism reconstructs a conventional community, a series of silences and ruptures signal a simultaneous recognition that the alienation and anxiety of the post-industrial age are inescapable.

Inconsistencies and contradictions begin to appear when the ideas of the novel's cynical characters are closely examined. There is little doubt that the reader is supposed to dislike the fatalistic and unproductive skepticism of Skane and Brocklehurst, yet the text has difficulty defeating the specific perspectives these characters develop. Skane emerges as an antagonist in "this antimodernist romance"; his willingness to betray his best friend and have an affair with Isabel is reprehensible (Willmott 1998, 67). But his interest in radio broadcasting and sales is clearly going to lead him into a secure economic future, while Carney and Isabel tie themselves to the dying technology of the wireless. Similarly, Brocklehurst is a sterile and emotionally crippled philosopher, but his vision of the country's economic system is more perceptive than that of the community-minded Mr Markham. Markham echoes the perspective of George Rawlyk, who attributed the protracted underdevelopment of the Maritimes to the exodus of the region's most adventurous and ambitious individuals, as well as to the population's "prevailing tenacious attachment to ... traditional values and the past" (La Pierre, McLeod, et al. 1971, 41). Unable to foresee the economic crisis, Markham can only react after the fact and attribute the failure of his enterprises to the lack of determined entrepreneurs and courageous bankers willing to take advantage of opportunities: "The bank calls this a dubious experiment ... Trouble is I'm living thirty years ahead of my time" (NL, 277). Brocklehurst is not a sympathetic figure, but he realizes that the East Coast is tied to the world's economy and thus vulnerable to Britain's "postwar inflation"; and he accurately predicts the economic crash that everyone else overlooks (NL, 278). The narrator disapproves of Brocklehurst, but once his materialist-socialist position is logically developed, an effective counter-argument cannot be found: Isabel simply suspends their conversations with the insubstantial rebuttal, "I just couldn't stand it anymore" (NL, 275). The novel's flight from the very confrontations it initiates is one sign that its faith in traditionalism is on self-consciously shaky ground.

Unable to defeat the forces of modernism through logical or systematic debate, the narrative attempts to mask its own weak points by adopting a prophetic tone and lunging into a series of near-hysterical attacks on twentieth-century urban culture. The confident hymns to nationalistic and paternalistic orders that conclude *His Majesty's Yankees* and *Roger Sudden* cannot be repeated in this text. Instead, in an odd metalyptic shift, Raddall overrides Isabel's usually contained perspective; as the *Lord Elgin* sails into the North Atlantic, the narrator systematically attacks the materialism and moral relativism of the postwar Maritimes with the intensity of a reactionary tract:

the dim bulk of the land slipped away behind the rain like a shadow, an illusion after all. With it went all those other illusions: the scrabble for cash that could not buy security, the frantic pleasures that could not give content, the pulpit-thumpings that could not summon virtue, the Temperance Acts that killed temperance, the syncopated noise that was not music, the imbecile daubs that were not art, the lavatory scrawls that were not literature, the flickering Californications that were not drama, the fortunes that grew upon ticker tapes, the statesmanship that was only politics, the peace that led only toward more bloody war, the whole brave new world of '21 that was only old evil with a mad new face.

(NL, 321–2)

This overdetermined attack on virtually every aspect of twentieth-century culture is symptomatic of the narrator's anxious realization that the traditional vision constructed around Isabel and Matthew may not survive in the face of the many changes sweeping the Maritimes.

Finally, the dominant ideology is threatened even as it is being constructed in the final chapters of the novel. While Isabel and Carney are envisioned as spending their lives in the happy embrace of Marina's traditional society, there are inescapable signs that their Eden will not endure. In the closing moments Isabel is supposed to have concluded her search for a stable existence, but her desire to be "a light for Carney" is not a convincing solution to her existential dilemma. The success of her project is dependent on her mate's suffering and misfortune; thus her worthy work also sounds an ambiguous note. Moreover, unlike Gershom Rock, the site of David Jung's successful regeneration, Marina is on the verge of being dismantled. In the technological advances of the 1920s, Marina's wireless station is becoming "obsolete" and will soon "cease handling commercial traffic" (NL, 293). Though Isabel hopes to teach and strengthen the community, the population of the island itself will gradually be reduced when someone takes "a cold look at that ancient setup" of lifesaving and lighthouse services (NL, 293). Beneath the dominant ideology of the novel there is a clear subtext that suggests that the couple's attempt to escape into the secure world of the past will only be temporary. O'Dell envies the two lovers for Carney's failing eyesight will allow the two to live in the memory of perpetual youth; but as Helen Buss has pointed out, Isabel is simultaneously tying herself to a "patriarchy going dangerously and permanently blind" (Young 1991, 55). Buss proceeds to read against the grain and sound a note of optimism with the suggestion that Isabel has an opportunity to "invent a new order to take the place of the old" (Young 1991, 55), but there is little evidence that the narrative is able to recognize, let alone endorse this position. The text's attempts to reaffirm the traditional communal structures that lie at the heart of its conservative ideology are challenged by the narrative's own recognition that the modernist condition of alienation and uncertainty is unavoidable and inevitable. Willmott argues convincingly that Isabel is contained within rather than liberated from the traditional order as she returns to Marina. As

Carney is reunited with her, we witness how "the lost paternalistic identity of manhood must rediscover the love inscribed in women and women's words, not sentimentally for love itself, but for the patriarchal purpose it imposes on, thereby reinstating the value of, male power (1998, 74). These ideological tensions do not undermine the novel; on the contrary the narrator's pervasive anxiety about the changes sweeping the region and the text's inability to construct a singular vision together sound a subtle note of tragedy that makes *The Nymph and the Lamp* Raddall's most intriguing and pleasurable work.

In his article "Thomas H. Raddall and the Canadian Critics" (1991), Alan Young notes that the reputations of Raddall's novels suffered between 1960 and 1990 as a part of a larger critical "denial of historical fiction and romance and the denial of the writing of regional and popular history as significant or valuable contributions to our culture" (34). This critical devaluation of regional romance could also be cited as a reason for the long neglect of Day's works, and perhaps has unconsciously lead MacLennan's critics to overemphasize the realist character of his texts. Reconsiderations of Day, MacLennan, and Raddall are overdue, however, for their novels are fascinating transitional texts. Constructed in the midst of the transformations of postwar Maritime culture, these fictions blend romance and realism to craft distinct ideological positions. All three Maritimers invoke the romance genre as a means of imposing a degree of coherence and continuity on their textual worlds, and in MacLennan's and Raddall's texts the romance is intricately connected with a conservative desire to affirm the value of traditional social hierarchies and communities. However, a series of ruptures or discrepancies in their texts indicate that their visions are not homogenous. Thomas Raddall, Hugh MacLennan, and Frank Parker Day play consistently on the border between realism and romance, and their texts successfully reconstruct the tensions of a vibrant, transitional age. Such subsequent writers as Charles Bruce and Ernest Buckler build on the legacy of these early pioneers as they incorporate realism more fully into their fictions and explore in even greater detail the region's longing for a stable past and its hesitation about the uncertain future.

3 Between Realism and Nostalgia: Charles Bruce

Strange to have found, in the dust of this late day.
The old faith and frankness, the shared sun ...

Charles Bruce, "Of this late day"

During his long tenure as a reporter, editor, and administrator for the Canadian Press News Service, Charles Bruce always managed to find time and energy to devote to his literary career. His creative output remains an impressive achievement. Recognized in his own lifetime for his four volumes of poetry – one of which, *The Mulgrave Road*, won the Governor General's Award in 1951 – Bruce is now best known for his short fiction and for his novel *The Channel Shore*. In 1959 Charles Bruce brought together many of the short stories he had produced during the 1950s and published them as a collection entitled *The Township of Time*. Like the texts of Thomas Raddall, Hugh MacLennan, and Frank Parker Day, these short stories combine a realist style with a core structure based on the patterns of the romance. The stories record the quests of solitary individuals, the defeat of villains whose values threaten the community, and the attainment of stable and idyllic existences.

Bruce's earlier novel about a community on the Atlantic coast of Nova Scotia, *The Channel Shore*, was published in 1954 following a seven-year period of careful writing and revision. A story chronicling the lives of three families over a period of thirty years, the book won praise from reviewers when it appeared, but then fell into almost complete obscurity for more than two decades. Only after *The Channel Shore* was reprinted by MacMillan as a part of the Laurentian Library Series in 1974 and later reissued by McClelland and Stewart in 1984 as a part of the New Canadian Library series did readers and critics recognize its importance as an example of regional realism.

Initial explorations have brought to the forefront a number of Bruce's chief concerns, including his vision of community and his sense of history; however, the assumptions that are embedded in the novel – the competing and contradictory ideologies that drive the narrative – still need to be fully considered.[1] In the texts produced by Day, MacLennan, and Raddall, the formal and ideological tensions sometimes manifested themselves in dramatic and abrupt ways. *The Channel Shore* is one of the first texts to reproduce, in a sustained and steady fashion, the tension between the conventions of realism and those of nostalgia; between a strong faith in the ideals of communitarian liberalism and historicism and an impulse towards a conservative idealism. While the traditions of realism govern the central elements of this novel, a strong nostalgic desire controls its representation of contemporary events, its shifting representations of women, and the development of its villain. If the resulting ideological patterns that inhabit the novel are to be appreciated, attention must be paid to the various ways in which *The Channel Shore* has been influenced by these traditions of realism, romance, and nostalgia, and consideration must be given to the ways the fiction addresses contemporary historical, social, and sexual experiences.

THE CHANNEL SHORE

Of the many discourses employed within *The Channel Shore*, the conventions and assumptions of the realist aesthetic are the most powerful. The stylistic features of realism are immediately apparent, as Bruce creates physically detailed settings through a profusion of visual and tactile images. At times the reader is guided tourist-like around Bruce's version of the south shore: "At the top of the hill the land levelled out. From there a person could look ... along the northern fields and pastures of almost all the places at Currie Head, separated by line fences and untidy hedges of young wild apple trees ... Or let your sight drift out over the down-sloping fields and clusters of pitch-roofed farm buildings to the stretch of sea they called the Channel" (*cs*, 12). Similarly, the novel is meticulous in its creation of a complex timeline. *The Channel Shore* covers a period of twenty-six years and incorporates a number of genealogies and time shifts, but Bruce is so fastidious that he makes sure that the news the local mail carrier reads in the *Halifax Herald* corresponds with the actual headlines of that particular date. Immersed in a physically detailed environment and guided by a omniscient narrator who tends to focalize the text only through the community's safe middle-class characters, the reader is invited to view the text's world as objective and knowable.

While Raddall and Day adopt a realist style but continue to adhere to the structures of the romance, Bruce constructs his central plots in accordance with the conventions of realism, and then ties these elements to the dominant communitarian liberalism that governs the heart of the text. In accordance with the realist tradition that writers "plunge [their] heroes ... deeply into time-conditioned dependency," Bruce immerses his characters in specific communities and promotes a communitarian faith that within these specific contexts the protagonists can still exercise their free will and develop as individuals (Auerbach 1946, 425). This celebration of freedom is articulated directly by the reliable voice of Bill Graham, who reminds the hero Grant Marshall that his deterministic vision has wrongfully neglected the "truth" that people's actions through history are a blend of freedom and chance: "Don't you think – well nobody's a copy of his father, good or bad. All kinds of things get scribbled in, from other people, other generations. Or edited out. You can't figure inheritance on a slide rule" (*cs*, 346).

The ideology of individual liberty within community responsibilities has its strongest presence as the driving force behind both the primary plot and the development of the characters. Each of the characters, whether it be a major figure like Grant or a minor presence like Eva McKee, slowly becomes aware that he or she is moulded by specific communal situations. These characters enact the central principles of communitarian liberalism as each person discovers that he or she "belongs to a network of family and social relationships and is defined by this membership, and each person seeks personal fulfilment through participation in the evolving social structures of this community, finds personal liberty in an expanded self-development cultivated through these activities, and honours a traditional complex of agreed-on commitments" (Daly 1994, xiv). Indeed, with the exception of the most negatively portrayed individual, Anse, the characters' lives and actions follow a single pattern. They realize that they are part of a large web of cause and effect, that they are afflicted by negative social forces, and that an act of free will is required in order for them to escape these constraints and establish a healthy relationship with the community. If the characters follow this pattern through to its conclusion, they are content. If characters refuse to accept that they are part of a larger system, or attempt to obstruct those who seek to exercise their freedom, they inevitably meet with misery and misfortune. The movement of the characters from a restrictive to an authentic community relationship varies significantly according to the age, sex, and social position of each individual, but the overall pattern holds firm.

For Grant Marshall the journey from repression to a sense of freedom and pleasure in the community happens several times. "Part One" of *The Channel Shore* is set in "Summer-Fall 1919" and introduces us to Grant as a recently demobilized soldier. Unaffected by the deep cynicism that followed the First World War, in which he was never called to actively participate, Grant returns home and is soon caught in a struggle between his sense of obligation to his puritanical uncle/guardian James Marshall and his romantic desire for a neighbouring Catholic girl, Anna Gordon. James is a "strait-laced and dry-footed" Methodist farmer who trusts only "hard work and careful figuring and virtue" (*cs*, 29,57). He functions as a domineering father-figure who binds Grant's search for freedom with restrictive demands. In contrast, Anna Gordon – sister and antithesis of Anse – represents everything Grant needs in order to align himself with the ideals of liberalism. Described as "friendly and casual," "careless" and "laughing," Anna possesses a measure of independence, which allows her to express herself freely to her friends and family (*cs*, 72). Grant is drawn to Anna's humanity, but he is bound by James's "pride ... iron kindness and sense of family," and without alternative versions of his own past, he is unable to free himself from his family context (*cs*, 108).

After Anna leaves the shore and dies in Halifax, Grant's world is shaken to the point that he begins his move towards independence. Having lost his love, Grant breaks from James, moves into Josie and Stewart Gordon's home, and immediately feels he has "reached a decision that made [him] a new man, gave [him] this sense of iron freedom" (*cs*, 132). That Grant has taken a significant step towards controlling his destiny is confirmed when the narrator makes him the sole character focalizer for the last quarter of the first section; however, it would be a mistake to assume that Grant has found complete security, for he has not yet developed the qualities that will allow him to communicate with and comfort those around him.

After moving in with Anna's parents, he realizes that Josie Gordon is afflicted by grief and a "continuing iron calm," but he cannot find a way to comfort her (*cs*, 156). The ability to approach Josie and reestablish his relationship with the community emerges after Grant talks to Richard McKee, an elderly fisherman/farmer. Devoted to maintaining the skills and crafts of the past, Richard acts as a touchstone of historical continuity. His ability to accept and preserve his past makes him both a beacon for the text's troubled characters and an emblem of stable individuality. From Richard, Grant learns about his biological father's pranks on a malevolent trapper and a domineering teacher, and the youth is able to revise his own heritage to include more emotional responses: "And in this at last he saw the face and heard the laughter of Harvey Marshall. Harvey, a Marshall, touched by the thing that pulsed in the Grahams ... the McKees ... The thing that was alive, that was not cold doctrine or property or measured pride, but simple feeling" (cs, 160). These revelations enable Grant to break his silence with Josie and learn that her grief does not come from her daughter's death, but from her son's love affair with Richard's daughter, Hazel McKee, and the resulting shameful pregnancy. In his desire to heal the wounds of the community he loves, Grant – in the last ten pages of the first section – decides to go to Toronto and marry Hazel. Later in the novel, after Alan has been born and Hazel has died, Grant recalls how he experienced a sense of freedom and a reaffirmation of his bond with humanity through his marriage: "In the end we both learned something. Not a damn thing matters but what people can do for each other when they're up against it" (cs, 208). Grant passes from a state of repression to one of freedom, but he must repeatedly struggle to keep his balance in the subsequent chapters.

The second and third sections shift from their exclusive focus on Grant and take on some of the characteristics of the bildungsroman, as we watch Hazel's son Alan mature through adolescence and young manhood. Having played the part of the freedom-seeker in part 1, Grant becomes increasingly worried about the stability of his bonds with Alan, his adopted son, and once again subjects himself to restrictive forces: he lets "a false sense of the importance of public appearances lead him away from the truth" (Seaman 1976, 29). Grant bases his relationship with his adopted son on the illusion that Alan is his biological child and repeatedly attempts to bury the truth, first by trying to send the boy away to a boarding school where he will be safe from local gossip, and, in the final section, by refusing to reveal the truth of Alan's parentage from fear that their emotional bonds will vanish. Only as Alan matures and learns to assert his own will is Grant released from his burdens and returned to the "kind of easy freedom and [the] gradual relaxed excitement" that this text often uses to signal a character's emergence as a secure and mature individual (cs, 268). Although Auerbach suggests that realism often traces the "problematic nature and the hollowness" of everyday life (1946, 433), Grant's rejuvenation lies within the traditions of realist fiction, for his renewal takes place within an elaborate web of cause and effect and is embedded in particular social and historical contexts.

The ideology of communitarian liberalism is further reinforced in the characterizations of Alan, Josie, and Eva. The second and third parts of the novel, set in the winter of 1933–34 and the summer of 1946 respectively, concentrate primarily on Alan's attempts to establish his identity. As the offspring of Anse Gordon and Hazel McKee's rebellion, but raised by Grant as his biological son, Alan spends his thirteenth Christmas trying to unearth his true parentage, and his first summer after the war trying to find a way to tell Grant he knows about his origins. Both undertakings involve a struggle to establish and then assert his own identity while remaining an integral part of the family and community. Alan's emergence as the most frequent internal focalizer in the second half of *The Channel Shore* reflects the text's interest in exploring an individual's struggle for freedom, rather than in dwelling on Grant's struggle to maintain a tenuous liberty.

From the beginning of the second section, the text explores Alan's desires and history and confirms that he is embedded and acts within a particular personal and social context. Just as Grant's emotional responses are rooted in James and Harvey, so the text notes how Alan consciously models himself after his adoptive father, wanting to walk the woods, cut out the roads, and "peel pulpwood ... sharing a man's work, Grant's work, a known enterprise on the Channel Shore" (*cs*, 182–4). Other community members, such as Richard and Josie, also have an impact on his personality, feeding his interest in the history of the Shore. Shaped by his environment, Alan also feels the need to function independently, especially when he decides to oppose Grant's decision that he must go away to finish his schooling. As he grapples with Grant's unilateral decision, he repeats a single phrase four times. The phrase, placed in italics by Bruce, resonates beyond Alan's life and repeats one of the text's central ideologies, that each person must struggle against the forces of determinism in order to pursue his or her own path: *"He never asked me if I want to go. He just said I'm going"* (*cs*, 219, 234, 261, 267). Grant's desire for "iron freedom" drove the plot of the first section, and Alan's resolution to make his own desires known governs the events of the second.

Like Grant, Alan must rewrite his past and reevaluate his relationships with others before he can articulate and assert his will. Like his father before him, the boy visits "helpers" who act as reservoirs of the Shore's history. While exploring the contents of the old trunks Richard has stored in the loft of his workshed, Alan's discovery of his mother's picture of Anse Gordon prompts his stepsister, Margaret, to ask: "Mrs. Josie – the Gordons, What's she got to do – Are they any relation? To us?" (*cs*, 245). Richard says little in this section, but his preservation of the past gives Alan his first solid clue to understanding his heritage. Armed with a few hints, Alan goes to Josie the next evening and confirms the "facts" of his parentage and the "truth" about Grant's love for him.

Having rewritten his history, Alan has the information he needs to assert his autonomy, but lacks the motivation to confront his father. Just as Grant was driven to take his final step towards freedom-through-marriage by his sensitivity to Josie's shame and the community's need, so in both sections Alan's determination to act is solidified only when he realizes that the happiness of others is also at stake. On the morning of New Year's Day, 1934, Alan finds the necessary sense of conviction only after Margaret reveals how much she wants him to stay. Able to act on another's behalf, Alan goes directly to Grant and with a voice "roughened by the resolution that had come to him with Margaret in his arms," declares, "I don't want to go to Halifax Academy in the fall either. I want to work here in the woods, with you; and take grade ten right here, from Renie" (CS, 267). The same pattern unfolds at the end of the third section. Throughout this final part Alan struggles to find the right moment to make his origins public without hurting Grant, aligning himself with Anse, or alienating himself from the people of the shore. The appropriate time comes when Anse insults the entire community, calling them, "A bunch of farmers. Sheep manure and sawdust," and then crudely refers to his abandonment of Hazel and Alan: "If I'd known I'd planted a crop here, I'd have stayed to watch it grow" (CS, 388). The episode is structured so that Alan is able to act on behalf of both the citizens and himself, reinforcing the ideal that independence and individuality must be established in cooperation with the interests of the larger community.

The minor characters of *The Channel Shore* also reproduce Bruce's liberal assumption that individuals can act freely within specific historical moments. In the first section of the novel Josie Gordon is described as an "ingrowing woman," unable to lay "bare her heart" to others or overcome her grief about Anse's rebellions (CS, 110). Hazel's example of openness and vulnerability is a "definite turning-point" that allows Josie to free herself from her pride, embrace Grant's family, and experience a "slow recovery, the achievement of a tranquillity that was inward as well as outward" (CS, 223). Governed by pride and fear of community opinion, Eva McKee is another individual who is so worried that her daughter's romance with Anse will result in "getting yourself talked about" that she cannot address Hazel's deeper need for independence (CS, 9). Only when she sees Hazel on her deathbed does Eva confront her "pride" (CS, 240) and begin to integrate her own life with Grant's young family: "in some manner the years had turned the tone's edge ... the eyes had learned to smile" (CS, 239). The actions of the minor characters in the text reinforce its dominant ideology about individual freedom in the social and communal context.

While characters aligned with the central vision of the text ascend towards peace, those who block the freedom of others or pursue their own interests regardless of its social impact become increasing unhappy. Hat Wilmot is the local gossip whose "edge of malice" complicates rather than facilitates other people's search for independence (*CS*, 9). Near the novel's conclusion, the narrator portrays her as a ridiculous figure comically asking how a sailboat moves: "You mean that's all there is to it? The wind pushes it along?" (*CS*, 380). James Marshall is another example of an almost villainous character who resists the ideals of the text. James distrusts "casualness, laughter, garrulity wherever they were found" (*CS*, 133), drives Grant from his life, and in the second section he has been reduced to a bitter old man who "argues with God" (*CS*, 248). Though the circumstances of Alan's birth prove to be the salvation of several families, the boy's face only reminds James of his lost "health and strength and the bitterest defeat he had ever known" (*CS*, 250). The aged and rancorous James appears briefly in the second section, but he then disappears from the novel with hardly a postscript.

The characters and events of *The Channel Shore* consistently reproduce the ideology that an individual's relations with his/her historical and social contexts are free. This set of assumptions also influences the way the text constructs a stable position for the reader through its careful ordering and retelling of Hazel's story. Hazel McKee dies after giving birth to Alan in the spring of 1920, just outside the time frame of the first section. Because no single individual was capable of recording all the details of Hazel's demise, some characters suggest that a full knowledge of the event is impossible. When Renie meets Bill in the third section and declares "You know the whole story, don't you, Bill? I thought you did," Bill corrects her saying, "Oh, no … How can anyone know the whole story? Of anything. You'd have to put together everything a lot of individual people know, and don't talk about. Each one of them knows something no one else does" (*CS*, 337). While the characters have to content themselves with incomplete information, the text is determined to provide the reader with the very "story" that Bill believes is unattainable. Using a series of internal focalizations, the narrator retells Hazel's story more than a dozen times from the perspective of at least seven different characters. The reader is able to assemble information from the memories of Grant, Renie, Eva, Josie, Richard, Bill, and Vangie Murphy – as well as supplementary images from Alan, James, and Anse – to construct an almost complete history of Hazel's demise and its effect on the community. By collecting all the versions offered by the members of the community, the reader discovers the whole "truth" and enters the only position of knowledge from which all the enigmas of the text can be resolved. Informed about the internal lives of the characters and involved in the process of assembling the story, the sympathetic reader is aligned with the dominant ideals of the text: the liberal commitment to individual freedom within a social and historical context. The position that is constructed for the reader ultimately reinforces the ideals promoted through the text's characterization and plot.

Realism is the dominant form structuring Bruce's fiction, but it is not the only driving force behind this text; *The Channel Shore* is also deeply influenced by a powerful nostalgic impulse. Charles Bruce disliked the term "nostalgia," calling it the "silliest word in the English language" (Wainwright 1988, 122), but there is nonetheless a strong strain of "homesickness" that runs through his work. Charles Bruce was born in Port Shoreham, Nova Scotia, in 1906 and spent his childhood there until going to Mount Allison University in Sackville, New Brunswick in 1923 (Wainwright 1988, ii). After graduating in 1927 with his Bachelor of Arts, he went to work in Halifax, where he joined the Canadian Press, which transferred him to Toronto in 1933. Though Bruce lived much of the rest of his life in Toronto, he never particularly liked the city and longed to return to the east: "The transformation of his childhood home, together with his long term absence from the Maritimes, made him eternally homesick for a way of life that had disappeared" (Kristiansen 1994, 240). As early as 1934 he was inquiring into the possibility of starting a paper in Sackville, and later he considered buying the Windsor Tribune in Nova Scotia (Wainwright 1988, 66–8). Though he never moved back to the Maritimes, he sent his children to Port Shoreham every summer, and, during the last decade before his death in 1971, Bruce himself made annual visits to the old homestead. This enduring desire for home coloured much of his poetry and all of his significant prose; however much he disliked the term nostalgia, it plays a significant role in his biography and his texts.

The Channel Shore is a text that is particularly enriched as Bruce blends the communitarian liberalism and historicism embedded in the novel's realism with the conservative idealism typical of the nostalgic impulse. The longing for an ideal past generates passages of lyric description, influences how certain occurrences external to the life of the Shore are represented, influences the portrayal of the female characters, and finally is responsible for the construction of the novel's darkest character: Anse Gordon. The nostalgic impulse is first evident in the representations of the rural world as a secure, productive, idyllic place where the modern urban reader can be reconnected with an older agrarian tradition. The text repeatedly dwells on the beauties of the rural world and often takes on an edenic aura of plenitude, stability, and peace. This longing becomes more powerful when the Nova Scotia environment is linked explicitly with the idea of memory: "Fall comes to Nova Scotia like the late fulfilment of a boyhood love, half forgotten for half a lifetime and then at once alive and golden, new and strange ... The days are crisp and clear, or windless under a mild clouded sky. The nights are those a man remembers, looking upward through the murk of cities, his instinct looking back. There are nights in the full moon of October when darkness is a kind of silver daylight, when the sea is a sheet of twinkling light" (cs, 139). Though the narrator usually directs the reader's eye towards immediate and simple physical details, this passage foregrounds the movement of time. Memories of the land – the fullness of the moon, the recollection of love, and the silver colours of the scene – are expressed in language drawn from the codes of romance. For the narrator, the Channel Shore is not just an arbitrary setting for a handful of characters, it is an idyllic place where one can experience the fullness of life and escape the ravages of time.

In addition to the recurring elegiac moments, the idealistic impulse can also be felt in the way the text represents places and experiences external to the life of the Shore. The narrative's few references to contemporary experience tend to be very selective. Bruce is careful to record the impact of modern technology on the Shore, including the demise of the sailboat, the arrival of Grant's portable diesel sawmill, and the use of cars and trucks. However, Bruce was not interested in turning his text into an economic or political treatise; in order to preserve a nostalgic impulse, many of the disappointments experienced by Maritimers in the twentieth century are not emphasized. Bruce's desire to retain a vision of the past as secure and stable moment is most evident when we examine his representations of the Depression.

The second section of the novel is set in 1933–34, but the only mention of the Depression, which had plagued the East Coast since early 1921, is Alan's observation that "Lumber's pretty low" (cs, 203). Far removed from the economic collapse of the region, Grant is presented as a prospering entrepreneur who can "take the old stuff, the country that's all around your feet ... and build something they said you couldn't ... something really new" (cs, 269). When Grant creates a mill industry, it represents a smooth fusion of traditional values and innovative energy: the mill is integrated into the rhythms of the agrarian life and the saws shut down when it is time to mow the hay (cs, 277). Bruce's desire to protect his image of the Shore is evident in other careful representations of historical experience. The collapse of the local fishing industry is not depicted as the result of a 50 percent drop in salt cod prices and the creation of a fresh and frozen fish industry that was centralized in three or four major centres like Halifax and Lunenburg (Brym 1979, 130–40); it is the result of a natural decline in fish stocks. Similarly, although Nova Scotia had an unemployment rate of 19.6 percent during the 1930s and a large proportion of the population required some form of financial assistance, the only impoverished character is Vangie Murphy, and her hardships are presented as self-imposed. The massive emigration of nearly 300,000 people during the 1920s and 1930s is neatly compressed into the figure of Joe McKee, who journeys out to Peace River, Alberta, where he seems unaffected by the dustbowl years.

If the Nova Scotian experiences of the Depression are transformed by the text, so is the province's long history. Early in the first section the narrator recounts the local history, recalling "one golden period, the forty or fifty middle years of the [nineteenth] century ... [when the Shore] prospered on the basic economics of salt fish, enhanced by ... vessel-building and coastal trade, cattle and sheep, and squared hardwood timber" (cs, 12–13). The narrator notes that such prosperity has long since passed, but explains that the economy failed because it was "based on circumstances that were not to last" (cs, 13). Except for occasional allusions to minor hardships, Bruce does not develop a detailed analysis of the economic downturns of the twentieth century, for such close explorations might endanger his nostalgic vision of the shore. Though Erik Kristiansen argues that Bruce is overtly critical of the emerging "commodity culture and of [the] unsatisfied desires [that] reenforce a sense of powerlessness in a changing world" (1994, 234), The Channel Shore is not as critical of modern capitalism as his article suggests. Indeed, Kristiansen himself notes that Bruce presents "the budding capitalist, Grant Marshall, in so favourable a light that any critique of urban capitalism is countered by a voice favouring some rural capitalist development" (1994, 239). Margaret goes even further and suggests that modern development is little more than an extension of the old prosperity, skills being organically transformed into newer, economic models: "And people still lived on the Channel Shore, people with other skills, newer crafts, that somehow were related to and grew from the old. The story of the Shore was the story of a strange fertility. A fertility of flesh and blood that sent its seed blowing across continents of space on the winds of time, and yet was rooted here in home soil, renewed and re-renewed"(cs, 353). Through a skilful recreation of contemporary experience, Bruce is able to produce an apparently realistic setting while retaining an idealism reminiscent of the nineteenth century's faith in the inevitability of progress. Janice Kulyk Keefer suggests that Bruce's nineteenth-century mentality is also indicated by "his concern for a knowable community, his belief that ... 'there were still people you must meet and talk to, relationships you had to make, customs you had to follow' (*cs*, 149)" (1987, 60–1).

A nostalgic impulse influences *The Channel Shore*'s representation of the Shore and its history; the same impluse affects the novel's gender assumptions and its representation of women. Most of Bruce's ideological vision is manifested in what the novel says and does; however, some aspects of the his ideology are not visible until those things the novel resists saying are uncovered. When these moments of repression are examined, the narrative's masculine perspective and its link to nostalgia become more evident.

Unlike Bruce's collection of short stories, *The Township of Time*, and much of the fiction of MacLennan, Raddall, and Buckler, *The Channel Shore* does not rely exclusively on gender stereotypes to develop its female characters. Indeed, many of Bruce's representations of women initially appear to resist the nostalgic aura and work within the traditions of historical realism. Hazel, Margaret, Renie, and Josie fit the traditional mould of wayward woman, young lover, wife, and matron, but they also develop beyond these confining roles, and the text does not suggest that their subordinate station in life is agreeable, necessary, or natural. For example, Grant's patriarchal practice of limiting the women's opportunities to work outside the home is carefully critiqued. While Grant and Alan help old Frank and Dan Graham bring in the hay, Renie must stay behind and pick strawberries. The internal narrator records her dissatisfaction with this discrimination and notes her anger as she explains the situation to Bill: "Renie felt a small resentment at being out of it. As a girl on Prince's Island she had handled a fork, stowing away, and a rake behind the rack, raking after. But now Grant wouldn't let either her or Margaret take a hand ... 'They won't let me make hay. So I left them to stew in their own sweat'" (*cs*, 336). Similarly, the fact that Margaret is allowed to help Alan and Buff Katen work in "Josie Gordon's hayfield" is one of the signs at the novel's conclusion that the emerging society is an improvement over the past (*cs*, 393).

The text also historicizes gender roles and demonstrates that, in some cases, the "progress" of technology in the twentieth century has limited rather than liberated the women of the Shore. In her book *The New Day Recalled*, Veronica Strong-Boag notes that while mechanization made some labour easier, it also isolated women from traditional work groups and further curtailed their lives outside the home (1988, 133–7). Bruce records the negative effects of the industrial age on the

Channel Shore by having Josie remember, with some fondness, the "rough" life of earlier days when she "used to help father with the fish" and by having Richard recall an earlier time when women were able to work with the men in the fields. By recording the shifts in work habits through history, the text affirms that confining gender roles are socially constructed, not universal and natural.

Yet if Bruce is able to go further than either Day, MacLennan, Raddall, or Buckler in producing nonstereotypical female characters, *The Channel Shore* also inscribes a patriarchal perspective, through its nostalgic desire to maintain the "ideal" character of the community. This vision comes to the foreground in several ways. The confinement of women within the house is questioned when a passage is being focalized through a character like Renie, but the external narrator rarely questions the privileged access males have to such "outside" economic spaces as the woods, the fishing ponds, and the fish huts. Margaret's wish not "to intrude in the man-world" of Richard's tool shed is presented as a natural courtesy, and not a mark of the Shore's constructed division of labour (*cs*, 244). At other times, Bruce seems to make a point of defending the economic hegemony of men. Renie is the local schoolteacher but the external narrator stresses twice that her work is "an incidental filling-out of life" (*cs*, 196, 219) and that she does her job "not for a living, but as a person who lived in the place, helping out because teachers were hard to get" (*cs*, 187). Affirming that Renie's true calling is to fulfill her nurturing instinct and that her "happiness was in the people who were hers," the narrator takes unusual measures to ensure that she is not perceived as a threat to Grant's dominance (*cs*, 191).

At a deeper level, the nostalgia of the text creates an ideological blind spot around the deeper systemic sexism that pervades the rural community. Though Grant and Alan are afforded a high degree of autonomy within the specific context of their community, the social structures of the shore are more restrictive for the women. Hazel McKee wants to break away from her mother's repressive attitudes, but she recognizes that as a woman her options are limited: "She would have liked to be a singer ... But it wasn't practical ... No. You stayed on the Channel Shore to work and marry. Or you got away from it to go into household service – but that was beneath a McKee. Or to do stenography or teach school. Not to sing" (*cs*, 10). The text accurately reflects the historic limitations placed on women and records that Hazel's sexual relationship with Anse is a "private rebellion" against her lack of opportunities for freedom, but it does not explore the larger implications of her search for "a secret dark independence" (*cs*, 24). After presenting Hazel's sexual expression as a result of a woman's desire for independence in a repressive society, the text never reexamines the issue. When her pregnancy is discovered, Hazel's fear, Josie's shame, and the community's disapproval are communicated by the narrator as a natural consequence of violating the moral code. The rigidity of the community is not subsequently implicated for its contribution to Hazel's "fall," and in this silence – generated as the narrator attempts to maintain a romantic vision of the rural world – the patriarchal perspective of the text is unveiled.

Vangie Murphy is another female character whose sexual rebellion crosses the limits prescribed by society. Again the narrator hints that the strict social taboos against premarital sex and illegitimate children are partly responsible for Vangie's miserable life, but in the end the social order is absolved as the narrator reveals that Vangie actually prefers her life of isolation and poverty: "She would have admitted to herself, had the thought occurred to her, that she liked best the role of road-walking sloven … On the road there was a hint of the carelessness, the freedom, that had coloured her younger days with a harsh excitement" (cs, 226). The confirmation that the text does not question the patriarchal structures of the Channel Shore is found in the opening list of "People of the Shore," which registers the family names of "Stileses, Clancys, and Lisles" – who hardly appear in the novel – but excludes the name of Murphy. The silencing of Vangie's membership among the people is a mark of the text's desire to suppress questions about the lack of freedom for women in a supposedly idyllic community.

In The Channel Shore the nostalgic impulse often operates at a slight distance from the realist conventions governing the heart of the text. Concentrated in the language of the external narrator and in the representation of the region, Bruce's conservative idealism is a pervasive part of the ideological conditions of the novel, but may seem limited in its power over the central actors and actions of the plot. When the most disruptive character, Anse Gordon, is considered, however, it is apparent that the narrative is deeply troubled by the implications of his corrupt nature. For a novel embedded in liberalism and historicism – committed to tracing the social context from which the various personalities emerge – the job of explaining the origins of a "villain" can be very difficult. If it followed its normal pattern of "realistic" character development, the text would have to explain Anse's malicious essence by tracing a dark line of cause and effect through the community's history. While tracing a villain's origins may not threaten a realist narrative, it certainly disturbs an idealistic text. In order to avoid creating such a "dark" heritage in the Shore community, the author uses the conventions of romance to construct the

novel's most menacing figure, so as to distance him from the nostalgic ideals of the text. The emergence of Anse as an emblem of evil to
be expelled, rather than a "three-dimensional" character who must
be integrated into the community, is an indication that the conservative nostalgic subtext stretches from the margins to the very core of
the text's "realist" action.

Throughout the novel, the narrator makes it clear that Anse is to be
distrusted and disliked. In a novel that resists putting its characters
into moral categories, Anse is an intensely codified individual and
becomes a one-dimensional character very much like the vice figure
from a morality play. He is present in less than a third of the text;
however, in that short time he is recorded repeatedly as being "sar-
donic" (CS, 311, 383), possessed by "contemptuous malice" (CS, 381),
"touched with mockery" (CS, 2, 312, 314, 323, 327, 388), and moved
by "contempt" (CS, 2, 14, 17, 42, 355, 388). Anse Gordon is a figure
created outside the conventions of "realism." This is confirmed by
the text's refusal to explore the origins of his cynicism and rebellion.
Josie cannot understand her son and recognizes only that there is a
mysterious quality in him that sets him apart from others: "something in Anse you couldn't reach ... Something unreachable." She refers to him as "the dark first child of their marriage," as if his sullen
character was predetermined from birth (CS, 49). That his behaviour
has no precedent is confirmed by Stewart who thinks of Anse while
mourning Anna's sudden death and says, "Queer, y'know. Not his
fault ... It's what you're born with. Restless" (CS, 135). Stewart is attempting to justify Anse's neglect, but there is more than a grain of
truth in his analysis of his son. Anse stands alone on the Shore; he has
no discernible heritage, and he leaves no tangible legacy. By constructing him as an enigmatic rogue figure from the romance tradition, Bruce introduces a source of conflict, while defending his text's
nostalgic impulse to idealize the community.

Anse is not motivated by any historical force recognized by the text,
but that does not mean his actions must be capricious or incompre-
hensible. He cannot be propelled by the forces of his past, so instead
this romance antagonist is driven, like many modernist figures struggling against a sense of alienation, by his need to secure a solid image
of himself. The novel's heroes, Grant and Alan, have a clear sense of
who they are, and they struggle only for the freedom to declare that
identity openly. Anse, by contrast, is a split subject, secure only when
his self-image is reflected back to him by an outraged or fearful community. When Anse appears in the first chapter as a returning soldier
from the First World War, he searches for a sign that would confirm his
sense of self-importance – "the evidence to himself of the power he

was" (cs, 15) – and finds his external confirmation in his seduction of Hazel McKee. Because Anse relies on the community's reaction to establish himself as a coherent individual, Hazel's humiliating public rejection of him destroys his self-image. Unable to bear seeing "the fact of belonging to Anse Gordon held worthless and disavowed," Anse retreats into an embarrassed self-exile. When he returns to the Channel Shore after a twenty-six-year absence, he resumes his role as a romantic, alienated antagonist. Like the sailboat he attempts to restore, Anse is unable to move under his own power and instead anticipates the reception he will receive from his suspicious neighbours: "There wasn't one of them, not one, who wouldn't stop when they met him on the road, recognizing, for all their holiness, the flare of something special. And all of them a little envious. Envious and cautious" (cs, 315). As his plans to secure a position in the Shore's eyes as Alan's true father collapse, Anse is again confronted by the fact that he is powerless. When he lashes out against the community, he is ritually expelled from the society's borders.

In the end, the text cannot accept a figure like Anse. As a spectre of tyranny and rebellion, he is too disruptive to be allowed into a textual world that values free will and affirmation. In addition, the text's careful balance of realism and nostalgia, of liberalism's celebration of the individual and conservativism's faith in the community, is threatened by Anse's appearance as a figure from the modern world. Touched with irony, disillusioned with tradition, and trapped in a search for identity, Anse represents what the novel is least able to accept: the self-destructive cynicism that is part of the postwar psyche. The expulsion of Anse accomplishes more than the resolution of Grant's family problems. It secures the text's double desire to represent the Channel Shore as a place of individual freedom and community involvement and as an idyllic region where traditional values can still withstand the spirit of the twentieth century. Through the construction of Anse and his final absence, the nostalgic impulse joins with the realist conventions to govern the centre of the novel.

Bruce's use of realist conventions to develop his core structure marks a significant development in Maritime fiction following the romance-realisms of Day, MacLennan, and Raddall. At the same time, Bruce's nostalgic impulse distinguishes him from Buckler, Nowlan, and Richards, who are more deeply embedded in the modernist spirit. Bruce's only novel is a complex fusion of forms and ideologies, and the preface of the novel is correct to suggest we will not find the "Shore, so named on any map or chart." Bruce's Maritime community is a field of competing and contradictory assumptions that make it, ultimately, "a country of the mind" (cs, v).

THE TOWNSHIP OF TIME

Early in the 1950s, Bruce began to write short stories about the early settlements at the head of Chedabucto Bay. In 1959 twenty different tales were collected and published under the title *The Township of Time: A Chronicle*,[2] Bruce's second and final volume of prose fiction. It explores six generations of characters drawn from a common family tree, covering a time span of more than 150 years. The collection's poetic description of rural Nova Scotia, and the Tidewater community's balance of an agrarian and fishing culture, initially seems reminiscent of *The Channel Shore*. However, as the deeper structure of the stories are examined we discover that Bruce's earlier liberalism has evolved into a more uniform commitment to the form of the romance and the ideological assumptions of conservatism.

Like Bruce's novel, *The Township of Time* employs the stylistic devices of realism as the narrator focuses on the material aspects of the objective world and provides careful accounts of the immediate concrete details of daily life. The stories reproduce the sensuous details associated with everything from the "wash" and "cluck" of the Channel's waves, to the way a boy "scraped a patch of turnip flesh into pale yellow fluff and knifed it into his mouth" (*TT*, 159). Even the cityscapes, which were generalized in the *Channel Shore*, appear with exactitude in such stories as "Duke Street 1896" and "The Pattern of Surrender 1933." Wainwright records that Bruce "walked the route his character would have taken from University College and consulted 1896 issues of *The Varsity* to see what students were wearing" (1988, 197). The stories also attempt to accurately reflect the local dialects, especially those stories set in the early pioneer days of the province. Without producing the "Othering effect" that is evident in Day's *Rockbound*, the story "Juniper 1813" employs six different focalizers all of which have slightly different speech patterns; the children are especially prone to the use of such slang words and colloquial contractions as "ain't," "comin round," "Ido' know," "evenin'," and "gettin'" (*TT*, 37).

If the tenets of realism influence the style, the conventions of romance govern the structure. In *The Anatomy of Criticism*, Frye argues that in the romance the "reader's values are bound up with the hero," who must attempt some difficult task, which he usually achieves and which is subsequently associated with the order, peace, and fertility of an "imaginative golden age in time or space" (1957, 186). The defeated villain functions as a representation of the darkness, confusion, and sterility that the idealist text invariably expels (1957, 187). In *The Township of Time*, Bruce repeatedly employs this romance formula as protagonists attempt heroic quests and move the larger community one step closer to an ideal state. In the opening story, "The Sloop 1786," Colin Forester, an eighteenth-century Loyalist soldier of the British legion, fills the role of the knight errant, he is dressed "like Robinson Crusoe," but nonetheless discovers and rescues a damsel-in-distress, Lydia Willoughby (*TT*, 4). In "Sand 1907," the bachelor Mel Somers overcomes his lethargy and his resentment of a manipulative neighbour and attempts a heroic rescue after Cam Sinclair falls through the ice. The stories' conclusions provide a clear indication of the collection's romantic impulse. Five stories end with idyllic images depicting a renewed and strengthened bond within the family or the community, and another six of the stories end with either the promise of marriage or a commitment to the forces of romantic love, whether it be Niomi's courtship of her teacher Francis in "Cadence 1834" or the renewal of Lewis's and Floras's relationship in "The Climate of Affection 1937."

While the protagonists are prone to heroic action, the antagonists of the fictions are venomous. Several stories feature opponents who embody attitudes and values that threaten the very essence of the community. In "The Sloop 1786," Aunt Delilah is an elderly woman whose "pinched refinement … was the central satisfaction of [her] life" (*TT*, 6). Unable to let go of the symbols of her former wealth, the aunt becomes a bitter woman whose aristocratic attitudes not only lead her to insult Colin Forester but also to threaten the very assumptions of equality that constitute the basis of the pioneer society. In the end, the reader recognizes that her pretentious order is doomed to fade away. Ben Farren, a merchant who wants to marry Willoughby, Colin and Lydia Forester's daughter in the story "Juniper 1813," is another despicable character. Even before it is revealed that he has betrayed Willoughby's true love, Angus Neill, by having him pressed into the Navy, Ben Farren is portrayed in a negative light as a man who treats others with "contempt," and views the object of his affection as a prize "to win" with "daring, audacity, force" (*TT*, 34, 36). His humiliation at the story's conclusion is welcomed by the audience who sees in Farren a threat to the civil and moral codes of the Shore. The one-dimensional characterization of these villains and their ritualistic defeat reinforce the romance pattern of the text.

The stories' repeated emphasis on the heroic individual's ability to determine his or her own destiny and simultaneously move the community towards more democratic paradigms would initially seem to suggest that liberal humanist assumptions, first evident in *The Channel Shore*, permeate the collection. Three of the stories – "The Sloop 1786," "Tidewater Morning 1787," and "Cadance 1834" – celebrate the dismantling of hierarchical social orders and note that traditional class structures "got kind of levelled off" in the new settlements, allowing free interaction between officers and soldiers, judges and farmers (*TT*, 59). Richard McKee notes that "in this country they rarely used the term ... servant." He does not hesitate to marry a woman whose only possession is "a shiny earthenware teapot" (*TT*, 16). The stories also reproduce liberalism's confident vision of the subject as an integral, unified self, and some of the protagonists even experience brief periods of transcendence when they ascend above the forces of history and gain a universal perspective on their lives. Though Andrew, a student in Toronto visiting his aged aunt Niomi in "Duke Street 1896," is in a situation very different from John Forester, who lies dying of radiation poisoning on a hospital bed in "The Wind in the Juniper 1945," both are spiritually rejuvenated through their contact with other people and both see time as a unity, "past present and future merged and continuing ... all part of the same thing" (*TT*, 122, 218). But the stories' liberal professions are connected only to the main protagonists, for the binary structures reproduced by the formal conventions of the romance ultimately bind the stories to a powerful ideology of conservatism.

The stories in *The Township of Time* reproduce a polarized version of Maritime community. As is often the case in romance texts, the boundaries distinguishing good and evil, order and chaos, success and failure, hero and villain, man and woman are clear, and, as the volume reorganizes its world into well-defined and hierarchically arranged camps, it gives voice to a set of hierarchical and conservative assumptions. Bruce's novel has a patriarchal perspective, but he moves beyond the conventional stereotypes of women to construct his heroines in specific historical contexts. The short stories, however, are built around a quest motif that focuses almost exclusively on male heroes, and represents women as subservient background helpers and assistants. Of the thirteen stories that have female characters, only ten of those stories provide the women with speaking parts, and only one story of the twenty – "Juniper 1813" – employs a woman as a focalizer. Moreover, the women are bound to the stereotypic roles of sweethearts, wives, mothers, grandmothers, or witches. Only three characters, Willoughby in "Juniper 1813," the elderly Niomi in "Duke Street 1896," and Chris in "People from Away 1917," break out of traditional roles to become characters with significant thoughts and desires, and even then Willoughby is portrayed as a primarily sensuous entity who is removed from the world of male intellectual experience. Undoubtedly, women were restricted to narrow roles in the nineteenth and twentieth century, but the stories represent these roles as universal and natural, and the women who fill them as a rather homogenous group, especially when compared with the many diverse males who are positioned as heroes. The heroes may advance democratic ideals, but the many female characters find their identity and security only as they merge their selves with the roles defined by the collective society. As Bruce celebrates this sense of communal hierarchy, he advances a conservative ideology.

OBVIOUS DIFFERENCES

The Channel Shore and *The Township of Time* display some obvious differences. In *The Channel Shore* various formal conventions of realism and nostalgia and the opposing ideological positions of communitarian liberalism and conservatism are held in a productive and balanced tension. *The Township of Time* is more embedded in the structures of the romance and the plots and characters are more firmly tied to a more conservative vision. Yet despite the different forms being employed, the two books bear the marks of having emerged from the same place and the same pen. In both the novel and the collection, the ideological tensions can be read as the product of a society that is itself tempted to use a nostalgic desire for a golden past as a guide to explore and to filter the hardships of present realities. Bruce's fictions, like parts of the Maritime region itself, resist the pull towards modernist visions of the world and the inevitable alienation that accompanies them. These shifting perspectives are also the product of an author who felt torn between his desire to pursue a career in an urban centre and his longing for the rural peace that characterized his youth. In the end, Bruce's best prose is a complex field that signals the region's and author's unease with the transformations of the twentieth century. Ernest Buckler, in *The Mountain and the Valley*, follows Bruce as the first Maritime writer to unflinching face these fearful disruptions.

4 Conservative Laments: Ernest Buckler

> The time began to go. This would be the last day; and the day
> before the going is shadowed with the going, so that there is no
> free time left.
>
> Buckler, *The Mountain and the Valley.*

When Ernest Buckler left his family's farm in the Annapolis Valley in 1925 to begin his BA at Dalhousie University, the community was on the verge of tremendous change. Like Buckler, thousands of youths across the Maritimes were leaving their rural roots and migrating to rapidly expanding urban centres in search of an education and higher-paying jobs. The sense of uncertainty created by this exodus grew as local Maritime products were unable to compete with goods from western Canada and the United States; smaller farming and manufacturing operations were eventually forced out of the marketplace. Of course, in the early stages of this economic restructuring, hopeful voices of protest arose. Advocates of progressive agriculture attempted to counteract or manage the transformations within their industry, and political groups like the United Farmers called for the implementation of such "practical measures as the building of more country roads to improve access to markets, the elimination of tariffs on imported farm machinery and fertilizers, and the further extension of electricity and postal services into the countryside" (Forbes 1993, 238). While the United Farmers party was never able to consolidate its political base and translate its popularity into votes or its platform into government policy, their demands were recognized and adopted by many of the province's mainline parties and were eventually echoed by the Royal Commission on Maritime Claims (Forbes 1993, 239). In short, when Buckler left the Valley, the traditional farm was under significant pressure, but there was still hope that small operations could survive and prosper.

After obtaining his Liberal Arts degree with a distinction in mathematics in 1929, Buckler went to the University of Toronto and completed his MA in Philosophy. He then spent five years doing actuarial work with the Manufacturers Life Insurance Company before his ill health and aversion to city life caused him to return home for good in 1936 at the age of twenty-eight (Pell 1995, 10; Young 1976a, 9). The Valley to which he returned was a radically different place from the secure community of his youth. Although farmers continued to organize marketing agencies and co-operative retail stores in an attempt to maintain their way of life, the economic collapse of 1930 had lowered the value of agricultural products 39 percent and many farms were reduced to subsistence operations. The optimism that fuelled the protest movements of the 1920s had been exchanged for a growing sense of doubt and despair. The Second World War bolstered the national economy and secured steady markets for some food stuffs, but enlistment and the demand for labourers in wartime industries further increased the out-migration of young people from rural areas. Even after the war the Annapolis Valley continued to experience change and hardship. The closure of the British market, which had absorbed up to 80 percent of the valley's apple production before the war, meant that many farmers "were obliged to uproot their orchards, close their warehouses, and nail 'For Sale' signs on their property" (Forbes 1993, 324). By the end of 1949, Valley farmers "counted half the apple trees they had possessed" at the beginning of the decade, and such a loss weighed heavily on the community (Forbes 1993, 324). The farmers, like Buckler, who chose to remain, made a passable living by adopting the technologies of the new mass-consumer culture, but many regretted seeing the "old order based on scarcity and hard work" disappear (Forbes 1993, 383).

Unlike Frank Parker Day who wrote his fiction before the traditional folkways were fully destroyed or Charles Bruce who spent his life in exile and thus was able to avoid encountering some of the changes sweeping his "country of the mind," Buckler was thoroughly immersed in the economic and cultural shifts of his time. His three works of fiction encounter and reproduce these social/psychological disruptions, and they continually register his anxiety about his homeland's metamorphosis. In his second novel, *The Cruelest Month*, Buckler confronts the modern era directly, and through his exploration of his urban characters – whose modern world is ultimately void of meaning or security – he sounds a note of alienation and uncertainty. In his third book, the elegiac fictional memoir *Ox Bells and Fireflies*, Buckler attempts to reproduce a conservative and idealized past, reconstructing a traditional world as a conscious escape from and critique of contemporary experience. However, his first novel, *The Mountain and the Valley*, combines the two impulses of his later work and creates his most sensitive and evocative exploration of the Annapolis Valley. As the members of the Canaan family move from an idyllic traditional way of life towards an isolated and ultimately modernist existence, Buckler reproduces some of the most powerful tensions of his era and creates a compelling and archetypal exploration of his region's demise.

As in the exploration of Raddall, the term "modernist" here signifies the broader cultural and historical shift in the twentieth century as postwar societies increasingly experienced a sense of alienation, fragmentation, and skepticism. Although Buckler was deeply affected by the cultural shift towards modernism, *The Mountain and the Valley* shows few signs that his formal or stylistic practices were influenced by the more narrowly defined literary aesthetic of modernism.

THE MOUNTAIN AND THE VALLEY

The Mountain and the Valley was written over a period of more than ten years (Dvorak 2001, 30). Incorporating elements from some of the short stories he was writing at the time, Buckler's book was first published in New York in 1952 and, after a series of favourable reviews, it sold well on the American market.[1] At first, sales at home were sluggish, and only "two hundred and fifty copies of the book were imported into Canada for publication under the Clarke, Irwin imprint" (Davies 1988, 36). The novel remained in relative obscurity until it appeared as part of McClelland and Stewart's New Canadian Library series in 1961, after which it rose to prominence selling 28,000 copies by 1972, emerging as one of the country's best-known regional studies (Dvorak 2001, 31).

Without doubt, *The Mountain and the Valley* is the most extensively critiqued of all Maritime realist texts. The novel was initially viewed as an exploration of the rural world and a celebration of the main character's ability to transcend his limitations and capture the essence of his community before his death. Douglas Spettigue, Greg Cook, Marilyn Chambers, J.M. Kertzer, and Alan Young all produced early readings suggesting that the text has an ultimately affirmative vision of the world. Subsequent critics have viewed the work as an ironic narrative depicting a fallen world, and such critics as Douglas Barbour, Gerald Noonan, E. Sarkar, and Barbara Pell have supported this position by focusing their attention on the failures of David, the central protagonist. To date, virtually no critic has addressed the complex and competing ideological tensions at the heart of the text. Yet if the work is a "minor masterpiece," as L. Doerksen suggests (1980, 56), its success is based on its unique attempt to combine a conservative representation of the Annapolis Valley's historical and social fabric, with a less overtly politicized modernist bildungsroman tracing David Canaan's psychological growth from a sensitive child sheltered in the midst of his loving family, to a solitary thirty-year-old man. These two aspects of the narrative are so intertwined that it is difficult to appreciate fully the significance of the narrator's depiction of David, without first exploring the conservatism that drives both the nostalgic representation of Entremont and the narrative's critique of the modernist forces that eventually overwhelm and destroy this idyllic world.

As Buckler celebrates his valley's "traditions," his sense of nostalgia is fused with a set of conservative assumptions that anchor his fiction. Conservative ideologies stress collectivist and hierarchical models of social organization, while at the same time emphasizing the importance of a strong sense of ethnic or national identity linked to a core of cultural traditions. Conservatives in general, and Buckler in particular, emphasize the importance of tradition and hold that "virtue, stability, and civilization" depend on the continuity of long established institutions and cultural practices; they are innately hostile to "radical social change" (Minogue 1967, 195–6). Within this framework, traditions are the "heritage of skills and attainments on which our present achievements are founded," and authorities or patriarchal structures must be empowered to "guard such achievements and traditions against the continual threat of human folly, laziness, blindness, and stupidity" (Minogue 1967, 197). Buckler is too skilled a writer to launch an obtrusive defence of these assumptions; however, in the first two sections of the novel, the world seems most idyllic when the characters suspend their individualist impulses and submerge themselves in nature or forge a conservative bond with each other through their mutual community, their traditional cultural practices, or their conformity to particular patriarchal structures.

The brief prologue quickly aligns the reader with the text's nostalgic impulse. Focalized through the lonely eyes of the older David as he views his wintering fields, the opening pages confirm that any sense of plentitude and joy has long since vanished from his life. If the orchards were once symbols of fertility, David now sees only "twisted apple trees and ... bushes along the line fence" that are "locked and separate ... all their life had fled" (*MV*, 8). To underscore the character's desire for a happier past, the prologue shifts to view the world through the grandmother's feeble eyes. Each member of the once-intricately fused family is introduced as Ellen fingers the scraps of their clothing, which serve to signify their absence. The opening six pages thus inform us that the rest of the text will not take place in an evolving present, but will unfold within a framed past, a type of sacred memory.

The nostalgic mood deepens in the opening, pastoral sections of the novel, particularly in "Part One: The Play," when the narrator pauses and lingers over the beauties of the rural environment. Most of *The Mountain and the Valley* employs a limited third-person narration, and Buckler refuses to "supply an omniscient objective judgement on his protagonists" (Pell 1995, 20). Occasionally, however, a more removed omniscient narrator does emerge to produce an overview of the community or natural setting. For example, in the opening pages of chapter 7, the farm's changing seasons are traced and the narrator notes that each is appearing in all its possible fullness and beauty:

All of summer they knew: the day of daisy-trembling in the still hypnotic air ... the day the mowing machine dribbled the shocked clover between its chattering teeth ... until the day was full of green to the last brimming: the white green of the poplars and the oat field and the river: the storm green of the orchard and the spruce mountain: the black green of the potato tops: the green-green of the garden. (*MV*, 47)

But if the text longs to recreate an idyllic intimacy with the rural world, the style simultaneously signals that such recreations are difficult. Numerous critics – including Warren Tallman, D.J. Dooley, and Gerald Noonan – have noted that Buckler's enthusiasm occasionally leads him astray into tautologies like "green-green" or the notorious sentence in which thirteen adjectives are strung together to describe Christmas eve: "In that instant it was suddenly, ecstatically, burstingly, bouyantly, enclosingly, sharply, safely, stingingly, watchfully, batedly, mountingly, softly, ever so softly, it was Christmas Eve" (*MV*, 59). While the narrator sometimes distances himself from young David, who is sometimes overly poetic in his description of his world, this particular passage is free from such an ironic tone and is meant to capture the experience of the whole Canaan family on Christmas eve. David Williams salutes this as "one of the most overwritten sentences in the language" (1991, 162). The text's overly "poetic" passages indicate that the narration is trying hard – sometimes too hard – to recreate Arcadia, and the overdetermined attempts to restore an ideal world occasionally collapse under their own weight. Nostalgia is so important to the ideology of the novel that Buckler is willing to risk occasional embarrassment in order to ensure that a foundation is established for his emerging conservatism.

The traditional rural life includes many episodes of pain and absence, but early in the text most inhabitants of Entremont can still connect with the transcendental absolute through communal or patriarchal structures: Buckler "celebrates the cohesiveness of an exceptionally close family in a stable, interrelated rural community in intimate communion with nature" (Pell 1995, 24). For example, when the whole village turns out to see the school play, there are several moments when the people recognize the beauty before them, suspend their petty differences, and fuse into a collective. The marginalized figure of Bess is alienated in her awareness that "no woman her own age was sitting near her," and it is not until Martha speaks of their children as a single entity that Bess feels fully accepted and can "scarcely answer for tears" (*MV*, 73). True joy arises not from individual experience but from a sense "of belonging to a community" (Dvorak 1994, 28). Thus, David precipitates disaster not simply when he egotistically asserts his own individual interpretation of the play, but when he does so in the face of community expectations. His violation of the conservative sense of self-subordination prevents him from sharing Bess's elation.

If moments of transcendence occur through contact with the community, they also occur when cultural traditions are observed and renewed. Buckler celebrates past social structures with a near spiritual enthusiasm, which leads Marta Dvorak to suggest that the novel is "steeped in a mixture of pantheism and neo-Platonism ... in which nature is the expression of a pervading, non-personal spirit of good, a universal soul closely linked with the Platonic prototype of the One" (1994, 30).[2] Such transcendence, and the ideological power of such moments, is evident in the Christmas scene described in the ninth chapter, which is particularly fulfilling as the family gathers around the decorated tree: "The tree was there. So still. So Christmas-still. For a minute no one moved. This was the tree of hope" (*MV*, 61). A sense of completion radiates through this passage as the essence of the holiday briefly crystallizes both for the young, innocent David and for the older family members. Though language fails to communicate their emotions and the characters struggle to converse through half-sentences, the traditional decorations and the ritual exchange of gifts become the family members' means of expressing their deep commitment to one another. However fleeting they may be, these moments of pleasure are important for they provide a standard of plentitude to which characters like David will aspire: a benchmark that can be reached only in the early stages of the text, so long as the traditional community and its structures remain intact.

The text's fusion of nostalgia and conservatism can also be discerned in its extensive and complex celebration of patriarchal hierarchies and in the sense of pleasure that characters experience when they fulfill their place in the social order. Not all patriarchs are revered: Ellen's husband Richard was a domineering father whose puritan sense of pride led to tyrannical acts of repression, including his demand that his wife sever her ties with her family: "He never let her write back home. Not a line" (*MV*, 25). However, such men are anomalies and the few references to Richard only serve to emphasize his son's virtue rather than developing into a comprehensive critique of the patriarchal family structure.

At the top of the family structure stands Joseph, the ideal father, who represents the essence of male power, which organizes and secures the community. The narrator depicts Joseph as a folk hero, and his pioneer strength epitomizes a type of heroism no longer present in the modern world: "his lack of fear ... and a kind of stubborn thoughtlessness to alter circumstances for his own ease were local legend" (*MV*, 20). Aptly named after the biblical father of Christ, Joseph represents the virtues Buckler feels are needed to ensure the family's survival (Doerksen 1987, 237–8). He is a selfless labourer whose sense of duty, practical wisdom, and spiritual integrity make him a source of strength for both his children and his community. Joseph fulfills the traditional archetypes of masculinity and the narrator ensures that his deeds appear as natural actions rather than as culturally constructed behaviours. For example, in accordance with the patriarchal convention, the women remain within the home while the novel's male characters inhabit the economically important external work places, which include the barn, the fields, and the woods. Joseph's "external" role is unquestioningly reproduced by the narrator who only uses Joseph as a focalizer when he is engaged in some form of labour, either moving rocks with David or packing meat with Martha. At such moments, when Joseph is conscious of his position at the head of an enduring family, he feels a deep satisfaction, which echoes in his homespun language: "My life tastes like bread. The days roll down the week like a wheel. Then it is Sunday and the wheel is still and we walk through the garden and try a hill of new potatoes" (*MV*, 151).

If Joseph represents Buckler's ideal man, Martha – whose name is probably a reference to the serving woman of the New Testament – is the text's strongest model of the feminine; she is happiest when she fulfills the role defined for her by the Victorian cult of domesticity. Although diaries, letters, and journals from the period between the wars indicate that women were still active in many types of farm labour, Buckler's representations are circumscribed; it is clear that Martha feels most content – most natural – when she stays within her maternal, restorative, nurturing role.³ As with Joseph, the narrator prefers to use Martha as a focalizer only when she is alone and attaining a sense of edenic contentment through her household chores: "The kitchen was the perimeter of Martha's whole life. She dressed it as carefully as she would a child ... when she was outside it she felt strange ... When the day's work was done and supper over the kitchen seemed to smile" (MV, 17).

Joseph and Martha are happiest when they are fulfilling their traditional gender roles. This rural union of man and woman – this depiction of a "new Adam and Eve [who attain] oneness in the new garden through work" (Dvorak 1994, 28) – becomes a touchstone to which the other less successful relationships are compared, and as such they function as an indispensable part of the novel's conservatism. However, just as Buckler needs this stable couple to establish the novel's ideological centre, so he must also extinguish the couple in order to fulfill his larger project of representing the disintegration of the rural world. Unlike Frank Parker Day, Hugh MacLennan, or Thomas Raddall, Buckler has no illusions that a single perfect couple can escape into a reserved paradise of their own. This paradoxical drive to both idealize and eliminate causes some curious problems for the narrative. While most of the characters operate within a careful historicist chain of cause and effect, Buckler invokes the device of chance, or perhaps more accurately fate, in order to avoid the realist critique that would trace a vein of inadequacy in Martha and Joseph and compromise their role as an ideal. As Martha and Joseph argue about how to divide the butchered hog and then separate to perform their distinct tasks, it is clear that the couple would have been reunited were it not for a number of incredible coincidences that seal their doom. Martha would have been able to call to Joseph and restore their sense of communion if she had not suffered a slight heart attack at that crucial moment and if her subsequent spoken attempt at reconciliation had not been blocked by "the wind [that] was blowing away from him" (MV, 213). Similarly, Joseph is not doomed by his refusal to adhere to a communal norm: he is killed because the wind happened to gust when he was standing in the wrong place. When David climbs the mountain and passes the spot where Joseph died, he senses the inevitability of the accident using the word "exactly" sixteen times in a paragraph to indicate that some events are predetermined and that his father was not responsible for an event that was clearly beyond human interference: "There is the branch of the tree growing exactly that way because it has stood there exactly that number of seconds and because its roots broke and wandered exactly as they did under the earth" (MV, 290). Both Joseph and Martha leave abruptly at the end of part 5. Indeed, they are so admired within the text that Buckler does not even want to directly represent Martha's miserable loneliness without Joseph. Within the experience of the reader, the two disappear at the same time. Once the secure patriarchal system they represent disappears, the novel quickens its descent towards tragedy. The couple are removed after the conservative values they symbolize have been fully appreciated, but before the full power of the modernist world could compromise their ideal state.

Buckler's conservatism provides the driving force behind the text's nostalgic impulse, but the narrative's energy is not exhausted by these reconstructions of the past. As the fabric of the rural community begins to unravel – as the characters lose their hold on their idyllic state and drift towards a modernist existence – Buckler attends closely to the historicist aspects of his realist narrative and carefully examines the forces that generate the tragic effects of alienation. Tracing the multiple pressures acting on each character, Buckler condemns the power of the encroaching urban environment and the failure of the villagers to uphold traditional practices of their community. By wedding his conservatism to a critique of these disruptive forces, Buckler ties his exploration of his region's past to the realist core of the text: his ideological assumptions begin to shape the very processes of cause and effect that drive the plot.

The threatening power of the modern urban world emerges slowly, but once the city makes its appearance, the reader is hard pressed to find a positive allusion to any "urban influence" (Bissell 1961, viii). When David flees the farm and accepts a ride with two "city people," he recognizes that they do not "permeate each other all the time, like his mother and father did. They were merely sitting there side by side" (MV, 162). The urban world, with its "shallowness and disunity" – its overemphasis on material goods – tends to isolate people from one another through the false categories of class, instead of fostering a more communal and cooperative spirit (Kristiansen 1994, 243). Even the railway, the highway, and the radio take on negative connotations as they signal the "encroachment of urbanization and technological progress" (Young 1973, 220).

This critique of the urban world that begins with these minor allusions is expanded through Toby Richmond, David's pen pal, and eventually Anna's husband. Toby is a likeable and vulnerable character, but he lacks the deeper qualities that are admired within this narrative. He is a young man with a short attention span, little memory, and a rather feminine delicacy that is attributed to his soft urban upbringing (McKay 1994, 255). When David, Anna, and Toby explore the community's abandoned homes, the city-boy displays a remarkable insensitivity, sporting old clothes, reading forsaken letters, and pondering a broken snowshoe, all of which he "promptly forgot" (*MV*, 248). He is unaware that he is within a place made sacred by the lost past it signifies.

Given the inadequacies of the urban environment and its inhabitants, it is not surprising that Anna is unable to make a satisfying life for herself in Halifax as Toby's wife. Buckler is particularly selective in his representations of Anna's city life. She first leaves for Halifax at the end of chapter 18; for several years afterwards, within the chronology of the narrative, she only reappears as a character when she visits the farm. Buckler does not focalize the text through her eyes as a Halifax resident until the thirtieth chapter and does not devote a prolonged section of the text to her city experiences until chapter 34. Even at this late stage the narrator restricts the descriptions of the city. Unlike Hugh MacLennan's *Barometer Rising*, which develops vivid representations of Halifax, *The Mountain and the Valley* never explores an urban work environment or includes a detailed cityscape. The narration provides descriptions only of Anna's dingy apartment building and a few disorienting nightclubs; the reader cannot help but notice that these limited urban settings compare unfavourably with the domestic and communal spaces of Entremont. In the end, the reader is left with negative impressions of a city of "cramped" apartments whose rooms "seemed to disown" their tenants. Anna must eventually "imitate" Toby's "nomadic ... carelessness" in order to endure her condition (*MV*, 228). Toby will, of course, be killed by the weapons of modern warfare, but if Anna survives we cannot imagine that she ever really "lives" once she has left her pastoral home.

The novel's characters are usually responsible for their own unhappiness, but the narrator does not blame Anna for her inevitable relocation to the city, nor does he condemn Toby for his recklessness. Rather, Buckler condemns the city itself for its dehumanizing power. In a passage echoing T.S. Eliot's "The Preludes" and Raddall's tirade against modern culture in *The Nymph and the Lamp*, the narrator describes those elements that seem particularly dismal to Anna, including: "The row of ashcans in the rain. The impersonal clink of milk bottles in the delivery boy's basket ... A foul word of adult knowingness from the mouth of a child in a narrow street. The laugh of a friend at some joke that only had a mechanical catchphrase humour in it. A little whirlwind drawing up the chewing-gum wrappers and scraps of newspaper from the sidewalk. The unembarrassed silence of the woman next door as they hung out their clothes from adjoining balconies" (*MV*, 229). Emotionally, spiritually, and stylistically, the urban world is a wasteland, and through Anna's unhappiness the text develops its critique of the shallow, superficial materialism that threatens the security and stability of Entremont.

The text also moves beyond its direct analysis of Halifax to explore the powerful economic or technological forces that extend out of the urban centres to disrupt the agrarian life of the valley. Kristiansen argues that, for Buckler, "the penetration of the marketplace into the countryside meant that rural Nova Scotia could no longer be truly rural, there seemed little hope that these areas would gain any of the advantages of contemporary urban life" (1994, 243). Glenn Willmott extends this analysis to argue that Buckler's novel reproduces a tension common to postcolonial texts. It represents the rural world as a place that is being reshaped to serve a dual purpose. Buckler emphasizes that his region is being treated as a differentiated other that is by turns ignored by capitalist interests and then exploited as a potential new market for urban goods and products (Willmott 1995, 306–7). Alienation inevitably results as the rural farms are gradually sold off to industries that seek only to reap raw materials while the people become cheap copies of the industrialized culture as they are corrupted by their desire for the new consumer goods. While Day underrepresented the suffering inherent in the cod trades and Bruce veiled the hardships of the Depression and the disintegration of the small communities in the postwar era, Buckler meticulously documents the economic transformations, reinforcing his conservative ideology by consistently pointing out that these shifts exact a tragically high cost: "a big timber company had bought these farms solely for their timber. The company had no interest in the houses or the fields. The people had moved to town. The houses just stood there. Their doors were open and their windows broken out by hunters. The walls were still upright; but the kitchen floors sagged toward the cellar, the plaster had warped and crumbed" (MV, 247). The text's bleak representation of industrial transformation is driven by the same conservatism that fuelled the idealistic representation of the Valley.

The novel does not restrict its analysis to those pressures that threaten the valley from without. Several individuals precipitate their own destruction by failing to reproduce the traditional cultural patterns that lead to contentment. Such is certainly the case with Chris and Charlotte. From his first appearance, it is clear that Chris is driven predominantly by physical desire; he is able to reproduce only a shadow image of his patriarchal heritage. Chris and Charlotte's sexual relationship reproduces the text's patriarchal assumptions – the young man acts as the aggressor while the young woman is sexually resistant, "negative and hidden" – but the narrator is critical when they fail to develop this physical experience into a more stable and complex relationship (MacDonald 1976, 199). Chris increasingly thinks of Charlotte only as a sexual object; his realization that "maybe there was lots of it. Maybe he could find it better somewhere else" (MV, 110) signifies a commodification of intimacy that is not viewed sympathetically by the narrator. The two are trapped into a "shotgun" marriage, and after Charlotte's miscarriage, Chris is reduced to a parody of his father, a kind of fallen Adam: "He circled around and around the cellar ... he reached down into the apple barrel. The apple was wilty and half rotten, but he bit into it and chewed it the same propulsive ludicrous way" (MV, 200). Having failed to reproduce the rich inner lives that characterized his parents, Chris is divorced from his heritage. His subsequent wanderings through war-torn Europe and the factories of western Canada accurately reflect his inner sense of alienation. Traditional models prove to be an avenue to contentment, while a transgression of convention leads to a sense of loneliness within the valley, every bit as intense as that produced by the city.

If a failure to reproduce traditional models leads to individual misery, a rejection of Entremont's shared patriarchal/communal customs undermines the very heart of the rural village. Initially, Bess Delahunt would seem to be just such a threat to family stability. Physically expressive and emotionally open, Bess "chins up" to the local men, becomes a pariah among the women, and the object of coarse humour in the community. Though socially ostracized, the narrator suggests that the condemnation is unwarranted and represents Bess as a sensitive, merciful woman whose motives are misunderstood. Bess's grief at her husband's death is genuine and her attempts to "mend his shirt cuff where the frayin showed" echo the pathos of her situation (MV, 37). Whatever her superficial violations of communal mores, Bess represents the deepest values of an ideal community: honesty, strength, and a sense of compassion. The narrator is protective of Bess, and extra steps are taken to inform the reader that she really does respect communal norms, having suspended all sexual licence after her second marriage. That Bess, in the final pages, should be divided from her second husband by malicious gossip before drowning herself in despair is a strong signal that a fine individual has been destroyed by a community that chooses to uphold superficial behavioural norms while ignoring the deeper values of the conservative position.

The narration, which works hard to vindicate Bess for upholding the deep communal values of compassion, works even harder to demonize Rachel Gorman. Throughout her first appearance in Martha's kitchen, Rachel's poison tongue works systematically to utter something negative about each member of the Canaan family, until Martha feels as if her "morning was tarnished" (*MV*, 32). Though she has the veneer of puritan restraint and self-denial that passes as virtue, Rachel is represented as a self-centered woman who sacrifices her friends and her own child to indulge her need for attention. Bess may have the reputation of subverting the village's moral code, but in the narrator's view Rachel is guilty of the more abhorrent crime of undermining the community's faith in the patriarchal order.

The narrator strongly implies that Rachel is such a domineering and therefore unnatural wife that clumsy Spurge Gorman is motivated to escape on the annual log drive, a decision that results in both Pete Delahunt's and his own death. As they return from the log drive with the news that Pete Delahunt and Spurge Gorman have drowned, one man remarks that Gorman "had no business on the drive, clumsy as he was. But the poor bugger always seemed so glad to git away" (*MV*, 34). Buckler thus suggests that Gorman is attempting to escape from his overbearing wife, and by extension the audience understands that Rachel has not worked to make her home a happy one.

Implicated in the death of her own husband, Rachel proceeds to ruin the happiness of the next generation as she prevents Chris from assuming his proper role as the centre of Charlotte's world. In a text constructed within patriarchal stereotypes, there are few roles for women outside the categories of nurturing mother or devoted wife. Unlike Day's character Fanny, or Bruce's character Renie Marshall, there are few women in *The Mountain and the Valley* who transgress gender stereotypes without being criticized for their difference. A tendency to polarize the feminine characters is evident as Rachel emerges as a villain in a novel that avoids overtly labelling most other characters. Twice Rachel earns the text's most vicious appellation and is referred to as a "bitch" (*MV*, 192, 288), and it would be difficult for the reader to find an interpretive position within the framework of the novel that would allow them to contest this judgement. Rachel eventually goes to live with her own mother in Beaverbrook. Her retreat to a matriarchal household outside the community signals that she is ultimately unable to exist within the "benevolent" patriarchy of Entremont, but her symbolic expulsion from the narrative comes too late. If the city threatens the valley from without, seditious forces like Rachel Gorman have subverted it from within.

The influence of Buckler's conservatism can be felt in the narrative's nostalgic and idyllic representations, as well as in its realistic attempts to trace the unhappy decline of the minor characters. These ideological assumptions permeate the text; whatever aspect of Entremont is being explored, the audience is able to interpret the events through the consistently recurring conservative framework. But if Buckler's conservatism becomes the central ideological force structuring the novel, it is not the only set of ideas at work here. Indeed, *The Mountain and the Valley* would be a disappointingly one-dimensional text if Buckler had not succeeded in interweaving his conservative critique with a remarkably sensitive internalized exploration of the modernist condition through the figure of David. As David changes from an innocent and optimistic child lodged in the bosom of his family to the alienated and empty figure who is alone in the final pages, it becomes apparent that the text is stepping outside its assured conservatism to address a powerful modernist despair. Given that so much energy has been devoted to constructing a unified formal and ideological position, it is intriguing that the novel also relies heavily on the techniques of subversion and irony to construct a main character who represents and momentarily recognizes the meaninglessness of contemporary existence.

David Canaan is the most thoroughly analysed character in Maritime literature. Commentators have approached this complex figure from a number of different directions with varying degrees of sympathy. Most would at least agree that in the first section David seems to have a particularly promising future. An unusually sensitive child, David is alert to all the possibilities of life. He loves the natural world; in the opening chapter he awakes excited at the prospect of exploring the "undulant hush of darkness" that covers the mountain (*MV*, 13). David – sensitive as well to his friends and family – attempts to comfort Effie after the death of her father (*MV*, 41), and he fully appreciates his family's Christmas traditions (*MV*, 55). He is not a perfect child and displays moments of arrogance as he views his family with a "surging, binding kind of pity" (*MV*, 50), but David's early life is rich and full, and he grows in the expectation that such moments of plenitude will increase in power and frequency.

But if critics agree that David is a child of great promise, there is less consensus about why this promise is not fulfilled as he passes through adolescence. Certainly, David's unsuccessful struggles to define himself and develop his innate abilities mark him out as a recognizably modernist character. His struggle for identity echoes the central concerns of many twentieth-century novels. But the critics have tended to focus their searches and examine narrow aspects of his personality or situation to explain his "failure" to achieve the transcendent experiences he desires. Operating within the not entirely reliable assumption that the events of David's life follow a logical causal progression, critics have examined his various weaknesses and his flawed relationship with his community in an attempt to understand why he has not fulfilled his potential as an individual man or as an artist. Claiming that he refuses to assume his proper role as a responsible citizen, Douglas Barbour is one of David's harshest critics, asserting that he "is too selfish to ever look at others for their own sakes: he sees everything in relation to his own selfish needs" (1976, 71). In a similar way, Barbara Pell holds David responsible for choices that have "retarded his innate artistic ability" and cramped his imagination so that it remains "narcissistic and solipsistic" (1995, 68). His failure to achieve his own mature identity has "crippled his ability to accept the relationship of a man and the responsibilities of an artist" (1995, 59). Others are less severe in their judgements, claiming that the hero is unable to attune his imaginative power to his own real needs or those of the community (Chapman 1978, 187), or that he is simply unable to separate himself from his community in order to fulfill his imaginative calling (Dooley 1978, 680). A few critics have also explored David's relationship with his community by considering the formal elements of the text. Leana Doerksen, for one, believes David is doomed because he is unable to successfully fulfill the bildungsroman model and complete his rebellion against his family and friends in order to establish his own identity and free himself as an artist (1980, 50). Certainly there is no shortage of evidence to support claims that David alienates himself from his community and family to pursue a self-centered course of action. When David coerces Effie into satisfying his sexual desire in a vain attempt to impress Toby, the narrator presents his actions as selfish and insensitive, and David himself is burdened by the knowledge of his guilt (*MV*, 141). Similarly, when David refuses to forgive Chris after falling from the barn rafter, the narrator clearly sympathizes with the elder brother and criticizes David for heartlessly thwarting his brother's search for absolution (*MV*, 188). For such moments of self-indulgence the narrative critiques David, and some of the isolation that he subsequently experiences is reasonable and just.

If some critics seek answers in David's relationship with his environment, others have explored his unique facility with language and have noted that his abilities actually seem to work to his disadvantage. As early as 1971, Richard Reichert had noted that David is unable to capture the language of the valley in the "language of the imagination" (20). E. Sarkar developed this point, noting that "David no longer uses language as a means of communication, but as an end in itself; he no longer participates in the infinite language of human relations, but rather allows language to substitute for human relations" (1979, 359). John Van Rys uses Bakhtin's paradigm to suggest that David fails when he refuses to enter the polyphonic discourses of the community and "withdraws into internal dialogue, monologue, and silence" (1995, 71). MacDonald is less quick to blame David and notes that he seems caught in an inescapable dilemma, declaring that his "tragedy is that he is attracted by the concrete, secure world of the farmer and feels a kinship to it, while living almost entirely in the world of words" (1976, 198).

Again the text validates these observations, for David's facility with imaginative language frequently isolates him from others. This sense of difference emerges when the local boys mock Toby for his refined speech, and David echoes his pen pal's elevated language, willingly alienating himself from his teenage friends: "It was never quite the same with the other boys after that moment" (MV, 138). As an adult, David is unable to use his imagination to form a meaningful connection with his rural environment, and his speech certainly separates him from his father as he lashes out against Joseph during the wood-cutting scene (MV, 159). The suggestions that David's final sense of misery and isolation is caused by his own inability to control his linguistic gifts or negotiate a stable place in his community are valid. Other forces, however, also disrupt his life, and the explorations of his character that do not account for these are incomplete.

If fate drives Joseph and Martha's final scene in order to preserve the idealized couple's conservative role within the text, chance plays a much larger role in the events that buffet David. So many of the moments that transform his character are a matter of bad luck that he seems driven more by arbitrary forces than guided by patterns of conservative stability. Certainly, David makes small decisions that initially divorce him from others and the narrator holds him fully responsible for their immediate outcome, but then chance steps in to make these chasms far wider than David had intended, ultimately leading him towards complete isolation. For example, David's guilt following his betrayal of Effie is a just punishment under the conservative code. His sense of sorrow and isolation, however, is then intensified by the young girl's death. Though the narrator informs the reader that she had contracted childhood "leukaemia" and would have died regardless of David's actions, Bess is unable to remember this medical term, and young Canaan "never knew" that he was not instrumental in her demise (MV, 146). Arbitrary chance transforms a regrettable incident into a tragic event that permanently scars the youth who is "never, even for a moment, all child again" (MV, 146). Similarly, David's refusal to forgive Chris reveals his self-centered desire to maintain control over his brother, but then fate steps in and Rachel's unexpected demand that Chris marry Charlotte forever removes the possibility that Chris and David will be able return to their small family unit.

As David enters adulthood, the narrative increasingly relies on chance to structure the events of his life and systematically isolates him from all he holds dear. The death of his parents and the growing senility of Ellen isolate him from his past. His bad heart prevents him from joining the army and divorces him from the significant events of his generation: "The war had gone around David. It was like all the rest of the things that happened to the others" (MV, 240). Moreover, Effie's death has robbed him of the marriage partner who might have secured his future in the community. While Buckler is careful to reconcile the misfortunes of the other characters within the dominant conservative framework, he repeatedly returns to this element of chance to structure the pivotal moments in David's life. He bears personal responsibility for a portion of his misery, but ultimately he is isolated by forces outside the normal chain of cause and effect. His existence becomes meaningless; there is no single interpretive framework he can invoke in order to decipher his experience. As a lonely and isolated figure, David is simultaneously unique in his community and representative of the modernist condition.

David eventually represents not a particular set of norms, but rather the impossibility of a stable code. Raddall's Isabel Jardine is able to conclude her existential quest when she finally discovers the secret that allows her to fulfill her role within the dominant conservative ideology as a lamp for Carney. David is unable to resolve his existential dilemma because there is no longer a stable community within which he can establish an identity. Even his lifelong search for moments of release or transcendence is affected. As a child, David stumbles effortlessly into moments of bliss in which he can imagine a future life of accomplishment. His childhood desires to be the "greatest general" (MV, 35), "the best skater" (67), "the greatest actor" (76), or the finest singer (135) in the "whole world" carry a kind of naive charm that simply signals the boy's optimism. However as David matures and his world begins to fall apart, his fantasies of being the "best [doctor] in Canada" (172), or the most famous "fiddler," "mathematician," "dancer" (284) or "writer" (293) become increasingly ironic. With his own health failing, his family and community disintegrating, and the world itself transformed by war and population migration, the later sections of the novel suggest that David is unable to attain his moments of transcendence or plenitude not because he is selfish, overly wordy, or disrespectful towards conservative norms but because the moments of transcendence themselves are no longer possible.

In the final chapter of part 6, "The Train," David himself realizes that he is alienated, alone, and trapped in a tragic life that produces neither meaning nor joy. The chapter opens calmly with David waiting in his field to wave at the passing train that carries Toby to Halifax. When Toby doesn't "glance once, not once, toward the house or the field" (MV, 268), David recognizes the symbolic weight of the moment; like the train, his own chance for happiness is pulling away from him, leaving him in a terrifying vacuum. The text is intent on communicating his emptiness, and the narrator draws close to the protagonist to record his thoughts for the next three pages. With a full recognition of his sense of pain, Buckler records David's realization that he will never have a close friend, a companion, or a child. David's loneliness breaks upon him in a "toppling moment of clarity" (MV, 268), and he recognizes all the conventional moments of intimacy he will never experience: "I will always be a stranger to everybody" (MV, 269). Yet when David then attempts to identify the forces that have lead to his despair, the narrator does not return to the conservative critique and blame David's fall on some rejection of conservative values. Invoking the conventions of tragedy, the narrative brings the hero to a full recognition that blind chance has contributed to his ruin and in a final Oedipal moment of self-mutilating rage, David slashes a row of parsnips; an attack on his own symbolic rootedness in the rural culture. In his subsequent attempts to pat "the torn flesh of the parsnips back into shape as best he could," we can read his resignation to his fate and the narrator's acknowledgment that he will never experience any measure of fulfillment (MV, 272). David can comfort Anna with the lie that Toby "waved to us," but he knows that his own life holds no such moments of recognition. He does not have a stable identity. The chapter closes with an image of David carrying a bucket of milk and enduring physical discomfort with the same "unbent" spirit as his father, but without any of the family or community ties that would give meaning to his heroic gestures. In David, the very forces celebrated by the text's conservative impulse prove unable to withstand the disruptive power of chance and change.

The text approves of the "hero" when he meets his fate honestly. In contrast, the narrator has little patience with David's final attempt to avoid the hardships of contemporary existence. When the epilogue records his ascent of the mountain and his simultaneous return to all the ideals and hopes that have already proven to be groundless, the scene is presented with a clear and biting irony. Even the setting of the epilogue is ironic for though David once hoped the mountain would be a place of beauty and harmony, it has always proven to be a place of foreboding and death for Anna, Martha, and Joseph. The reader anticipates David's failure the minute he begins his climb.

As David makes his way through the mountain woods, he relives the most intense moments of his life, and in a response to these memories he decides to write a book recording the essence of his family and village. A few early critics suggest his sudden desire to be a writer is an authentic discovery of his true identity. Douglas Spettigue (1967, 49) and Alan Young (1973, 224) both believe that David achieves a personal triumph by successfully fusing his past and his present. Clara Thomas (1973, 84–6), Marilyn Chambers (1975, 196–8), and J.M. Kertzer (1975, 82–3) go further and see David's final vision as an aesthetic awakening that signals his entrance into his role as an artist. This view was even restated by Elroy Dermert in 1994, when he argued that "we are encouraged to believe [that David] is capable of fathoming the great pastoral ideals of community, of family, and of peace with one's self and one's land. We are even lead to believe that he could articulate these things in writing if he put his mind to it" (144). As David ascends to the top of the mountain, however, it is clear that his dreams are illusions. Unable to truly merge with his subject matter, David is quickly distracted by a self-aggrandizing dream that his "book" will win "the prize" (Barbour 1976, 73). Even more problematic is his hope that his stories could capture the community's "single core of meaning" and "make a light shine kindly" on them all (*MV*, 293–5). Contrary to suggestions that David anticipates the novel Buckler actually writes, David's literary vision is the exact opposite of Buckler's text. While David longs to produce a novel that would heal all familial wounds and close all communal gaps, Buckler's text demonstrates that these absences and lacunae are permanent, inevitable parts of the modern condition. David hopes to restore "the best people in the world," and Buckler demonstrates that these people have already vanished.

When the final ray of idealism shining forth from David has been buried under the deadly snow, only Ellen remains, a lone emblem signifying that the traditional life lauded in the opening is soon to close. Ellen is at least able to complete her artistic projects and her rugs function as material histories of the family unit, but, even in this closing moment, the narrator's modernist sense of despair is uncompromising. Ellen's rugs are woven from the community's past and act as intelligible histories so long as the weaver herself can recall and articulate the memories behind each strand of fabric. By repeatedly stressing that Ellen is slowly losing her mental faculties, the narrator indicates that, however beautiful and functional the rugs are in themselves, they cannot maintain their role as community records once

Ellen has died. The concluding pages carry a strong self-reflective echo, for the narrative seems to be admitting to itself that even the finest artistic expressions cannot recreate the richness of the past. Though we as readers have been given the stories associated with each colour and texture in Ellen's rug – each echo and nuance of Entremont life – and though we become enduring repositories once Ellen and the community have passed away, this store of memory only allows us to recall a dead culture. The traditional rural life, Buckler admits, will never be restored.

This central tension between the conservative desire to return to the past and the modernist recognition that such a return to a time of meaningfulness is necessarily doomed locates *The Mountain and the Valley* in the very vortex of the cultural transformations sweeping the Maritimes in the 1940s and 1950s. As Buckler watches his beloved traditional lifestyle disappear around him, he writes in protest against the forces of destruction and launches his strained quest to return to a bygone age. But at the same time Buckler recognizes that destruction is irreversible, and in the end he must explore how new voices will exist within the wasteland. His ability to intertwine the two ideological perspectives prevents the novel from becoming a monotonous condemnation of change; instead, it becomes the region's most complex reproduction of Maritime culture just before it slips permanently away from its rural roots.

STRAINS OF NOSTALGIA

If Buckler's first novel succeeds because its ideological tensions facilitate its examination of a complex cultural context, then one of the reasons his subsequent fictions are less successful is that their ideological assumptions tend to be too unbendingly monolithic to allow a satisfying exploration of the characters' or the region's struggles. Given Buckler's deep conservatism, it is not surprising that he did not spend his life exploring a variety of political perspectives. Thus, unless he wanted to repeat the patterns already developed in *The Mountain and the Valley*, there are a limited number of paths available to him within his conservative framework. On the one hand, Buckler could investigate the communities that remained after the last vestiges of the traditional rural world had been extinguished. This exploration of postwar anxiety dominated his second novel, *The Cruelest Month*. On the other hand, Buckler could return to his idealized representation of the past, developing a series of portraits depicting the region's edenic existence before it was swept by the forces of change. These vignettes became the regional idyll *Oxbells and Fireflies*.

The episodic *Ox Bells and Fireflies*, published in 1968, isolates the strain of nostalgia first evident in the opening of *The Mountain and the Valley* and extends it into a prolonged celebration of the rural community. Buckler ignores such realist conventions as the separation of subject/object and the reproduction of a clear chain of cause and effect, presenting instead an idealized version of the traditional farm community that contrasts with the negative view of the distant city. Nearly all the text's anecdotes end in the type of affirmation typical of romance. At the text's conclusion the disparate tales begin to fuse together into an organic and complete whole: "And there were songs the color of poppies and roofs the sound of sleep ... and thoughts the taste of swimming ... and voices the touch of bread ... and fireflies and freedom ... And fireflies and freedom" (*OBF*, 302). The stories celebrate the unifying power of a little town named Norstead, a community that returns to and relies on the rituals of past generations to mark each individual's progression through the cycles of birth, education, marriage, family life, old age, and eventually death. Yet if Buckler's reminiscences recreate an idealistic past, the ideological frameworks that drive his realistic and ironic fictions are still very much in force. The importance of a single body of cultural traditions, the need to connect the individual to the expectations of the collective, and especially the reliance on a clear patriarchal hierarchy to maintain stability are all stressed in this fictional memoir. The text's masculinist impulse is so strong that, although the narrator frequently adopts a first- and second-person voice in order to draw close to the reader, a feminine point of view is rarely employed and the depictions of women are never presented in anything but the remote third-person voice. Indeed, the text must veil a whole series of religious, political, economic, and sexual conflicts in order to achieve its ideal vision, and the textual community is as distinctive for the rural experiences it excludes as for the actual incidents it represents. This third fiction is an intriguing web of tensions; however, in this study of realist, texts Buckler's second novel has a greater claim to our attentions.

THE CRUELEST MONTH

Shortly after the publication of *The Mountain and the Valley*, Buckler informed his literary agent, Harold Ober, that he was thinking of writing a "sophisticated novel, with a background of Greenwich's Belle Haven District," where he had spent his summers in the 1920s earning his university tuition (Young 1977, vii). Nine years later, *The Cruelest Month* was completed and subsequently published in 1963.

This is an ambitious work: the allusions are complex, odd mathematical metaphors are abundant, and elaborate symbols abound. The text confronts modernist experience and modernist literature directly, and as Alan Young has pointed out the four-part division of Buckler's novel is deeply indebted to T.S. Eliot's "The Wasteland": the first two parts of the novel record the memories and backgrounds of each character, the third part depicts their attempts to break from their pasts, and the fourth movement represents their individual departures to their new lives (1976a, 39). Buckler explores a wide spectrum of the contemporary world and develops a "sustained and sceptical gaze at modernity," but his basic plot structure remains simple (Kristiansen 1994, 248). Eager to examine the "tortured sensibilities of an educated, urbanized elite" who are deeply embedded in the modern era, but uncomfortable using the urban world as a backdrop, Buckler solves the dilemma by conveniently transporting his anxiety ridden subjects to a tourist home in a rural setting (Kulyk Keefer 1987, 228). At "Endlaw," the farmhouse/resort owned by Paul Creed and maintained by housekeeper Letty, five damaged characters arrive for a few weeks in April 1951, searching for a little peace and quiet wherein they can reevaluate their lives. In the course of the narrative each of the characters confronts his or her biggest personal weakness – one that has invariably been made more painful by the modern or urban environment of their daily lives – and through some form of intuitive reconnection with the natural world surrounding Endlaw, all resolve to change some part of their lives in the hope of achieving happiness. Buckler's conservative ideology is evident both in the narrative's exploration of how each character's problems are rooted in modernist society and in its constant assertion that none of these characters – try as they might – can be content in a contemporary world divorced from the only true source of peace: the traditional rural culture and environment. As the final chapters repeat the same ironic conclusion in each character's life, Buckler, like Eliot, steps away from the possibility of renewal and denies the affirmation of the wasteland archetype. As the city folk seek renewal in a pastoral setting, it may initially seem that Buckler is reproducing Thoreau's *Walden*, a text Paul self-consciously gestures towards with his anagram "Endlaw." But, unlike Thoreau, Buckler is ironically aware that rural rejuvenation is ultimately impossible (Marx 1964, 247–62).

Each of the novel's characters represents a single aspect of the human condition, and the seven characters together produce a comprehensive critique of the modern era. A "startlingly handsome" soldier, Rex Giorno is the most superficial of the characters, and represents the urban world's obsession with physical appearance and the beauty of the flesh (CM, 47). Of the five visitors, he appears least frequently; the narrative seems to exhaust quickly its descriptive powers, noting that he is "like a child" a monotonous sixteen times before he drives back to the city (CM, 48, 52, 86, 88, 127, 141, 144–5, 195, 206, 216, 219, 223, 236). Rex has willingly played the role of a material, if beautiful, commodity within his society, but he is unable to confront his own ghosts – which include the self-inflicted wound that allowed him to escape the front. He spends his time at Endlaw either drinking or sleeping in the "shape of a question mark" (CM, 163). Nature provides this urban figure with little solace, since the only time he recognizes the presence of the rural world is when he uses a tree for target practice (CM, 144). His wife, Sheila, emotionally exhausted after five years of marriage to a hollow partner, is a more substantial character. Her affair with Bruce and the emotional rebirth it produces would seem to be pointing towards a happy ending for this lost woman; however, just as she seems ready to commit herself to a rich new life with the native Nova Scotian, she mistakenly interprets Rex's accident with a rifle as a suicide attempt, and her emotional bond to him rekindles in a sudden flare of protectiveness (CM, 244–6). Though Rex and Sheila Giorno drive down the highway to start a new family, the narrator leaves no illusions that their desperate, loveless relationship has improved. In a final symbolic moment, Rex's discarded cigarette starts a forest fire that nearly destroys the natural world neither was able to fully appreciate. The text's conservative critique of the high-society world that produced these two reified entities could not be more pointed.

Kate Fennison and Morse Halliday reproduce "the fragmented self of urban modernity" and inhabit the realm of the mind and the intellect rather than the domain of the body and the emotions, but, for all their linguistic and cerebral skills, neither finds security (Kristiansen 1994, 251). A failing writer, Morse arrives at Endlaw seeking a release from his writer's block. He is a perceptive person who accurately identifies the weaknesses of each of the guests, but – as Kate notes – his observational skills are untempered by any sense of compassion (CM, 238). His cynical perceptions are deeply rooted, and the reader tends to place little faith in his sudden conversion to Kate's optimism. His sense of elation at the novel's end is only another peak before another fall: "Morse on the side of the angels! It would sound absolutely false" (CM, 284).

Kate also settles for less than her ideal. In love with Paul Creed, she compromises her emotions and commits to Morse for practical and intellectual reasons: "I was going to ask you to marry me ... Nothing romantic. A bargain pure and simple. A contract. For one year less a day ... I know I could get you really writing again" (CM, 159). Driven by her desire to embrace a bit of life before she grows old, her decisions are rushed; she fears that "he'll have no more use for me once he's wrung the story out of me" (CM, 256). The realm of the intellect gives this couple a more hopeful future that the Giornos and their mutual commitment allows them to safely pass through Rex's forest fire unharmed, but it is far less than the ideal love that was once possible in the vanished traditional world. Buckler criticizes intellectual powers that are ungrounded in a conventional humane community.

Paul Creed is the central figure of Endlaw, and his sense of "immediacy" helps put people at ease with themselves and the natural environment, yet Paul himself remains an empty entity. Having spent his life migrating around the world, Paul is a sophisticated and intensely private individual who is shocked to discover that he is in fact completely alone: "He saw what his life had been, a refusal to visit inside the house of anyone's spirit because if the visit were returned he must always speak to them from the doorway of his own" (CM, 63). Without a stable community to which he can reveal his innermost fears and dreams and on which he can rely when he discovers that he is suffering from chronic heart disease, Paul discovers that he is "absolutely lost ... invaded by an absolute loneliness" (CM, 171). He becomes an emblem of alienated modernism, and like his predecessor David Canaan, Paul's final sense of transcendence and clarity is tinged with irony. In the final chapters, Creed renounces his attempts to maintain his personal independence, destroys the many notebooks that "encapsulated the lessons of a lifetime" (CM, 272), and turns to an intimate relationship with Letty as a source of comfort and rejuvenation. Kristiansen notes that Buckler's novel is, ironically, deeply suspicious of written language, a form of expression that he views as displacing and corrupting the ideal spoken language of pre-modern culture: "On the one hand, writing is connected with the fragmented self, alienation, a competitive impersonality, social inequality, and entrenched hierarchies. On the other hand, we have speech, which is related to the small rural community, the immediate presence of other people, authenticity, integrated personalities, community solidarity, and social equality" (1994, 254).

While the union of the worldly traveller and the illiterate housekeeper works within the symbolic system of the text, it is also an uneven match that cannot last. After their first night together they hardly know how to address each other. Paul may attempt to abandon his modern use of language, but he discovers that he is unable to resurrect the spoken culture of the pre-modern world and his attempt to leave his modern world is unsuccessful. Unlike David, Paul's sense of loneliness results not from arbitrary misfortune but from a long string of personal decisions. His sense of alienation is thus his own responsibility, a conclusion that aligns the resort owner with the text's larger critique of modernist influences.

If Rex, Sheila, Morse, Kate, and Paul represent the problematic aspects of the modernist world, Bruce Mansfield and Letty are characters who originate in the rural environment, but must then attempt to renegotiate their place in the new world. Bruce is an anomaly within the text: unlike the other characters, his personal history is recorded in detail by the narrator, including the childhood he spent at Endlaw when it was still his father's farm, his early affection for and eventual marriage to Molly, and his subsequent troubled relationship with his son, Peter. Bruce is governed by his feelings of guilt, which originate in his neglect of his family, and are presented as the natural consequence of an individual's decision to misalign himself with the commodifying forces of the modern world. His overwhelming despair when Molly and Peter are killed in a car accident perfectly represents the inevitable destruction that follows anyone's attempt to abandon their rural heritage to pursue the illusions of urban opportunities. As the only historicized figure in the novel, Bruce seems out of place in *The Cruelest Month* and would be more at home in *The Mountain and the Valley*; indeed, as the novel progresses he reconnects himself with the rural virtues celebrated in the opening sections of Buckler's first novel. Bruce and Peter's conflict-filled relationship was first developed by Buckler in his short story "The Rebellion of Young David." Given that it was published a year before Buckler's first novel, the sense that Bruce, as a historicized character, has more in common with the complex figures of *The Mountain and the Valley* than with the linear actants in *The Cruelest Month* is not without justification.

The longer Bruce immerses himself in the natural world, the stronger he becomes, until the narrator recognizes that he is once again "fluent in the earth, he had the true countryman's rock-bottom sturdiness and masculinity that no other can match" (*CM*, 132). Healed by a natural world that is the very antithesis of the deadly urban environment, Bruce is able to confront his own past: when he makes love with Sheila in an appropriately Arcadian setting, he is returned to a state of wholeness. As he drives away from Endlaw, he sees a young deer and remembers the mystical sense of wonder such sightings produced in his own childhood. He vows to become a "children's psychiatrist" in order to save "the ones who held their bodies like a weapon" (*CM*, 268). Bruce is the only character whose sense of regeneration is unmarred, but if he varies from the ironic disappointments that govern the fates of the other characters, he only confirms the conservative ideology that has a structuring influence throughout the text.

Finally, there is the figure of Letty who, more than any other character, plays a central symbolic role. Letty embodies the very forces of nature that the others have to varying degrees ignored. As an illiterate country woman Letty is immune to the transforming power of the modern age. She dislikes the enclosed and insensitive nature of town life and comments that the useless language games Morse loves to play "wouldn't amount to a fart on the plain of Arabia" (*CM*, 10). As a woman of the earth, Letty speaks only through her labour, and her unpretentious lifestyle leads to an unusual degree of contentment: "I don't think she has ever lost a thing. She's one of the few people I've ever seen that time didn't turn porous and leaky" (*CM*, 118). As an emblem of the old-fashioned world, Letty is central to the values embedded within *The Cruelest Month*, but the novel itself seems to recognize that she cannot really exist in the same modernist milieu that surrounds the other characters. Letty is the novel's only undamaged character, but she is largely isolated from the main action. She appears in only five of the thirty-three chapters – only twice as focalizer – and as a result her symbolic importance is far greater than her actual textual presence. The narrator admires the marginalized Letty as the sole voice of untainted tradition and uses her to critique the errors of the lost postwar generation, but the text leaves little doubt that her stability represents an insufficient reply to the overwhelming disruptions represented by such figures as Rex, Sheila, Morse, and Kate.

Buckler's *The Cruelest Month* has long been ignored as the inferior younger sibling of the more acclaimed *The Mountain and the Valley*, and in a sense the lack of attention is justified. Buckler's attack on the empty modernism that swept the Maritimes is subtly executed through a wide variety of characters, but it is still a song of protest that sounds in a single register. Buckler is consistently critical of the materialism, superficiality, heartless intellectualism, and simple loneliness that characterize contemporary existence, but unlike *The Mountain and the Valley*, *The Cruelest Month* does not attempt to view that modernist experience from within. The sense that each of the characters is inevitably trapped within his or her own modernist context produces a sense of unrelenting "nihilism" and "bitterness" (Young 1976a, 43) and, as Buckler himself admitted, the novel is "too deliberate … themes get in the way of movement" (Orange 1970, 55). Still, if the novel fails to fully engage the reader, it does stand as something unique in Maritime fiction: it is the first sustained critique of modernism that is divorced from the optimistic romance patterns that had dominated the texts of MacLennan and Raddall.

TURNING POINT

Ernest Buckler's fiction represents both a culmination and turning point within Maritime realism. As part of the last generation to emerge from the traditional rural culture and having experienced that community's transformation and disintegration, Buckler was also the last writer to chronicle, eulogize, and elegize the rich heritage of the Valley. After Buckler, no writer could return to the fading rural world with quite the same intense sense of longing and celebration. Ernest Buckler then turned his eye to examine what the Valley was becoming, and his texts push further than any before him to meticulously reproduce the emerging influence of postwar era, while continually announcing that the transformations are both tragic and ironic. By addressing a wider range of contemporary experience, including its sorrows and failures, he blazes a trail for such writers as Alden Nowlan, Alistair MacLeod, and David Adams Richards who represent the disruptions of the 1960s and 1970s while presenting a less idyllic vision of the past.

5 Writing in the Dusk: Alden Nowlan and Alistair MacLeod

> The house was old and after a few hours of emptiness the kitchen smelled of age and abandonment. These smells lay dormant while there was life and movement in the house, but when the fire died and the doors and windows were closed, the rooms filled slowly with mustiness.
>
> Alden Nowlan, "In the Finland Woods"

In the final three decades of the twentieth century, Maritime realist texts began to cast longer, grimmer shadows as a series of writers focused on the inequities, struggles, and hardships that some earlier novelists tended to marginalize or soften. From this period, Alden Nowlan and Alistair MacLeod have both emerged from and reproduced a Maritime culture that is very different from that experienced by Buckler or Bruce. First of all, both Nowlan and MacLeod grew up in communities that had been deeply affected by the economic downturns of the 1920s and 1930s. Nowlan grew up in Stanley, Hants County, Nova Scotia, a small village on the fringe of the more productive Anapolis Valley characterized by its seasonal lumber industry and small subsistence farms. Raised within a culture of poverty, Nowlan brings to his fiction a deep interest in economically and socially marginalized individuals. Similarly, MacLeod's adolescent experiences in Cape Breton exposed him to the island's harsh economic realities, which proved to have a formative influence on his early fiction. Just as they were both raised in communities familiar with adversity, both writers produced most of their fiction after the Maritime region itself was reshaped by the wave of economic reforms in the late 1960s. Both writers saw their communities transformed in a fundamental way as federal-provincial equalization payments, governmental assistance programs, and a new focus on regional disparities led to the creation of a modern welfare state. Some of the worst social inequities experienced by Nowlan were addressed by the processes of modernization that targeted the region's educational, health, and social services. But while the impoverished conditions of their childhood communities were unlikely to lead Nowlan and MacLeod to reproduce a sense of nostalgic longing, the social transformations did mean that the writers were cut off from their difficult pasts by all paths except that provided by memory. Thus, at least in the early fictions of these two Maritime writers, the nostalgic impulse is less evident, and a sense of hesitation – and even alienation – rises in prominence. Tentative resolutions that emphasize the power of memory to ease the experience of estrangement, do not emerge until these writers produce their later, fully mature texts.

ALDEN NOWLAN: NIHILISM AND THE SELF

Of all the writers who have emerged from the Maritimes, it would be hard to identify one whose early life was more difficult than that of Alden Nowlan. The grinding poverty of his community, the remarkably unstable nature of his family life, and his own sense of being unusual provided the threads of "neglect and abandonment" out of which Nowlan wove his life (Toner 2000, 24). If Nowlan was sometimes careful to adopt and use aspects of his difficult past to self-consciously craft his image as the "people's poet," Patrick Toner's biography confirms that he did not, in most cases, exaggerate the loneliness and misery of his childhood in Hants County. Abandoned by his mother, estranged from his father, and raised by a number of family relations – particularly his grandmothers Emma Nowlan and Nora Reese – Alden left school between grades 4 and 5 and worked as a labourer while he nursed his "haunted imagination" and educated himself in the writer's trade (Toner 2000, 29). He thought of himself, first and foremost, as a poet and received a Governor General's Award for *Bread, Wine, and Salt*, the sixth of his twelve collections of poems. By the time his career was cut short by his untimely death at the age of fifty, however, he had also received recognition as a journalist, columnist, playwright, screenwriter, novelist, and writer of short stories.

Nowlan did not produce a particularly large body of prose fiction. His first novel, *The Wanton Troopers*, was written before he was thirty, and it remained unpublished during his lifetime. He wrote numerous short stories for both literary and popular magazines, and forty of these were collected into two volumes, *Miracle at Indian River* and *Will Ye Let the Mummers In?*. Published in 1973, *Various Persons Named Kevin O'Brien* is Nowlan's only other long piece of prose, and it is a curious fusion of short fiction and memoir. If Nowlan's fiction received comparatively little attention during his lifetime, critics have recently acknowledged that it opened new imaginative territories. Such writers as Raddall, Bruce, and MacLennan examined the problem of poverty and violence, but placed these problems on the edges of their fictions. Nowlan made the concerns of the marginalized and the impoverished the focal point of his work. Almost without exception, all of Nowlan's fictions are anchored in rural or small-town settings in which harsh living conditions threaten or confine the central protagonists. Nowlan often examines the miseries of characters who exercise a small measure of choice as they attempt to shape their own identities but are unable to dramatically transform or improve their lot. While previous Maritime writers tempered their disquiet with the salve of nostalgia, Nowlan's early work, particularly *The Wanton Troopers*, develops an unusually strong sense of fatalism and even despair. Only in the later *Various Persons Named Kevin O'Brien* does this sense of fatalism begin to relax as Nowlan investigates the possibilities offered to the alienated individual in the midst of the modernist condition.

The Wanton Troopers

The Wanton Troopers is Nowlan's first long prose work. Supported through part of 1961 by a $2,300 grant from the Canada Council, Nowlan took a nine-month leave from his duties as a reporter and editor for the Harland *Observer* and "made and kept a promise to himself to write one page per day until the novel was finished" (Toner 2000, 150).[1] Hoping to establish his reputation as a novelist as well as a poet, Nowlan sent his manuscript to both Ryerson Press and McClelland and Stewart, neither of whom elected to publish the work (Toner 2000, 124). Nowlan did not record his reasons for not approaching a third publisher. He may have worried that the text was still a bit raw, for although he was willing to show the manuscript to Anne Greer, an academic researcher, the novel remained unpublished until after his death.

The Wanton Troopers is stark, but it is far from amateurish. A thinly veiled version of the events and turmoils of the author's own youth, the novel is a bildungsroman that chronicles the childhood years of Kevin O'Brien, who negotiates his troubled relationships with his family and community as he grows up in a repressive and rural backwater named, appropriately enough, Lockhartville. Certainly, the text brings to Maritime literature a shaper, harder style of realism then had previously been employed. The novel features short chapters, each of which recounts a significant moment in Kevin's development as his sensitive nature reacts to his harsh environment and as he watches the gradual disintegration of his parents' troubled marriage. The style is sparse and direct; the short, crisp sentences resist abstract philosophic speculations; and the text focuses on immediate, sensuous, and concrete experience. The narrator does not adopt a poetic voice; in contrast, the third-person narration is focalized through the boy in order to provide a "straight forward naturalistic narrative of Kevin's earlier years" (Milton 1998, 42). As one of the subgenres of realism arising late in the nineteenth century, naturalism took the historicist impulse to its logical conclusion, claiming that characters are irrevocably caught in a web of cause and effect dictated by environmental forces and internal stresses over which they can exercise little if any control.

When Kevin crosses a neighbour's field, Nowlan does not use the opportunity to create a lyrically pastoral image of the land, instead the natural landscape mirrors the child's bleak and fragmented existence: "He ran up the hill. Beyond the fences, on either side of the lane flocks of sheep were grazing, their fleeces the colour of dirty white shirts. They blatted at him as he ran by kicking up red dust, the old ram blatting first, then all the ewes echoing him. Kevin was not fond of sheep. He disliked their sour, vomity odour and their stupid trusting eyes ... The back dooryard belongs to the farm. Here there were weeds and thistles and discarded tools and odds and ends of harness, and if Kevin did not watch his step he was likely to step in hen dung or cow manure" (*WT*, 43).

Having developed a gritty style of discourse, the text proceeds to trace the gradual maturation of young Kevin – an alter-ego for Nowlan himself – and examine how his personality is shaped, or more accurately warped, by a society that has almost completely collapsed. Though Kevin begins the text as a sensuous child who adores his troubled mother and indulges in escapist flights of imaginative fancy – including the desire to be "Tarzan King of the Jungle" or the "King of Nicaragua" – these impulses are curbed as he grows older. He does not become a carbon copy of the previous generation, but his innately open and free spirit is buried beneath a powerful sense of self-doubt, skepticism, and loneliness. The text traces and critiques the processes by which Kevin's familial and social culture crushes his sensitive character, but while these processes are viewed as tragic they are also presented as inevitable and inescapable. The novel pays particular attention to Kevin's parents, who function as the victims of their society's repressive culture and the conduits through which those same values are impressed upon the next generation. Nowlan does not demonize Judd and Mary O'Brien. Indeed, his sensitive analysis of the ways in which the parents are as trapped and bound by their ideological and cultural assumptions as their child explains why Nowlan dedicated the novel "To My Mother and Father In Forgiveness."

Judd O'Brien is, at least on the surface, a brutal patriarch and the "product of the repressions visited upon him by class and religious background" (Milton 1995, 63). He has a sensitive and artistic side and spends the occasional evening drawing the horses and mules he recalls from his "harvest excursions" to Saskatchewan, but he has internalized the community's codes, which read such expressive practices as childish. He quickly burns his papers as "damn foolishness" (*WT*, 57–8). Judd's sense of freedom and even his sense of himself have been warped and reshaped by the endless bouts of drinking, by the hopeless poverty that necessarily attends his work as a labourer, by the sense of determinism that stems from his puritanical past, and by the community's rigid gender codes, which force each man to reject his emotions as feminine and weak. The consequence of such a surrender is the emergence of a powerful, mercurial anger that breaks upon Kevin and his mother without warning. When a mortgage bill arrives and reminds Judd that his wages as a millhand are insufficient to fulfill his role as a breadwinner, he vents his frustrations by viciously beating Kevin for imagined acts of disobedience. His reactions to his wife Mary, whose open character functions as a constant reminder of his own emotional stagnation, are even more violent. Increasingly suspicious that his wife is preparing to leave him, Judd erupts in misogynist attacks on the farm's representations of the feminine; he grabs a "pitchfork" and drives its "three tines into the cow's side" while declaring her to be a "dirty bitch," and then proceeds to behead his wife's pet cat declaring the animal to be a "god-damn cheatin' whore" (*WT*, 85, 88). As in *The Mountain and the Valley*, there is no doubt that the O'Brien family is dominated by the father, but whereas Buckler represents the separation of the gender roles as natural and benevolent, Nowlan insists that the rigid codes governing masculinity and femininity are constructs of the broader culture: they are upheld only at a tragic cost to the individual and the community. But the codes, if harsh and destructive, are also unalterable, and by the end of the novel Kevin has absorbed enough of his father's sensibility to respond to his girlfriend's desire for an expression of his emotional commitment as "silly," and, after he "wrench[es] her hands," he views her as a Satanic temptation (*WT*, 162–3). Kevin's alienation from Judd has not prevented him from reproducing his father's values and assumptions.

If Judd represents one of the figures through whom the society's assumptions are transmitted to Kevin, his mother, Mary, represents the futility of attempting to resist the dominant ideologies. While

Milton argues that Mary represents a positive expression of playful-
ness in her search for liberty and her plans to escape the community,
such a reading underestimates the degree to which she has also
been damaged by the forces she attempts to oppose. Unable to construct a role for herself as an independent woman, she can only
stage a warped retreat back into childhood. Unable to function as
Kevin's protector or provider, she attempts to find other roles to
play in his life. This bending of roles produces some odd moments
for Kevin, as Mary treats him as a playmate, a companion, a confes-
sor, and even sometimes a suitor: "Oh, you say sweet things sometimes, Scamper. You really do" (*WT*, 86). Mary is less an example of
Nowlan's vision of how to escape the community's restrictions, as
she is an example of how resistence to the community only produces a set of alternately warped roles. By the end, she is forced to
flee her family: her escape, a final betrayal of young Kevin's needs.

Fred Cogswell once observed that in Nowlan's own world there
was a "considerable degree of sexual segregation," and he argues
that the writer himself was governed in his personal life by these
rigid roles and a fear of women (1986, 219). In *The Wanton Troopers*,
Nowlan assumes that this segregation exists and then proceeds to develop a sophisticated analysis of how gender and social divisions are
constructed within the region's culture. He looks beyond the immediate family and explores the failure of the overly codified society to facilitate the individual's struggle to realize his or her potential.
Certainly, Kevin's relatives offer no relief to the sense of repression he
experiences at the hands of his father. His grandmother is presented
as a one-dimensional character whose Calvinist vision of sin and
judgmental condemnations of others invokes a sense of doubt and
fear: "The presence of his grandmother O'Brien sometimes filled him
with a vague, unsettling dread, akin to that nighttime fear" (*WT*, 89).
There are no welfare or social institutions to offset the family's
destructive influence. The only community system Kevin encounters,
the school, is even more overtly repressive than his home life.
Taunted and beaten by the older boys for his odd ways, Kevin eventually fights back. He achieves membership in the local fraternity of
violence, but feels only a sense of guilt as he learns that the boys enjoy the violence for its own sake: "Kevin realized that his school
mates did not care who was the tormenter and who the tormented"
(*WT*, 101). By the end, as his family begins to disintegrate, the narrator
uses a combination of free-indirect discourse and internal monologue
to capture Kevin's inner confusion as he contemplates the collapse
of his world. His recurring sense of sexual guilt, religious fear,
emotional anxiety, and childish pleadings conclude in a fragmented

prayer: "Make them stop God. I promise I won't ask you for anything else. I'll never ask you for anything else. Please God" (*WT*, 171). By now, of course, Nowlan has provided ample evidence that God does not listen to the residents of Lockhartville.

Nowlan's first novel is grim, and its politics are ambiguous. The narrator is deeply committed to the value of the individual, and Kevin's independent, inner life is examined with great care. Kevin can recognize that his family and his community are deeply troubled, and, although he cannot quite articulate how a better alternative might be shaped, his resistence to his father's violence and his longing for a stable and enduring relationship with any other person become the touchstones of the text's value system. But if Nowlan's interest in the individual echoes Bruce's communitarian liberalism, it is also more complicated. In *The Wanton Troopers* individuals can only realize their inner vision and sense of identity within a supportive society and culture, and, since that community is warped, the individual who must grow up in a regional context is put at risk. The O'Briens are unavoidably, irredeemably damaged and lost, and though Nowlan documents the specific forces that oppress them, he does not suggest that their environments could ever be altered enough to transform their destinies. The narrative produces a deep sense of disillusionment about life in the Maritime region and denies the possibility that either a liberal, conservative, or even a revolutionary ideological perspective could relieve the prevailing sense of fatalism and determinism. The lack of alternatives offered by the text breeds a kind of nihilism, which Nowlan did not begin to modify until his later texts emerged.

Two Collections of Short Fiction

With the completion of *The Wanton Troopers*, Nowlan was freed from the most powerful of his autobiographical ghosts. In the spring of 1961, while working on the novel, he wrote to Fred Cogswell and noted that there "has been a strange movement in the mind and heart, purging and strengthening. As if every thing were being cleaned away to make room for something new" (Toner 2000, 115). In the years that followed, Nowlan returned to his work as a writer of short fiction, and in the mid-1960s Greg Cook proposed that they assemble and edit fifteen stories into a collection that would be published under the title *Glass Roses* (Toner 2000, 133). When Cook could not find the necessary resources to publish the book, Nowlan took the project to Roy MacSkimming at Clark Irwin (Toner 2000, 170). MacSkimming selected eight of the stories from Cook's collection and added ten of Nowlan's more recent stories to assemble the eighteen-story collection *Miracle in Indian River* (1968). Nowlan continued to write stories for a variety of markets, but he did not attempt to compile another volume of short fiction until the early 1980s. Just before his death in 1983, Nowlan put the final touches on a second collection, entitled *Will Ye Let the Mummers In?*, which drew from materials written in the previous three decades. Indeed, Nowlan's final collection of prose relies heavily on his early material: of the twenty two stories in *Will Ye Let the Mummers In?*, at least twelve were written before 1973. In short, of the forty stories published in his two collections, three quarters were produced before *Various Persons Named Kevin O'Brien* was completed. The short fiction thus acts as a bridge between his first novel and his final long prose text.

The affinities between Nowlan's short stories and his first novel are immediately apparent. Like the chapters in *The Wanton Troopers*, Nowlan's short fictions are carefully focused and typically brief. Like *The Wanton Troopers*, the stories are also characterized by a blunt style: short sentences, gritty diction, and either an external narrator who focalizes the text through an isolated, often male, character or an internal narrator who is young or remembering his youth. Moreover, in his short stories Nowlan continues to explore the experiences of individuals "who are alienated from themselves and from their real feelings" and whose difficult lives become microcosms through which he can reflect on the state of the larger society (Hinchcliffe 1985, 167). Some of the short stories continue to mine the writer's own past. "Walking on the Ceiling"and "Notes Toward a Plot for an Unwritten Short Story" take an autobiographical turn as Kevin O'Brien relates his traumatic experiences in a hospital setting, experiences that echo Nowlan's own battle with cancer in the late 1960s. More often, Nowlan turns away from personal experience and turns towards the wider community for his subject matter.

The characters of Nowlan's short fictions are often drawn from the lower classes or under classes, and typically they struggle with the limitations imposed by their harsh work environments or impoverished home lives. Most of the characters in Nowlan's stories are trapped in situations that are "abominable and intolerable"; sometimes they are locked in violent marriages or brutal jobs, sometimes in broken bodies or, as is the case in two stories, in mental institutions (Kulyk Keefer 1987, 166). Whether the characters are behind literal or metaphoric bars, they are rarely able to exercise many options or choices, and not surprisingly there are few happy endings possible when an "open consciousness [is] pitted against the crude, closed mentality of place" (Kulyk Keefer 1987, 166). Characters like "the

Polack" in "Glass Roses" may have once experienced a broader and more sensitive culture, but the foreign woodsman's memories of his mother's beautiful "little glass roses" cannot free him from his harsh circumstances in the lumber camp or transform the recurring nightmares that plague his sleep (*MIR*, 59–60). In "Love Letter," the poor young wife follows her own irresistible need to escape her dismal "two room apartment" and enjoy a moment of simple human contact, but she ultimately betrays her husband, who has joined the army and gone off to Europe (*MIR*, 63). In "Anointed with Oils," the young factory worker, would love to escape her constricted life and flee to the glamour of the urban setting, but as her dysfunctional family reaches out to claim her attention, she realizes that she will likely never escape the conditions of her birth and childhood: "that smell would not go away" (*MIR*, 51). Whatever their situation, Nowlan continues to explore the marginalized sectors of Maritime society.

As Nowlan uses his short stories to expand his representations of the individuals who live on the edge of their community, he returns to his ideological debate about the threat of determinism within the regional context and rearticulates the fatalism and nihilism of *The Wanton Troopers*. The grim narratives chronicle the community's "dirt poverty and its attendant ills," and they examine "the brutalizing of human relationships, [and] the extinction of hope for anything brighter or better than brute subsistence" (Kulyk Keefer 1987, 166). Sometimes the loss of an individual's unique potential is presented as inevitable, given the rigidity of the class system. In "A Call in December," a middle-class man is accompanied by a younger narrator as they make a charitable visit to the community's poor and deliver a few groceries to a "shack right smack in the middle" of a marsh (*MIR*, 29). The visitors are shocked by the squalid conditions and appalled as well by the inbred passivity that seems to limit the young "foxlike" mother and doom her "hidden baby" (*MIR*, 29). The mother is unable to reach beyond her suspicion of the welfare systems that might threaten to remove her child, and the charitable visitors are unable to make the imaginative leap needed to understand her desolation. The older man's final question conveys to the reader a compelling sense of his confusion and despair: "Why in hell does a man have to build his house in a bog hole?" (*MIR*, 32). In other stories, the protagonists are bound by the region's familial and gender roles. In the story "Skipper" – which was first published in 1962 and later collected in *Will Ye Let the Mummers In?* – Nowlan examines a young mother's attempts to shape her youngest son into a sensitive and caring individual who might someday grow up to "be a clean, sober man who would wear a white shirt and a necktie to work" (*WMI*, 19).

Though the child initially hates his violent father and vows to be different, he inevitably follows the "old, brutal pattern to its conclusion," takes a job in the local mill, enters the masculine culture of drunkenness, and, in the closing paragraphs, joins his father who is "laughing at the other end of the house" (*WMI*, 19, 22).The codes that govern the social structure and the sphere of the masculine, claim young Skipper just as surely as they claim most of the other characters of Nowlan's short fiction.

Various Persons Named Kevin O'Brien

Given Nowlan's determination to examine the sometimes brutal experiences of individuals on the margins of Maritime society, he did not find it an easy task to craft an ideological position capable of countering the sense of nihilism that emerges in the early work. He eventually found a plausible solution, not by calling for a transformation of the larger – sometimes oppressive – social systems, but by turning inward to study the subjective realm of the individual in greater detail than before. Nowlan's key work of fiction examining this subjective territory is *Various Persons Named Kevin O'Brien* (1973).

Various Persons Named Kevin O'Brien is actually a rather curious fusion of literary forms. The resulting work is truly heterogeneous. Initially, *Various Persons Named Kevin O'Brien* seems to be mining the unpublished manuscript of *The Wanton Troopers*. Kevin O'Brien returns as the central protagonist, though the child has now matured into a journalist whose return visit to his home town triggers a series of memories that unfold in a roughly chronological sequence. Nowlan echoes his first novel as he structures many of the incidents of the narrative around the boy's encounters with his repressive father Judd; he even reintroduces some of the memorable characters of the earlier novel, including the crew of abusive schoolyard boys, the sadistic teacher with the anti-Hitler fantasies, and the difficult, puritanical grandmother. One important figure in *The Wanton Troopers* who does not appear in *Various Persons named Kevin O'Brien* is Kevin's mother. Paul Milton, in his 1995 article "The Psalmist and the Sawmill: Alden Nowlan's Kevin O'Brien Stories," asserts that as the playful and transgressive character of the mother is excluded from the later text, Nowlan introduces instead a much stronger sense of textual play in order to resist the naturalist discourse of the text: "Play is incorporated through the non-linear, contradictory structure of the narrative which signifies possibility rather than fatal necessity. I would suggest that the absent body of the mother, the site of the child's play in the early novel, returns in this text in its idiosyncratic structure" (67).

At other times, the text echos the collections of short fiction. The separate chapters of *Various Persons* were initially published as short stories, and then reassembled and linked one to another through a series of introductory segments that tie each section back to the reflections of the adult Kevin. A few chapters of *Various Persons* – including "The Imaginary Soldier" and "Life and Times" – are actually informal essays constructed from the protagonist's casual remembrances of childhood anxieties. As a whole, *Various Persons Named Kevin O'Brien* is certainly episodic; occasionally anomalies appear demonstrating that the editors did not fully integrate the disparate narratives. For example, the sawmill, which "has been permanently shut down" on the first page, is miraculously back in production in the section entitled "Night Watch," as the narrator examines "the figures on the gauges, noting that the water tank is only half full and the steam pressure has fallen to less than eighty pounds" (*VP*, 107). Ultimately, Nowlan's text is more than a collage of anecdotes, something different than a collection of short stories, yet not quite a cohesive novel. Having produced what would now be identified as a mosaic,[2] Nowlan himself seemed hesitant to classify his text and provided the subtitle "a fictional memoir" as a label for the work.

The first indication that *Various Persons Named Kevin O'Brien* represents a transition in Nowlan's development as a prose writer is evident in his attempt to stretch the defining features of realism. The narrative remains anchored in the immediate and concrete details of Kevin's past and present, but the structure itself is more complex: the external narration that is prevalent in the opening stories shifts to an internal, first-person narration in several subsequent chapters. Moreover, while most of Nowlan's earlier fictions are constructed according to a clear, traditionally realist sequence of cause and effect, *Various Persons Named Kevin O'Brien* is built on associative connections as it follows Kevin's thoughts as he drifts from present to past and back again. This structural technique is one of the first clear signs that the narrative foregrounds the subjective experience of the character and narrator. Indeed, the text is important because this attention to the variability and instability of the subjective state – emphasized by the title's insistence that there are various persons named Kevin O'Brien inhabiting a single self – represents both a new style of fiction for Nowlan and a break from the ways in which Maritime texts have represented individuals in the past.

As Kevin and the reader become increasingly aware that the self is a complex entity and that the investigation and articulation of the individual's many selves is an important project, we can sense a shift or a clarification in Nowlan's ideological position. If asked during his lifetime about his political stance, Nowlan would have undoubtedly identified himself as a conservative, pointing to his long-time association with the provincial and national Conservative party and his close friendship with long-time premier, Richard Hatfield.[3] But if he was comfortable with his ties to the Conservative party throughout the 1960s and 1970s, his own set of ideological assumptions are not as easily identified. He shares the kind of conservatism evident in MacLennan, in that he recognizes the centrality of the society's influence on the individual and argues that individuals cannot escape being shaped, for better or for worse, by the traditions and conventions of the larger community. But as his literary career developed he was less interested in the condition of the larger society and more attentive to the potential complexity and power of the individual to react within and perhaps even refashion his or her immediate context. Nowlan's interest in the shaping power of the individual's subjective state is first evident in his poetry, which shifted from the early work's commitment to a kind of naturalist imagism to the confessional mode of his later verse. As Nowlan explored the power each individual has to reshape the fragments of their inner experience, even if they are unable to alter their surrounding environment, a liberal ideology began to emerge, which would grant primacy to the interests and struggles of the free individual. Or more accurately, as Nowlan shifted towards the tenets of liberalism it is clear that he addressed the modernist challenge that had been offered to Maritime novelists since Frank Parker Day penned *Rockbound*. Since Maritime writers first adopted realism, with its attention to the complex and multifaceted protagonist, they have struggled with the problem of how to examine the inner lives of characters who have been deeply influenced by the modernist condition, without threatening their wider, often nostalgic, vision of the region. Nowlan is the first to embrace the ambiguity of the modernist condition in an affirmative fashion and investigate its possibilities, even if one of those options is not the opportunity to find happiness.

Nowlan's attitude towards Kevin O'Brien's attempts to "contemplate without bitterness one's own essential absurdity" – is often misread by critics (*VP*, 5). Kulyk Keefer seems uncertain when she claims that Kevin is both the "prisoner of a past he is unable either to accept or reject" (1987, 167), while at the same time she claims that "written language" has provided him with "his very means of escape" (167, 169). Kulyk Keefer's uncertainty as to whether the hero is free or bound is echoed in Michael Oliver's assertion that Kevin's central purpose is to unify his multiple perspectives: he "must acknowledge his feelings about his family and attempt to understand his relationship with his heritage before he can define himself" (1976, 54). But

Nowlan is not interested in having Kevin either free or define himself. The point of the narrative, and the reason why *Various Persons Named Kevin O'Brien* constitutes a breakthrough in Maritime literature, is Nowlan's assertion that Kevin is able only to identify his plurality of selves. The "multiple Kevin looks upon himself as a fragmented creature" (Milton 1998, 48) who is able to simultaneously speak "the language of the region, the language of the metropolis ... and the language of the mass media" (43). Thus, the text recognizes the complexity and multiplicity of the subject as a possible, indeed a necessary, condition of the modern era, even if such a plurality of selves is not experienced as a triumph: "The teenaged Kevin O'Brien that the twenty-five-year-old Kevin O'Brien remembers was piteously young for his years, whereas that person considered himself to be unusually mature; there were even times when he thought of himself as an old man. The matter is complicated further by the fact that none of these former selves will die until the final Kevin O'Brien is dead" (*VP*, 24).

Kevin's awareness of his multiplicity of selves is anchored in his recognition that identity is a construct of memory. Memory is not dependent on the actual events of the past, as much as it is the product of an individual's facility through language to reconstruct the past: "it is possible for one deliberately to alter the course of events that have already taken place" (*VP*, 24). The Kevin of *Various Persons* is no more able to escape the restrictions and confining assumptions of his society than was the Kevin of *The Wanton Troopers*; but by exploring the ways in which identity is constructed through memory and language, he can shape his responses to that childhood. The multiple selves that Kevin proceeds to construct prevent him from descending into the tragic circumstances that doom the modernist figures of his earlier texts.

The exact mechanisms Kevin uses to recognize and shape the multiple aspects of his identity vary. As the older Kevin wanders through his community, he relives some of the defining moments of his past. But, as Kevin looks back, the reader immediately recognizes that, unlike in previous Maritime texts, there is a surprising lack of nostalgia. While the tone of the separate chapters is less bitter than that of his earlier fiction, his "wry – and often rueful – compassion" does not lead him towards an idealized vision of his past (Gibbs 1992, xvii). For example, while Grandmother O'Brien, in *The Wanton Troopers* was "totally soured on life" (Gibbs 1992, xvi), the grandmother in "There Was an Old Woman from Wexford" is a more complex and sympathetic figure. Yet, despite the change, she never becomes the kind of repository for an idyllic past found in the grandmother in Buckler's *The Mountain and the Valley.*

Instead of reconstructing his childhood as a time of plentitude, Kevin repeatedly focuses on the most traumatic moments of loss, the moments that reinforce his own alienation as an individual and his own ability to simultaneously inhabit several roles. Kevin's defining memory of his time with his schoolyard chums is recounted in "Rumours of War," in which the village boys dramatize their own version of the Second World War and torture a younger child. The chapter demonstrates that the children are eager to act out the same sadistic fantasies that Kevin initially repudiates when they were presented by his teacher. As Kevin retreats from his friends – physically revolted by the brutality he has witnessed – the narrative rejects the notion that there is an idyllic memory in the past waiting to be recovered. There is no preliterate, founding experience that can help locate the narrator. Instead, there is simply the acknowledgement that he can play out his role as a "Junior Commando" who is "an authority on military jargon", even when this brutal role represents the antithesis of his own private values (vP, 19). Similar moments depicting a plurality of selves are recounted in the chapter "Kevin and Stephanie," in which Kevin becomes aware of the brutal power games that are located at the heart of any family relationship. Kevin learns that he is capable of frightening his sister when he pretends to be "an old man in a black mask" (vP, 68), but later he must submit to her vicious blows because he is also "Lebuba," the little brother who cannot strike back because "you aren't big enough. Not by a long shot" (vP, 71).

Perhaps the incident that best demonstrates Kevin's ability to inhabit several selves at the same moment occurs in the final chapter, entitled "His Native Place." The chapter is unique in the book, in that Kevin in not recalling a distant memory as much as he is recording a current event, notably his decision to attend a local dance, where he responds to his cousin's attempts to force him to readopt the rigid masculine code of the community. Paul Milton accurately notes that Kevin has lost contact with the local cultural norms as he has left the region and entered into the assumptions of the metropolitan and popular culture, but he is slightly off target when he argues that Kevin's final decision to fight and defeat the abusive intruder Bob D'Entremont "surely demonstrates his connection to the world of Lockhartville" (Milton 1998, 47).[4] While Kevin does momentarily return to his earlier role within the village and submits to Lockhartville's violent norms with a sense of ease and relief, which is recorded in his observation that "he never felt better," even this deep identification with a single aspect of his identity does not demonstrate that he has been "reabsorb[ed] into the community" (Milton 1998, 48). As the opening paragraphs of the chapter remind us, his entire reconnection to his community is only temporary, for the events themselves are being remembered by Kevin as he flies away from the region. His moment of identification is thus framed by his position as the narrator who recognizes that his return to his home place has been "largely imaginary" and partly "ridiculous" (VP, 129). Kevin has not rediscovered his true self, as much as he has demonstrated that his identity is made up of several selves, and his ease with this recognition indicates a surprising level of comfort with the modern condition.

In *Various Persons Named Kevin O'Brien,* Nowlan examines the deterministic forces that defeated the characters of his earlier works. In his later fictional memoir, the protagonist escapes being buried beneath the forces of determinism by recognizing the instability of the self and using the possibility of multiple identities to forge a response to his oppressive environment. The modern instability of the subject is not a comfort in itself, but it affords the individual the opportunity to construct several responses to the pressures of his immediate circumstances. None of those selves are freed from their contexts, but neither are they defeated; thus Kevin is able to fly away from his home knowing that he must carry the burden of his past with him, and that it is a burden that can be carried. In embracing aspects of the modern condition, Nowlan extends the work begun by Buckler and opens up a territory that will also be examined by Alistair MacLeod and David Adams Richards. MacLeod will initially examine many of the issues confronted by Nowlan, though he ultimately develops a more conventional and conservative vision of the traditional community in order to resolve his initial sense of alienation. Richards will push further than either Nowlan or MacLeod in his exploration of the isolated individual, though he too will shift his style in order to retain a sense of the subject's integrity and independence.

ALISTAIR MACLEOD: REALISM, FREEDOM, AND TRADITION

"Don't forget to come back James," he says, "it's the only way you'll be content ..." I offer him my hand to shake and find it almost crushed in the crooked broken force of his ... And I have a feeling for a terrible moment that I may never ever get away or be again released.

Alistair MacLeod, "The Vastness of the Dark"

In some ways Alistair MacLeod does not fit the profile of the typical Maritime writer. Born in North Battleford, Saskatchewan, in 1936, MacLeod spent his childhood in the coal-mining area of Alberta. In the mid-1960s, before he was thirty, he began his doctorate at the University of Notre Dame. He subsequently taught at the University of Indiana, before moving to Southern Ontario in 1969, where he has spent most of his working life as a professor of English and Creative Writing at the University of Windsor. For most of his career, only during the summer months was he able to return to his family home in Broad Cove Parish, Cape Breton. Compared to the years spent away from the Maritimes, MacLeod's time in Cape Breton may seem brief. But if the time was brief, it was also formative. Like Thomas Raddall, he moved to the Maritimes at the age of ten. He spent his adolescence on his family's farm in Inverness County, Cape Breton, and, after graduating from high school, he remained in the region for another ten years in order to pursue his education.[5] During these years he worked as a miner, a logger, and a teacher in small country schools in order to pay for his studies (Nicholson 1985, 91). MacLeod's personal experiences as a youth and his family's deep connection to their Gaelic heritage formed the templates of his creative vision, and all of his texts, with the exception of "The Golden Gift of Grey," are set, at least in part, in the harsh environment and beleaguered community of his island home.

By any account, Alistair MacLeod is a slow writer. Through the 1970s and early 1980s he averaged one short story a year, resulting in only two collections, *The Lost Salt Gift of Blood* (1976) and *As Birds Bring Forth the Sun and Other Stories* (1986), each of which contain seven stories. These volumes were reissued as a part of McClelland & Stewart's widely available New Canadian Library series, and then both collections were brought together and published as *Island: The Collected Stories*. Released in 2000, this latest compilation places the earlier stories in chronological order and includes two additional stories: "Clearances," a new work, and "Island," which was previously only available in a special volume published by Thistledown Press in 1989.[6] Between 1989 and 1999, MacLeod published very little, as he devoted himself to writing the novel *No Great Mischief*. MacLeod's short stories and novels are carefully crafted, and his work has been greeted enthusiastically by critics. Twice, his stories have been included in the prestigious anthology *Best American Short Stories*; several of his stories, most notably "The Boat," have been widely anthologized; and while Maritime writers of short fiction have often been overlooked by the academic community, MacLeod's work has been examined in more than a dozen full-length critical articles. As tends to be the case when scholars examine collections of short stories, critics have adopted one of two approaches when exploring MacLeod's fiction. Some, like James Taylor and Simone Vauthier, have focused on particular stories and examined MacLeod's imagery and symbolism or his complex reshaping of space and time. Other critics, including Colin Nicholson, John Ditsky, Janice Kulyk Keefer, Francis Berces, and Andrew Hiscock, have examined the body of work as a whole, and identified the formal tensions, thematic concerns, and philosophic issues that recur in the texts.

The broad overviews of MacLeod's fiction have generally been productive, and this is due in part to the fact that there is a relatively high degree of uniformity between his short stories. Nearly all of MacLeod's stories are related by or focalized through male narrators who either are young or are remembering a critical moment of their youth. These male protagonists are inevitably threatened by such deterministic forces as a daunting environment, economic hardship, chronic poverty, or cultural narrow-mindedness. Compelled to compromise their value system, the heroes usually make decisions that establish their identities and set them, tentatively, on their path into the future. Given the grim tone of MacLeod's fiction, it is not surprising that Arnold Davidson should argue that it is anchored in a "poetics of loss," an aesthetic in which "displacement, substitution and elision ... give these stories a characteristic elegiac tone ... a present awareness of a past heritage of loss, a continuity, so to speak, of dispossession" (1988, 41).

Not only does MacLeod tend to return to similar themes and characters, he also relies consistently on a single literary form: throughout his career, he has unwaveringly followed the tenets that govern the genre of realism. MacLeod's commitment to the realist aesthetic is evident, most immediately, in his elegant and precise style. Characterized by its lack of linguistic self-reflexivity, a realist text keeps the role of language and questions about its own fictionality in the background, and once the style has been established it rarely calls attention to itself. Though critics have occasionally suggested that MacLeod's highly "literary" style moves his short fiction towards a postmodern aesthetic, there is little support for such an argument. MacLeod carefully effaces any of the inter- or intra-textual allusions that might suggest that the stories are self-conscious ventures into the realms of textual play, and even the extraordinarily elegant and precise style of the narration is justified within a realist framework, for the narrators are often highly educated. The narrator of *No Great Mischief* opens the text with an allusion to Keats's "To Autumn" and then periodically refers to such writers as William Wordsworth and Margaret Laurence, but such allusions make sense given the speaker's extensive university education, which not only gives him access to the literary canon, but also allows him to cast his quotations from the

Romantic writers in an ironic light. The sophisticated style of the stories is never examined in the self-reflexive fashion that characterizes the metafictional texts being produced by some other writers after the 1970s.[7]

Characterized in part by their traditionally clear and direct style, MacLeod's realist texts also assume that the individual is enmeshed in the contexts of history. Given his initial interest in exploring the lonely struggles of individuals who achieve only an incomplete sense of connection to the larger world, it is not surprising that MacLeod should feel an affinity with realism, which often foregrounds the integrity of the speaking subject by focusing on a single central protagonist in order to chronicle his or her maturation or development. More importantly for MacLeod, realism is a genre that is deeply embedded in the assumptions of historicism; each of his fictions is committed to tracing the relentless forces that press upon his multi-dimensional protagonists, whose experiences and decisions are situated in a complex web of cause and effect. Hiscock notes succinctly that MacLeod "chooses not to position his narrating heroes in the midst of a fully-fledged post-modern environment of relentless social fragmentation, unstable utterance, vigorous self-referentiality and the collapse of historical fixity ... His stories ... greet the metanarratives of ... Self, Meaning, and History ... as organizing (if not comforting) principles of human existence" (2000, 68). Of course, MacLeod's realist texts can never provide a "truthful" record of history, any more than they can provide a complete and faithful reflection of reality, but, nonetheless, the assumptions arising from historicism have had a deep impact on his early fictions.

But if MacLeod employs realism to repeatedly examine similar themes and issues, it would be a mistake to assume that his texts are built on a single philosophic or ideological paradigm. He consistently addresses questions of identity and examines the threatening power of external forces, but between the early stories and the subsequent fictions there has been a distinct epistemological and political shift. Compared to the persistent note of skepticism, doubt, and uncertainty that characterizes the work published in the late 1960s and early 1970s and brought together in *The Lost Salt Gift of Blood*, the later stories and his first (and so far only) novel signal a clear and confident epistemological shift towards certainty. Such early fictions as "In the Fall," "The Vastness of the Dark," and "The Boat" sound a note that echoes in the early work of Alden Nowlan, as MacLeod focuses on the lonely trials of isolated individuals who exercise their limited personal freedom to achieve only an incomplete sense of connection with their larger society. The more recent texts, "The Closing Down of

Summer," "The Tuning of Perfection," "Vision," and *No Great Mischief*, concentrate on the ways in which individual protagonists are tied more firmly to a larger community.[8] This later emphasis on communal structures is attended by an ideological shift towards more conservative and patriarchal constructions of the "real."

In the stories of the late 1960s and early 1970s, MacLeod explores the forces that threaten the individual and then articulates a subtly convincing liberal vision of individual freedom. MacLeod's interest in the possibility of individual freedom is clear in the early stories, and his commitment to a liberal position is thus evident. However, in these texts, human freedom is so circumscribed by the limiting cultural and environmental conditions, that we do not see the characters achieve their independence, and thus it is difficult to determine whether MacLeod would advocate for an individualistic or a communitarian version of liberty. Therefore, this analysis attributes to the texts the general term "liberal" without attempting to identify a more specific form of that ideology.

In his early work, MacLeod fuses two branches of realist fiction as he blends a psychological realism – which attends to the inner lives of his emotionally and spiritually anxious protagonists – with a naturalistic tendency to explore and chronicle the impact of the environmental forces on the individual. Indeed, environmental conditions are at times so powerful that the texts approach a kind of determinism, with their insistence that individual freedom is subsumed in the numerous pressures of immediate circumstance: "His characters are critically vulnerable to if not determined by environmental conditions ... and are well within reach of devastating economic poverty" (Berces 1991, 116). Many separate forces act upon MacLeod's heroes. Most immediately apparent is the harsh natural environment that daily threatens the fishers, miners, and farmers of Cape Breton. There is nothing in MacLeod's world that would approach Charles Bruce's romanticized celebrations of the humane farmlands of *The Channel Shore* or echo Ernest Buckler's nostalgic hymns to an idealized natural landscape. MacLeod's early stories document nature's ability to bend and warp the vulnerable human, as is evident in "The Boat," when the narrator recalls the ocean's effect on his father's body: "My father did not tan – he never tanned – because of his reddish complexion, and the salt water irritated his skin as it had for sixty years. He burned and reburned over and over again and his lips still cracked so that they bled when he smiled, and his arms, especially the left, still broke out into the oozing salt-water boils as they had ever since as a child I had first watched him soaking and bathing them in a variety of ineffectual solutions" (*I*, 20). MacLeod's fictions are populated by numerous older characters, whose scars testify to the harsh power of the world (Berces 1991, 117). If the individuals are lucky enough to escape external scarring, the environment may exact an emotional or spiritual toll as numerous characters take to drink or fly from their Cape Breton homes in a futile attempt to escape their fates. The environment is not demonized, but the natural world is unrelenting, dangerous, and devouring. The raging seas, and unstable mines make manifest the force of chaos that underlies nature's drive to assimilate and extinguish. As Berces astutely notes, "Two factors exerting constant nihilistic pressure are the proximity of most characters to survival conditions and, secondly, death itself, the final elemental darkness threatening to reduce all hopes to one uniform and meaningless conclusion" (Berces 1991, 116). The sense of hesitation that characterizes the region's cultural landscape in the postwar era is manifested in the difficult settings of the texts.

As if the harsh environment were not enough to convince the reader that a sense of fatalism underpins these early stories, the protagonists are also keenly aware of the economic forces that shape or rule human choices. In the story "In the Fall," James, David, and their father would like to save their faithful and loyal pony from the slaughterhouse. But the family's poverty not only forces the father to leave the island for long periods of time to work in Halifax, it also necessitates that they sacrifice any sentimental feelings for an animal that will "probably die in March after we've fed him all that time" (*I*, 101). Economic pressures threaten to overwhelm MacLeod's characters and force them to read their lives as meaningless. Interestingly, MacLeod tends to represent the economic and the environmental forces in similar ways; they are viewed as inevitable, natural conditions beyond the sphere of influence of the local community. This economic determinism is not accompanied by a politicized analysis of capital or class, and the texts would not fit comfortably into the genre of social realism that emerged in the early twentieth century. Certainly, MacLeod presents the miners, fishers, and farmers as figures with an inherent worth and dignity, but Marxist frameworks have little currency in his fiction. He is more interested in the workers as individuals than as representatives of the proletariat.

Even more powerful than the natural and economic forces are the cultural expectations that dictate the behaviours of the protagonists. In "The Vastness of the Dark," James mistakenly accepts his father's claim that he is "free to go if you want to" and underestimates the cultural ties that will bind him to his Gaelic, industrial, familial past (*I*, 39–40). By the story's end, he realizes that he cannot easily escape his family, which has "somehow endured and given me the only life I know for all these eighteen years" (*1*, 56). The tragic power exerted by these deterministic cultural forces is also evident in the character of the father in "The Boat." Though he longed to go to university, his past work, his family ties, and his obligations as a father and husband, chain him to a life for which he is personally unsuited. The best he can do is sacrifice himself in order to ensure that his children have the opportunity to escape their restrictive heritage, even if he is unable to slip those cords.

MacLeod traces the impact of various environmental forces, but even the temporal realm – made manifest as the weight of the past and the burden of the future – restricts the options available to the individual. In his overview of MacLeod's fiction, Nicholson mistakenly argues that in the early stories the temporal realm can be shaped by the individual subject: "In Alistair MacLeod's writing, our past is recuperated in a continuous present: uncertain, jeopardised even, but open still, and still possible" (Nicholson 1987, 93). Nicholson is correct to suggest that the past is always immediate and present to the self-conscious individual, but he underestimates the restrictive power of time. In "The Vastness of the Dark," James realizes that he has been guilty of "oversimplification ... through this long and burning day, but also through most of my yet young life" (*1*, 55). This realization does not free James, as much as it leads him to submit to the cultural practices that constitute his past; thus he joins a group of miners who are driving off to pursue the very occupation that James swore to leave behind. MacLeod's characters feel linked to the generations and eras past, but this "interfusing [of] past and present" tends to define and confine the protagonists, rather than enabling "an extension from concrete immediacy out towards timelessness" (Nicholson 1985, 95).

The textual world constructed in early stories is clearly hard, threatening, alienating, and meaningless, but MacLeod does not suggest that the human subject should therefore submit to these harsh forces and accept annihilation. Nihilism has little force in his stories. MacLeod's early texts are ultimately driven by a strong commitment to a liberal vision of the independent individual. Hiscock argues that "very few if any of his narrators light upon an authentic sense of self unhampered by past illusions and obligations," but if unhampered self-fulfillment is impossible, the stories invariably describe a moment when the protagonists do confront the forces that oppress them (2000, 67). Through their free choices and their reactions, they are able to address their circumstances and secure a degree of personal integrity. Triumph is not an option, but the stories do reproduce a hesitant and tentative hope.

The pervasiveness of his conviction that individuals should oppose overwhelming circumstances is apparent when we examine his depiction of the characters who fail to resist the dehumanizing forces that threaten them. The villain in "In the Fall" is undoubtedly the drover, MacRae, who carries with him the "odour ... of countless frightened animals that have been carried on the back of his truck" (*1*, 105). He is a reprehensible character, not because he has come to collect the family's pony in the expectation of being able to turn him into "mink-feed," but because he has so completely submitted himself to the raw and animalistic impulses of life. MacRae is a cardboard character who stands as a warning of what could happen to any of the family members should they align themselves with the harsh rhythms of nature. Similarly, the salesman who gives James a lift to Springhill in "The Vastness of the Dark" is completely divorced from the legacy of self-sacrifice, integrity, and honesty, which is Nova Scotia's real heritage, and his selfishness shocks James and makes him feel as if "this man has left footprints on a soul I did not even know that I possessed" (*1*, 57). Such figures recur throughout MacLeod's early fiction, and they become manifestations, albeit in reverse, of the writer's moral code and ideological position. MacLeod opposes any attempt by individuals to escape the hard choices presented to the self-aware individual by submitting too quickly to the deterministic forces that sweep the textual world.

Characters from urban centres are often depicted as selfish and self-centered. This pattern is played out by such negative actants as the travelling salesman, the overly protective and snobbish mother in "The Return," and the selfish children who are at the airport to greet their father at the end of "The Lost Salt Gift of Blood." But the rural world is just as capable of producing self-centered characters and the reader must avoid concluding too quickly that MacLeod, as a Maritimer, is reproducing a hinterland's bias against the urban centre.

The essence of what it means to be a human being is, in MacLeod's work, the ability of the individual to articulate and secure a sense of the self even as he or she recognizes the powerful forces that press from without and within. Identity is not just a matter of reinscribing the self into an enduring narrative, of turning a "live history" into a "narrative history" (Nicholson 1987, 85). The character must act, or at least attempt to act, in order to establish a self. The early stories echo the liberal humanist vision of the individual that anchors Charles Bruce, but as was the case with Nowlan, MacLeod's vision of liberalism is shadowed by his acceptance that in a modernist condition; only a gesture towards the ideal of freedom may be possible. When a protagonist does make a gesture towards freedom, MacLeod's insists that it constitutes an instance of grace. Although he is not developing or advocating a particular theological framework, he views such moments of choice with a kind of awe: an awe felt in part because they are moments of possibility and in part because they often arise only through the great sacrifice of another individual.

There would seem to be little to celebrate in "In the Fall." As the beloved pony goes to its death, the youngest son, David, expresses his outrage at his parent's betrayal by slaughtering his mother's prized chickens. If David's assertion of his own values in the face of his harsh environment reflects the passions of his youth, the reactions of his parents are more affirming in their subtlety. In the closing image of the story, the father "puts his arms around my mother's waist," and she removes the combs from her hair so that "it surrounds and engulfs my father's head" (*1*, 117). The evils of the world cannot be defeated, but the sufferers can be fully cognizant of their traumas and still find comfort and strength in each other's presence. The older son recognizes that in a deterministic world uncertainty and compromise are inevitable, but if the losses are authentically recognized a deeper humanity can be retained and even strengthened.

The best example of MacLeod's determination to maintain at least a tentative sense of individual integrity and freedom in the face of a deterministic world appears in "The Boat." The narrator finds that he must choose to betray one of his parents. He is trapped between his sense of obligation to his demanding mother, who feels her son will be "untrue" to his family if he leaves his village to pursue his education, and his sense of duty to his sacrificial father, who has given him the chance to leave by allowing himself to be washed overboard during a storm and lost at sea. He is "a traitor whether he goes or stays" (Kulyk Keefer 1987, 234).

Readers are sometimes uncertain about the father's motivations at the moment of his death, for the narrator reveals only that he turned to look at his father "and he was not there and I knew even in that instant that he would never be again" (*1*, 23). Suicide is the most likely option. Earlier in the story, the narrator carefully recounts how he vowed that he would fish with his father "as long as he lived," and his father only "smiled" and cryptically replied "I hope you will remember what you've said" (*1*, 22). The passage is carefully planted by MacLeod and the "resonant admonition" would make little sense, unless we admit that the father is planning his own death in order to allow (or even force) his son to abandon the boat and seek a new life (Stevens 1996, 270). Indeed, it would be difficult to explain the narrator's torturous nightmares unless we conclude that he, at least, is convinced that his father's death was not accidental.

Given his impossible situation, it is not surprising that the narrator cannot find happiness. Though he does take up the opportunity afforded by his father's untimely death and becomes a teacher at a "great Midwestern university" (1, 2), he is haunted by his choice, and often wakes in the middle of the night so "afraid to be alone with death" that he seeks solace in the nearest "all-night restaurant" (1, 2). In a grim world, no path can take the individual towards happiness, and since joy is not an option in MacLeod's existential fiction, it is vital that the protagonist have a hand in choosing his or her own misery. Francis Berces draws on Camus and argues in a similar vein that the "very harshness and simplicity of their living conditions ... all provide ... a Sisyphean context in which the human spirit is seen striving to affirm its most basic values rather than submitting to the weight of necessity" (1991, 115–16). Kulyk Keefer argues that the stories in MacLeod's first volume, *The Lost Salt Gift of Blood*, reproduce a tragic paradigm, but he does not fulfill the full tragic form; his protagonists are not destroyed by the cruel choices they are forced to make. Indeed, the very opportunity to make a choice allows them to fortify their sense of identity and survive in their otherwise tragic situation.

The emphasis on the fate of the individual and the recognition that only tentative bonds link the protagonist to the larger community, breeds a kind of egalitarian vision in the early texts. There is little question that MacLeod is representing a social structure that is anchored firmly by patriarchal traditions and assumptions. But MacLeod does not always treat the primacy of the male, and the family's dependence on the man's economic power, as either natural or good. Just as Nowlan recognizes and critiques the harmful effects of constrictive gender roles, MacLeod's fictions often demonstrate that individual happiness and family stability are threatened by the patriarchal traditions that value only male work; when that worker is injured or killed – as they inevitably are in MacLeod's fiction – the rest of the family descends into terrible poverty. Moreover, in several stories the struggle of the individual is still central enough that several female characters undertake the existential struggle to define themselves. "The Road to Rankin's Point" is a particularly good example of this egalitarian ideology as the grandmother struggles against time, old age, and the oppressive good intentions of her own children, in order to maintain her independence. Driven by the stoic realization that "no one said that life is to be easy. Only that it is to be lived," she is still determined to stay on her own land (1, 172). The moment her ability to continue resisting the whims of fate is compromised, and it seems that she may have to move to a retirement home, she willingly dies. She thus is a complex character who is as constrained and doomed as any of the male characters in early texts. Such independent figures must be balanced against the many stereotyped shrews and Madonnas/mothers who populate MacLeod's stories, but if the early fiction is predominantly masculinist in tone, it is not exclusively patriarchal in its construction. The roles assigned by gender are set aside in the early texts as MacLeod emphasizes the centrality of the individual.

The later short shorties, including those brought together in *As Birds Bring Forth the Sun*, mark a significant departure from MacLeod's earlier work. The change in tone was first recognized in an early review of his second collection. Michael Dixon notes that "despite the constant pressures of emotional and physical violence," the protagonists experience a "sense of profound serenity and faithfulness" as they reclaim a "collective past" and a "collective memory." Kulyk Keefer agrees that while the later stories are anchored in the same oppressive environment, the characters are "freed of any fierce sense of closure" (Kulyk Keefer 1987, 236). The sense of ease, which both critics perceive, is the first evidence that MacLeod is moving towards an epistemological sense of certainty. There are, of course, numerous ways in which a writer can construct a solid philosophical ground on which to stand. Nowlan responded to the sense of determinism that dominated his early texts by attending more closely to the fragmented subjectivity of the individual and the possibilities to be found within the modernist condition. In contrast, as MacLeod's vision of the world has matured and developed, he has increasingly linked the lost individual to the image of the community with its stable, traditional, and patriarchal systems. This emerging sense of certainty and security, and his growing sense of assurance regarding the individual's place in the world signals a philosophic shift towards a more conservative perspective.

Many aspects of the world represented in the stories from the late 1970s and throughout the 1980s are just as harsh as those seen in the earlier stories. In such stories as "The Winter Dog" and "As Birds Bring Forth The Sun," the environment remains dangerous and threatening. Indeed, in these texts the forces of nature seem almost to be plotting actively to betray the human characters, whether it be the ice fields that tempt the young boy to explore the shifting flows, or the wild dogs who are driven by "blood-lust or duty or perhaps starvation" to kill the vulnerable and kind man who lands on their shores (*1*, 314). Economic and cultural constraints remain strong as well. In "To Everything There is a Season" the family depends on the money earned by the eldest son, who works the "long flat carriers of grain and iron ore" that sail on the Great Lakes (*1*, 213); and in "The Closing Down of Summer" MacKinnon's elite team of miners must ply their trade in Africa, far from the exhausted mines of Cape Breton. Perhaps these oppressive forces are not as merciless and overwhelming as in the early stories, but they still threaten rather than support the individual.

A more substantial shift becomes apparent when we note that MacLeod's later texts are less concerned with the individual's existential quest for freedom and an independent self. The later stories rarely attend to the individual choices of the protagonists, instead the protagonists of the later stories discover and secure their identities by fusing themselves with a larger community. This move towards a conservative ideology, in which the individual must be linked to a larger social body, which is itself maintained through its commitment to traditional hierarchies and modes of expression, is evident in each of the stories. For example, in "The Closing Down of Summer," the miners recognize that their sense of identity is forged and strengthened by their work as a collective unit and by their joint experience of their Gaelic heritage that has shaped them "unconsciously through some strange osmotic process while ... growing up" (*1*, 194). The miners, who function as an interdependent working collective as they travel to mines all over the globe, have "gone back to Gaelic songs because they are so constant and unchanging and speak to us as the privately familiar" (*1*, 194). The essence of the individual can thus be established and interpreted only within the traditional community, and, in a very real way, MacLeod insists that identity is tribal in character.

The confident conservatism of the later texts is also evident in the way MacLeod changes his representation of time, for the temporal world of the later stories is considerably less imposing than in the earlier texts. The characters are still embedded in their cultural heritage and their specific local past, and their lives are still influenced by the hand of fate, but that past is less restrictive: death remains omnipresent, but it is not sealed. Throughout these texts, mysticism plays a role as superstitions, second sight, and dreams allow the protagonists to connect with the past and converse with forces beyond the grave. Life and death are not represented as binary opposites, but rather as a continuum along which particular individuals can move freely. Protagonists who are able to connect mystically with the past are able to resist and even reshape the present, and so individual identity is no longer anchored exclusively on ambiguous gestures of freedom, but on the movable ground of a community's inherited cultural memory.

In "The Tuning of Perfection," the central figure has been alone for most of his adult life. Although he feels vulnerable and isolated from his daughters and the wider community, he will not compromise his integrity as a folk singer and modify his music to meet the demands of a television producer, even though he alienates his entire clan with his stubborn behaviour. Archibald anchors his identity in the past, and his dream of his long dead wife – a dream that affords him access to a past community – reaffirms his sense of identity and reinforces his commitment to his artistic heritage. "Vision" has an even stronger vein of mysticism. This complex story examines a family of five generations that is haunted, almost literally, by a scandal that originated in the grandfather's decision to marry a woman while fathering twin daughters with his sister-in-law – who is is eventually betrayed and destroyed. The family suffers collectively from its cursed past and its shameful legacy of "uncertain" parentage. Each generation encounters the betrayed sister-in-law's spirit and one by one the men of the clan are disfigured. But if the individuals are physically wounded, the apparition of the woman also has a positive function, in that she makes appearances to warn her descendants of danger. The story suggests that mystical forces at work in the family more than compensate for physical losses by endowing the family with a greater kind of prophetic, visionary power. The narrator feels that he is a "child of uncertainty," but when compared to the protagonists of the earlier stories, he is able to reach into his past and build upon his heritage to discover a strong sense of identity. He cannot "see and understand the twisted strand of love" that binds his family, but he does not doubt the existence of the bond (1, 368).

The characters of MacLeod's later stories anchor themselves in their traditional community, either the immediate community that surrounds them or the community that is accessible to them across time; as the role of the stable community is emphasized, its enduring structures, hierarchies, and gender roles are also valorized. Thus, while his early work tends towards an egalitarian perspective, the later fiction tends to stress the importance of maintaining the traditional gender roles in order to preserve the heart of the society. There are a few attending mothers and the occasional wife speaking from the wings, but few women emerge, like the grandmother in "The Road to Rankin's Point," to assert their place as individuals within the communal tradition. The one exception would be the "Island," in which the central protagonist, Agnes MacPhedran, defies the communities standards that govern sexuality and through a process of happenstance forges her own identity as "the madwoman of the island" (1, 406). But even in this case she is represented as a rogue figure who is interesting because she has abandoned the conventional gender roles, not because she has refashioned them to the benefit of the larger community.

MacLeod's patriarchal construction of gender roles is evident as his various male characters attempt to secure their identity and anchoring themselves in their culture by connecting with or contrasting themselves against a woman who embodies, and sometimes entombs, the essence of the community's heritage. The feminine is thus presented as passive space; a functional and necessary supplement to the masculine drive towards identity. In the story "Vision," the betrayed woman is represented with considerable sympathy, but she is less an individual than an abstract mythic figure who appears only in a series of recollections and occasional visions. She is always described by a third party, and the narrative is not focalized through her perspective. She is the anchor for the grandchildren and great-grandchildren who identify themselves as the "sons of uncertainty"; but little attention is paid to the identity of the woman herself.

"The Tuning of Perfection" also depicts the feminine as the essence of the local culture. Throughout the story Archibald is anxious about his role, for the values and practices of his folk world seem irrelevant in the new industrial and mass-media society. But despite his general desire to preserve his old-fashioned ways, he cannot find the courage to defy his family and refuse the chance to perform his music on television, until his wife appears in a dream and sings "with a clarity and a beauty that caused the hairs to rise on the back of his neck even as the tears welled to his eye" (1, 304). In this context, the vision of the dead wife functions as a touchstone of authenticity and integrity; an icon of cultural stability who enables Archibald to defend his culture. Not only does the dead woman reach beyond the grave to play out her role as a supplement to her husband, but as the benchmark of feminine perfection she contrasts with the modern women who have accommodated the demands of the twentieth century and become myopic in their vulgarity and materialism. Archibald's granddaughter drives a pick-up, which testifies to her crass character with its bumper sticker, "If you're horny, honk your horn" (1, 286). Not surprisingly, she cannot fully understand Archibald's desire to maintain the integrity of his culture and his soul. She remains insensitive to the community's deeper heritage, the possibilities offered by the past, and the importance of the traditional gender identities. In his later short stories and most recently in his acclaimed novel *No Great Mischief*, MacLeod celebrates each of these forces as he responds to the uncertainty of his early work and develops a more mature sense of stability, a more conservative and patriarchal ideology.

MacLeod's Novel: No Great Mischief

In the late 1980s, MacLeod announced that he was writing a novel tentatively entitled *No Great Mischief if They Fall*. Given the pace at which the short stories were produced, it is not surprising that the novel grew slowly.[9] Finally published in 1999 under the title *No Great Mischief*, it garnered praise from reviewers, struck an immediate chord with readers, and remained in the top ten of bestsellers lists for much of 2000. The novel has also won an array of prizes, including the Trillium Award, the Canadian Booksellers Association Libris Awards for Author of the Year and Book of the Year, the Dartmouth Book Award for Fiction, the Thomas Raddall Atlantic Fiction Award, the CAA-MOSAID Technologies Inc. Award for Fiction, and, most impressively, the International IMPAC Dublin Literary Award (worth $172,000).

For the fans of the short stories who had waited eleven years, *No Great Mischief* felt like familiar ground: MacLeod chronicled the experiences of the narrator Alexander MacDonald, who goes to visit his derelict brother Calum and in the process remembers not only his family's history but the complete mythology of the "clan Mac-Donald." Indeed, the ways in which the novel echoes and borrows from the short stories suggests that MacLeod not only relied on the technique he developed as a writer of short fiction, but he was also guided by a similar sensibility and vision. MacLeod's first novel reproduces some of the structural and thematic qualities that defined the short stories. The chronicle of their grandpa's misadventures on the ice when he almost froze, the account of the brothers' parents and their untimely death, and the story of the three elder brothers and their life on the old family farm are carefully structured and could stand alone with any of MacLeod's later fictions. At points, the novel repeats some of the specific images and patterns employed in the short stories: the narrator of the novel, like the speaker of MacLeod's first story, "The Boat," is a modern, academically gifted individual who is tortured by his sense of guilt for having abandoned his family's roots; the main narrator/character, like the narrator of "The Golden Dog," is anticipating the death of a near relation, which will occasion his journey back home to Cape Breton; and Calum Mac-Donald and his clan of miners function very much like MacKinnon's crew in "The Closing Down of Summer,"including their sense of affinity with the Zulu tribes of South Africa, whose identity is preserved through their vibrant folk culture. But most importantly, in his novel MacLeod returns to and carefully develops his central conviction that the tightly knit, traditional family unit within a fully integrated communal society can provide a sense of identity, purpose, and security that is simply unavailable to the alienated individual in the fragmented, urbanized, industrial, modern world.

In *No Great Mischief*, MacLeod uses his two main characters, the narrator Alexander MacDonald and his eldest brother Calum, to extol the value of the traditional social order exemplified by the clan system. The importance of the clan in this novel cannot be overestimated; through this familial and even natural image MacLeod articulates, without becoming stridently ideological, a compelling conservatism. He contends that individuals must anchor themselves in their immediate community in order to attain a sense of identity. *No Great Mischief* begins its celebration of the *"clann Chalum Ruaidh"* by reviewing the trials of the immigrant Calum Ruadh, who left his Highland home, endured the miseries and privations of pioneer life, and replanted his family on the shores of Cape Breton. Ever after, his descendants form a contained community to which they can connect themselves if they choose to do so. The family is linked most obviously by its common physical and genetic heritage; its characteristic "predisposition to have twins," and its unique colouring of "red hair" and eyes "that were so dark as to be beyond brown and almost in the region of a glowing black" (NGM, 30). But the clan also anchors and completes the emotional personalities of its members, as is the case with the narrator's two grandfathers, who are radically dissimilar, even opposite individuals, but who "throughout their lives … were each a balance to the other" (NGM, 264). The clan even binds individuals at a deeper level through a kind of spiritual communion; the narrator's sister returns to the ancestral lands in Aberdeen, Scotland, and finds an immediate almost mystical sense of belonging within her ancient community:

She met the woman face to face, and they looked into each other's eyes.

"You are from here," said the woman.
"No," said my sister, "I'm from Canada."
"That may be," said the woman. "But you are really from here. You have just been away for a while." (NGM, 160).

MacLeod insists so much on the importance of the clan that he has his characters repeat such calls for loyalty as "Blood is thicker than water" and "Always look after your own blood" more than ten times in the course of the novel (*NGM*, 14, 35, 38, 58, 70, 110, 203–4, 262, 277). The calls for clan solidarity, and the novel's careful use of blood imagery verge on overdetermination, but MacLeod takes that risk in order to secure his central ideological vision.

The values of the clan are best exemplified in the character of Calum, who eventually emerges as the main repository of the text's value system. Named for his ancestor, the eldest brother becomes the leader of his immediate family after the death of his parents. Eventually, he also becomes the leader of the MacDonald clan when they become an internationally known, hard-rock mining crew. He embodies the clan's history and experiences such a bond to his community that he feels guilty when any family member suffers a hardship that, had he been present, he might have been able to mitigate. The identity of the clan is anchored in three concepts that he epitomizes: memory, loyalty, and fearless opposition to an enemy. David Williams notes that the phrase "Do you remember … reverberate[s] throughout the whole of the narrative" (2001, 52), and certainly Calum anchors his identity on the family stories that have been passed down to him through his grandparents. The opening chapter of the novel, when Alexander visits Calum in his Toronto rooming house, provides a good example. Calum repeatedly asks "Do you remember …" in an attempt to reestablish contact with his youngest brother. Memory compels Calum in nearly all he does, including his sudden decision to drive seventeen hundred miles from a hard-rock mine in Timmins to Chalum Ruadh's Point, where he constructs a memorial for his parents by drilling their "initials into the face of the rock" (*NGM*, 213). Calum is haunted by the past, and eventually this powerful sense of remembered history passes to Alexander, who recollects the stories that form the novel and thus fulfils the "traditional Celtic role of a 'guardian of memory'" (Jirgens 2001, 89). While memory is the cornerstone of the clan's identity, loyalty to that memory is a force that binds the clan together.

Just as the ancient clan was fearlessly loyal when called to battle, so Calum is the essence of loyalty in all he does. He quits his job and leads his crew away from a profitable contract when it conflicts with his obligation to honour his cousin who was killed in the mine. He willingly finds work for the undeserving American cousin simply because he is a MacDonald. Indeed, if he is forced to choose between defending the immediate clan, which provides and sustains his sense of identity, or conforming to the dictates of the large modern society, Calum does not hesitate to choose the former. His defence of the clan's reputation leads him to strike and kill Fern Picard and bear the burden of the manslaughter conviction. It is entirely appropriate that he is the source of a story about a tree that is "severed at its stump," yet it does not fall because its "upper branches were so densely intertwined with those of the trees around it that it just remained standing. There was no way it could be removed or fall unless the whole grove was cut down" (*NGM*, 239). This parable about family loyalty functions as a kind of gospel for the novel, and as such it articulates one of MacLeod's central values.

If the identity of the clan is anchored, in part, in the concepts of memory and loyalty, then the clan also identifies itself through moments of opposition and its clear memory of instances of betrayal. The ancient MacDonalds remembered the battle in which their struggle against the English oppressor was lost because "the boats ... from France" did not arrive (*NGM*, 162). The clan's heroic identity is solidified further as family historians recall – on two separate occasions – how Wolfe betrayed his Scottish troops even as he employed them in the assault against Québec City, not because he knew they would succeed, but because they "are hardy, intrepid, accustomed to rough country and no great mischief if they fall" (*NGM*, 109, 237). Whether the clan system is anchored in positive values or strategic oppositions, the identity that is constructed for the family member is far more complex, secure, and stable than anything offered in the modern world.

MacLeod's defence of the traditional community is so clear and powerful that he is placed in a rather difficult position. Having rejected the modern world and placed his hope in the traditional and conservative vision of society reproduced within the clan system, he must, in the narrative itself, acknowledge that the old social structure has not only diminished, but is in the process of disappearing. When Calum MacDonald approaches his family's land and quietly dies, Alexander reaches for "his cooling hand which lies on the seat beside him," and the reader recognizes that not just a man, but a way of being, has been brought to a tragic end.[10] The assumptions reproduced in *No Great Mischief* have, by the narrative's own admission, already receded from the experience of the millions of readers who have so eagerly engaged with the novel. As MacLeod celebrates an ideology that he also presents as doomed, his novel adopts an overtly nostalgic mood and employs a sense of melancholic longing that ties it to earlier Maritime fictions.

In their early texts, Nowlan and MacLeod represent the hardships experienced in the region and reject opportunities to idealize the past. MacLeod's early stories are, as has been noted, entirely free of a nostalgic impulse. In *No Great Mischief*, MacLeod commits himself more deeply to the social structure of the past, and he exhibits a clear longing for the pre-modern, pre-urban community. His novel echoes some of the tensions evident in Buckler's best work. The narrator admits that the past cannot be recovered, but Alexander does insist that his memories, or more precisely his recorded stories, can preserve a shadowed memory of that past that can then be projected into the future. In the opening pages this nostalgic tone is sounded as Alexander retreats from Calum and is "surprised to realize" that his brother's music is "no longer coming from him but from somewhere deep within me: "There's a longing in my heart now / To be where I was / Though I know that it's quite sure / I never shall return" (NGM, 17). This nostalgic impulse does not dominate the narrative, as it does Buckler's first novel, but there are moments in which we can sense that an idyllic quality was evident in the clan's past and simultaneously recognize that such moments have disappeared forever. By the novel's conclusion, the grandparents have died, the clan's leader has perished, and even the narrative itself begins to break apart. The closing page abandons the traditional narration, and employs a series of poetic images, traditional proverbs, and allusions to the tale just told. The reader senses that the old continuity has literally fragmented and left only remnants behind. *No Great Mischief* is certainly the product of the Gaelic Diaspora, but in its fusion of hesitation and nostalgia it can also be read as a distinctly regional and Maritime text.[11]

No Great Mischief anchors its ideological vision on the clan and the traditional world that system evokes, but the text's conservatism also influences the representation and critique of the modern world in interesting ways. The narrator, Alexander, is the text's most completely developed example of the modern man. Though he comes from a tightly knit clan, Alexander has abandoned the traditional work of his ancestors, capitalized on his intelligence and academic abilities, and become a orthodontist in a large city in Southern Ontario. He is a success according to the standards of his urban contemporaries, but he is plagued by his sense of disconnection from his past: his admission early in the novel – that he is a "twentieth-century man ... *whether I like it or not*" (NGM, 17) – reveals his ambiguity about his modern condition. From his sense of alienation from his Cape Breton roots, to his feelings of guilt about his own profession as a dentist who attends to and improves the superficial appearances of people, the narrator feels tainted by the corruption that infects the modern world.

Nor is the narrator's suspicion that the modern world breeds an inferior type of individual left unsubstantiated by the text. Citizens of the modern world prove to be arrogant oafs on numerous occasions. When the Alexander goes to a dentistry conference, he is appalled by the American blowhard who dismisses his own heritage and his family's past. To reinforce this general suspicion of the modern era, the cousin from San Francisco, who wears a "Celtic ring upon his finger" and pretends to adhere to his Gaelic heritage as he relies on the clan to help him dodge the draft, ultimately proves to be a selfish individual (*NGM*, 223). He brings shame on the family by stealing Fern Picard's wallet, and he violates the code of honour again when he abandons the clan in its hour of need and flees from the final fight between the Calum's crew and miners from Québec (*NGM*, 255). Modernity is critiqued in the text because it reproduces the conditions of loneliness and alienation that inevitably ruin the individual.

MacLeod's anxiety about the demise of the traditional world he longs to defend and his suspicion about modernity are so intense that they breed one of the few stylistic weaknesses in the novel; the narrator's memories of the past are aesthetically satisfying, but whenever Alexander explores the present, he produces didactic moments that lack the subtlety that usually characterizes his work. For example, MacLeod is overtly opposed to the modern condition, and, when Alexander visits his sister's home in Calgary, he communicates his aversion for contemporary decor by simply dismissing her home as a "modernistic house" on four occasions (*NGM*, 93, 96, 165, 167). Similarly, as Alexander drives to the city to find Calum, he passes a group of anti-nuclear demonstrators who are confronting a counter-demonstration by fervent nationalists, but the whole scene seems rather contrived and is crafted simply to highlight the fragmented nature of the urban setting. In a more obtrusive fashion, on five separate occasions the narrator observes the rich farmland; he travels through in Southern Ontario and comments on the two groups of people who are harvesting the crops. Some of "the pickers" are migrant workers who are anchored in the folk cultures of Central America and who are sustained in the midst of the loneliness and poverty of their transient lives by the language and music of their homes and families. The narrator casts these migrant workers in a heroic light, and the migrants become the contemporary equivalents of the wandering Cape Breton miners. But in these moments the narrator also describes and attacks a second group of pickers; the middle-class families from the local suburbs. In a novel that usually strikes a compassionate stance, the narrator adopts a sarcastic tone, reminiscent of Raddall's antimodernist tirades in *The Nymph and the Lamp*. He depicts the modern families as materialistic, spiritually impoverished whiners who cannot appreciate the wealth and opportunities afforded them: "The children of the families are even more weary now and close to open rebellion. They long for their rec rooms and their video games and iced drinks and for long telephone conversations with their friends in which they can express the anguish of their pain" (NGM, 168). The mini-sermons are the product of the text's anxiety that its central ideology is already languishing; they feel forced and heavy handed. Alexander's strident tone reminds us that MacLeod is uncomfortable with the tragic losses he depicts, and No Great Mischief continues to blame and demonize the modern world that has abandoned his conservative communal vision of the world.

Ideological Shift

Alistair MacLeod has been celebrated as a "one of the finest practitioners of the short story" and as a teller of "brilliant" tales. Doubtless he deserves such praise, for the meticulous precision and elegance of his style has allowed him to create short stories that are unparalleled in their complexity in the tradition of Maritime literature. But MacLeod's most important contribution has been his ability to remain flexible, for he has not simply retold the same tale in story after story, rather his Collected Stories and No Great Mischief reveal that his art and his ideological positions have varied over time. Over the last thirty years, MacLeod has moved from a fusion of liberalism and existentialism in his early exploration of the individual, to a more focused and conservative exploration of the role community and memory play in the life and consciousness of the individual. The reasons for MacLeod's ideological shift could be diverse. After a period of skepticism and uncertainty, MacLeod may have become more personally committed to the notion that communal and traditional hierarchies help to steady and stabilize the individual. Or, as has been the case with another Maritime writer, David Adams Richards, a prolonged exploration of the grimmer aspects of Maritime experience within a realist framework may have propelled him towards more salutary, less naturalistic forms through which he can produce a more confident representation of the region. Nor should we ignore the possibility that MacLeod may be responding to his own decision to develop his professional career outside the region, with a corresponding recognition of the importance of memory, history, and community within his later texts. Whatever the reasons for the shift, he has, throughout his career, attempted to articulate and illuminate his Maritime heritage, and like the lighthouse that Alexander sees as he approaches his ancestral home bearing Calum's body, MacLeod's fiction itself "sends forth its message from the island's highest point. A light of warning and perhaps of encouragement" (NGM, 283).

6 Hard Bargains:
David Adams Richards

> The house was ablaze before anyone knew about it, and ashes
> and boards fell or blew onto the road below. The smell of it
> scattered like crumbs throughout our whole area, and we could
> taste it for days after- as a reminder … And the Christmas tree
> that had been thrown into the yard sometime before, burnt like
> the burning bush.
>
> Richards, *Road to the Stilt House.*

Born in Newcastle in 1950, David Adams Richards lived on the
Miramichi river until the early 1970s, and since that time he has used
the river and the surrounding area as the setting for each of his novels. The small towns that dot the river flourished during the timber
boom of the late nineteenth century, but in the late twentieth century
these communities experienced a period of decline; underemployment was rampant, and many people emigrated. Like the Maritime
novelists who preceded him, Richards has produced texts that are
embedded in a culture caught between its painful experiences as a
modern, industrial society and its sense of an earlier traditional order.
Like Alden Nowlan, in particular, his fictional explorations of individual struggles against social disruption and economic crises are not
deeply influenced by idealistic "memories of a shared community."
Just as Nowlan is one of the first writers to examine closely the social
and economic problems that plagued the region in the decades following the Second World War, Richards is the first novelist to address
directly the social and cultural problems that have arisen in the Maritimes since the 1960s. Haunted as they are by the effects of the region's traumatic transformations, his fictions display a set of interests
and tensions that have not been seen before in Maritime literature.

That Richards has developed a distinct response to his region is
evident when we examine the ways in which he departs from the literary traditions that precede him. The first defining feature of Richards's prose is the almost complete absence of a nostalgic impulse.
While MacLeod's work initially rejected the vein of nostalgia that

flows through Maritime culture, he eventually returned to a more idyllic sense of the pre-modern era. Richards work never views the past through the lens of idealized memory, and like Nowlan he remains consistently aware that the preceding era does not constitute a golden age. Indeed, identified as a bleak writer who attends to "an intolerably dreary, foreclosed reality" (Kulyk Keefer 1987, 170), David Adams Richards is "as far from writing regional idylls as a writer can be" (Connor 1986, 270). Produced in a area that has continually struggled with poverty and chronic underemployment, his texts are deeply suspicious of any effort to romanticize the past. As Susan Lever notes, his "fiction does not express a nostalgia for some past rural community, but places questions about the perceptions of individual experience firmly in the present" (1994, 88–9). His narrators rarely turn to elderly characters or traditional emblems in the hope of finding solutions or inspiration for the present. Indeed, few representations of the community's past are left alive or intact. In his second novel, *Blood Ties*, the MacDurmot family spans three generations, but the eldest family member, Irene's mother Annie, is "incontinent, senile, helpless," and completely disconnected from her community (Summers 1992, 358). Reduced to a vegetative state, she makes a "soft unmistakable gurgling in her throat, the only voice she had" (*BT*, 16), and is thus unable to recall, let alone pass on, the types of family histories that Ellen Canaan communicates in *The Mountain and the Valley* or grandmother MacDonald recalls in *No Great Mischief*. In *For Those Who Hunt the Wounded Down* (1993), few figures are older than forty-five, and those who have survived into old age are hardly sources of wisdom. In the midst of his chaotic existence, Jerry Bines attempts to care for his sick grandmother, but rather than being a guiding force in his life, she has "been drunk as a loon the last three days" (*HWD*, 109). The narrators of all Richards's fictions are aware that the characters are ungrounded and disconnected from their roots, but since past traditions are as alienating as the community's current value systems, such disconnections do not represent a significant loss.

Just as Richards divorces himself from the strand of nostalgia that weaves its way through Maritime realist texts, so his fiction distinguishes itself from its predecessors though its grim representations of nature. In contrast to the restorative experiences of the natural world granted to various characters in *Rockbound*, *Barometer Rising*, *The Nymph and the Lamp*, *The Channel Shore*, and *The Cruelest Month*, Richards's characters are rarely able to achieve an intimate connection with the "natural" world. Their immersion in the alienating post-industrial conditions of the region undercuts any flight towards nature. Constructing the fields and forests through a naturalistic rather than a romantic discourse, the narrator of *Blood Ties* presents nature as harsh, unforgiving, and unable to comfort, sustain, or transform Orville. Haunted by the violent spectres of Mallory's spirit, the woods are a frightening space within which Orville acts out his most violent impulses and then returns home with rabbit carcasses to "loop over a beam that ran above the window … grotesque and stiff their cold forms leaving blood traces on the pane" (*BT*, 139). An appreciation of nature's grace and beauty cannot stifle Orville's aggression and anger.

Richards's representations of nature shift slightly in his later texts. Joe in *Nights Below Station Street*, Ivan in *Evening Snow Will Bring Such Peace*, and Jerry Bines in *For Those Who Hunt the Wounded Down*, all share a near-mystical ability to read the woods. Joe's intuitive skills as a woodsman lead him to Vye, the hopelessly lost urbanite, while Ivan's deep sympathies with the natural world compel him to sacrifice his own life in an effort to save a beloved horse. Jerry Bines is so closely attuned to the natural cycles that he is able to make his way effortlessly through the tangled Miramichi woods in order to pay secret visits to his sick child, and in fifteen minutes he is able to find the wounded moose that had eluded other hunters an entire afternoon (*HWD*, 75). If some later novels feature protagonists whose special sense of independence, self-reliance, and integrity makes them prone to heroic gestures, it is important to note that nature provides the stage on which they demonstrate their abilities without imparting these special abilities to any other characters. Few individuals gain access to nature's secrets, and the woods remain alienating and dangerous to all other characters.

Finally, while such writers as Raddall, Bruce, Buckler, and MacLeod expressed varying degrees of confidence about the individual's ability to develop and maintain his or her identity in the association with various community institutions, Richards focuses on the possibility of individual freedom while remaining deeply suspicious of community organizations, which he views as flawed and dangerous entities. Throughout his fiction, Richards maintains a sense of opposition to both conservative and communitarian visions of the world. His fiction is consistently opposed to the notion that the individual must either subsume or connect the self to the social networks and traditions of the community. In a separation of personal identity and state structures reminiscent of the individualistic liberalisms that predate their modern pluralist permutations, Richards presents marginalized outcasts with great sympathy, while criticizing the formal institutions that confine or oppress them. In the early novel *Blood Ties*, the schools and churches are represented as devitalized and spent institutions that punish and control without encouraging or facilitating the growth of the individual. Social agencies are actively destructive in *Road to the Stilt House*. The social worker, identified only as Juliet, means well but her attempts to integrate Arnold's family back into society's mainstream produce disastrous results. When Randy follows her suggestion to join the local "cub pack," his obvious status as an outsider makes him a target for abuse and ridicule by the "cub-master" and the other boys. The welfare department cannot address the family's most basic needs, and even the family's church – ironically named "Our Church of the Gladdened Heart" – is unable to provide spiritual or emotional consolation. After issuing the empty platitude "Each man must get along with himself" (*RSH*, 13), the priest resorts to the random violence Arnold casually expects: "Father Billy came here to slap me in the face, but that's his right" (*RSH*, 128). In *For Those Who Hunt the Wounded Down*, Richards once again takes aim at religious and judicial systems, and some the novel's sharpest criticisms are saved for the academic institutions represented by Vera Pillar. As she writes her self-serving sociological study, "The Victims of Patriarchy (and Its Inevitable Social Results)," Vera not only uses and misrepresents Jerry Bines, but she preys on the very violence she claims to condemn. A "parallel [is] drawn between the sociological feminism of Vera and the physical menace of Gary Percy Rils": both stalk "Jerry Bines like a hunter" (Armstong 1997, 10). Throughout his fiction Richards makes sure his characters are carefully grounded in specific familial and local contexts, but no outside institution, traditional practice, or social hierarchy imposes or effects positive change and this degree of disaffection with social systems is unique in Maritime fiction.

Richards's simultaneous devotion to the concept of individual freedom and suspicion of state and community institutions aligns him with the assumptions of individualist liberalism. Deeply committed to the principle of human equality and a belief that "society can safely be founded on the self-directing power of an individual's will and self control," Richards's texts echo Locke as they assert that true liberty arises only as individuals are freed from the restrictions and demands of the state (Grimes 1964, 66). By separating the local community from the state and by curtailing the power and influence of the latter, Locke establishes a stream of liberalism that is consistent with Richards's views. The laissez-faire character of individualist liberalism "places a very high value on individual life" and advocates an opposition to "habitual actions done in slavish imitation of ossified tradition," while at the same time casting a suspicious eye on institutions that may confine or threaten the citizen (Minogue 1963, 25–6). From the celebration of individual liberty, to the assertion that freedom remains "something spontaneous and unpredictable in human affairs" (Minogue 1963, 173), this ideological position corresponds to many of the central concerns of Richards's fiction. Indeed, Richards himself has repeatedly asserted his faith that the most important aspects of an individual are those that emerge from within the isolated individual and are entirely divorced from the larger community. He has frequently declared that "spontaneous action always frees you" (Scherf 1990, 160) and "only spontaneous action is good action" (Vaughan 1993, 17); many of his most memorable characters accomplish their goals by following their impulses.[1]

Attracted as he is to the ideal of freedom, it would be a mistake to suggest that Richards's novels generate simplistic quest structures. Some liberal theorists may hold that complete emancipation is possible, that the future is not determined but created by the present, and that "all options are available" (Minogue 1993, 30), but such boundless optimism is difficult to maintain in a region as economically limited as the Miramichi and in a style of fiction as embedded in historicism as Richards's realism. As often as some characters win a degree of liberation, others approach the brink of a deterministic fatalism. Richards's desire for individual independence has always been in potential conflict with the tenets of naturalism that have influenced his early texts. As shall seen in the remainder of this chapter, Richards's fiction has evolved over the last three decades; he has become increasingly anxious about the difficulties involved in maintaining his individualistic-liberal ideology, and though he initially employed a series of narrative shifts in order to defend his perspective, his later texts move away from the realism that defined his early work. The early novel *Blood Ties* attempts to employ a standard naturalist discourse while still maintaining a vision of the free individual. Any assertions that the individual is independent prove to be more uncertain in *Road to the Stilt House*. By the time Richards produces *For Those Who Hunt the Wounded Down* he has started to defend his ideological position through a formal shift towards the conventions of the romance, and this transition is largely complete with the publication of his latest novels. In *The Bay of Love and Sorrows* and *Mercy Among the Children*, imposing protagonists cast in the heroic mold defend his, now paramount, vision of the individual.[2]

BLOOD TIES

Richards's first three novels, *The Coming of Winter*, *Blood Ties*, and *Lives of Short Duration*, are usually identified as forming his first Miramichi trilogy; in these, he forged the initial expression of his central ideals. In the second novel, *Blood Ties*, individual characters are carefully constructed so that their struggles to establish their identities become the focal point of the narrative. The individuation of each figure is facilitated by the use of an unspecified external narrator who consistently focalizes the text through the eyes of the sympathetic characters, provides flashbacks of their formative experiences, and distances itself from the more violent or repressive figures who threaten to confine them. These subtle techniques of narration encourage the reader to draw close to the main characters – Cathy, Orville and Leah – and in each case the reader sympathizes as they struggle to free themselves from their confined traditional roles. As each individual struggles for liberty, we can sense that the text's desire to represent the central figures as independent characters is occasionally threatened by the naturalist-historicist impulse to document how each actant is enmeshed in an imprisoning web of cause and effect. The more historicized the character, the more difficult is that character's struggle for liberty. Yet, though various events threaten to trap each figure within a destructive deterministic cycle, the text's commitment to a concept of free will is evident as protagonists are eventually granted a measure of independence and a chance to change their lives.

Cathy's attempt to redefine herself dominates two sections of this three-part novel. Her longing to escape her confining status as an adolescent and emerge as a free and self-sufficient adult is apparent in the opening pages, as she argues with her brother Orville and longs for greater authority in her family. The first two sections thus echo the conventions of the bildungsroman, as Cathy leaves the confines of her family to search for a sense of power and is drawn to the reckless, untamed, and apparently free young men who move around the boundaries of the community. "Wild like the wind," John Delano resists all forms of confinement and all conventional codes of behaviour (*BT*, 81). Whether he is jumping off the town wharf at night to see if he can touch the river bottom or refusing to enter the internal domestic space of the MacDurmot home, he appears to be a young man capable of transgressing the expectations of the community. Yet if John functions as a detached individual, Cathy's association with him only leads to new forms of confinement. Because John affirms his own sense of independence by continually crossing social and cultural boundaries, Cathy is absorbed into his life not as an equal partner in his transgressions, but as a stable point against which John can measure his "wildness." When they go to the exhibition on their first formal date, Cathy anticipates a romantic encounter only to discover that John enjoys scaring her by rocking the rides. Just as Cathy feels compelled to play the feminine emblem of constancy to support John's instability, so she also feels herself slip into the role of the jealous, demanding girlfriend continually awaiting her man's return. Cathy intellectually rebels against this confining role and imagines bluntly rejecting his advances, but when he drops by the school for a visit, her emotional attachment overwhelms her desire to assert herself and she asks, "Ya wanta go for a walk?" (BT, 194, 196).

Cathy's longing for a genuine degree of autonomy is not satisfied until she begins to resist the restrictive gender codes that reinforce the notion that she needs to attach herself to a man to find a sense of purpose. Indeed, as she follows a path of self-transformation, *Blood Ties* reproduces a feminist perspective with far greater sympathy than is present in Richards's later texts. Increasingly uncomfortable with John, Cathy begins to act for herself as she attends a high-school winter-carnival dance and recognizes her own expressive abilities as a dancer. Ceasing to be self-conscious about her body, she feels an unusual sense of pride and self-confidence as she is absorbed in the music: "She forgot John and the way he was moving and only felt the need for the way she was moving – because the music made her move that way ... she felt it all so well, she felt all the sounds inside her, all at once, so well. When she looked about at the people she thought: 'No-one's dancing as good as me,' and inside at that very moment she felt none were" (BT, 273–4). Cathy's attention to her inner responses and her confidence in her abilities make her especially impatient after John is expelled from the dance and her demand – "Dontcha ever ... make fun of me like that" – signals a permanent breach in their relationship (BT, 280). Almost immediately after demonstrating that Cathy has learned to assert her will against the confining forces of her life, the narrative shifts to examine Leah's struggles for liberty. In the third section, Cathy rarely appears except to announce that she has decided to leave the shore and move to Toronto. To fly from the East Coast and search for opportunity in central Canada is hardly an original gesture of independence, but in Cathy's context it signals a significant redefinition of her sense of self.

Unlike his sister, Orville initially appears to have already broken from the confining expectations of the local community. From the opening page when he stays ahead of the family during the walk home and chooses to brave the rain storm rather than "turn to notice them," Orville cultivates an intense sense of privacy that even his few friends find odd (BT, 7). The reader's sense of his isolation is reinforced by the narrator's practice of rarely focalizing the text through Orville unless he is alone. When he is with a group of teenagers on the beach, walking to school with Karen and Cathy, or playing games at the church picnic, his experiences are almost always mediated through another character's eyes.

But if Orville has sequestered himself from the expectations of the community, he still does not function as a free and independent individual. Self-conscious about his missing eye, Orville does not withdraw from social contact in the name of freedom, but because he is imprisoned by his inner fears and insecurities. In a text that frequently uses flashbacks to construct the complex character of Leah, it is significant that one of Orville's few childhood memories focuses on his intense fear of being seen as different. Orville struggles throughout the text to liberate himself from his fears, seeking release through his hunting expeditions and his private candle-burning rituals. But it is only as he confronts his insecurities directly, in the closing pages, that he attains a kind of heroic stature. Though Orville has been particularly shy around the older boys whose physical skills emphasize his own "lack," Orville steps forth in the final scene to drive John from the house. Orville's demand that the drunken John "go on out of my house – leave my sister alone, leave my sister alone, you go on out of my house and leave my sister alone" (BT, 355) is greeted with scorn, but this incomplete protective gesture signals that he is able to move beyond his insecurity to protect those closest to him. Liberation for Cathy means a departure from her family; emotional freedom for Orville comes with his vocalized commitment to his blood ties.

Leah is the third member of the MacDurmot clan who attempts to free herself from the roles that have thus far shaped her life. Her attempt to free herself from her violent marriage with Cecil dominates the third and final section of the novel; indeed, Cathy's earlier quest for independence is a kind of prelude to her half-sister's more difficult and complex search. Of all the novel's characters, Leah is the most thoroughly enmeshed in a specific historical context. Using a variety of flashbacks focalized through each family member, the narrator constructs a fully developed background for Leah, exploring her gradual submergence in the complex web of burdens and obligations typical of a determined naturalistic character. From Maufat's recollections of Leah's awareness of herself as an "illegitimate" child, to Irene's memory of Leah's rebellious adolescence and her expulsion from a convent school, we learn not only that the young woman sought to break from confining social roles, but that her attempts to resist conventional roles have met with little success. Given her complicated past it is not surprising that the older and more insecure Leah should have difficulty breaking free from her community to find a new identity and a sense of independence. For a time, her deeply historicized character even seems incapable of attaining freedom.

The degree to which Leah feels fatalistically trapped by her circumstances is apparent in the opening chapter when, despite the fact that Cecil has thrown their son, Ronnie, "against the stove as if he were a goddamn dog," Leah feels compelled to return to him the next morning (BT, 38). Nor is this attack on Ronnie a unique occurrence within Leah's marriage, for Cecil's violent outbursts are emphasized throughout the first three hundred pages. The narrator completely avoids using Cecil as a focalizer, and his few recorded conversations with friends like Shelby are blunt:

"So then, where are all the women you always say you always have here?" [Cecil]
"None here tonight."
"None here ever ya bastard."
"Don't believe me if you don't want to," Shelby said. He was looking about for an ashtray.
"Oh except squaws – I'd believe you'd stoop to squaws."
"Don't believe me if ya don't want to."
"Shit."
"Don't believe me."
"I don't."
"Don't." (BT, 56)

Only after a series of deadening sexual assaults is Leah able to flee from Cecil and address her deep longing for freedom with the chant, "I'm goin – I'm goin; now – now" (BT, 282–5). Despite a lingering sense of guilt, and despite her own sense of insecurity signalled by the belief that she "was only emptiness in a dark room," Leah, finally deciding to break not only with Cecil but with her own family, vows to go west (BT, 292–3).

Leah is bound to her tragic situation by innumerable threads, but Richards ultimately affirms that even in the most deterministic circumstances, liberty is possible. The search for freedom is so important that the text's representation of Cecil dramatically shifts in the closing pages in order to facilitate Leah's flight. Watching Leah mourn the end of their relationship, Cecil suddenly emerges as a sympathetic figure who can recall his own sense of agony when he carried a dead infant from the scene of a tragic car accident and "held it and held it – as if to keep it warm until the ambulance came" (BT, 312). This abusive husband, whose internal life is ignored through much of the text, is reconstructed in the closing chapters as a sensitive and lonely figure who tells Leah to "get a good job" and gives her his only watch just before she boards her train (BT, 313). Cecil does not undergo a complete metamorphosis, but the narrator attempts to grant us a deeper understanding and more compassionate insight into his violent character, at the very moment when such a revelation will facilitate the ideological development of the text. Leah's drive towards freedom is so important that the text makes a special effort to restrain its naturalist impulse and ensure that she is able to overcome her confining past. For his part in facilitating her release, Cecil himself is rewarded with a feeling of being "sheltered and warm" (*BT*, 313).

A strong faith in the possibility of freedom governs the structure of *Blood Ties* and is an essential part of the central characters' development, but it does not have an exclusive hold over the events of the text. Both consciously and unconsciously Richards's text illustrates that confining power structures can only be resisted to a point, and then they reform to absorb and confine the subject. A variety of narrative gestures remind the reader that within the realist discourse and in a troubled Maritime community, freedom is a dicey proposition. Leah and Cathy successfully negotiate their way towards different identities, but the novel's heroines will have to continue resisting the power structures that define them, as is apparent when Orville teases Cathy that Mallory, the destructive spectre of the woods, has "moved to Toronto" (*BT*, 352). The women will carry the ghosts of the community with them, and the world they flee towards will be as deterministic and repressive as the one they leave behind (Connor 1986, 173). Even if Cathy and Leah manage a tentative escape, the few children represented in the text appear doomed to follow the restrictive paths that their elders flee. Young Ronnie has his own idealistic dream to "get myself a horse," but instead he walks into the church and declares – just as Orville did a decade earlier – "I want to be an altar boy" (*BT*, 346–7). Subsequent generations will struggle with the same traditions and restraints that have governed the local community for centuries.

Nor does the narrative style of *Blood Ties* produce a seamless celebration of the idea of freedom. Unlike the more focused defences launched in his later texts, Richards's second novel is imbued with a degree of ambiguity. In John Delano's impossible quest for liberty, we see that Richards sometimes checks his thematic drive towards independence, if the community is directly threatened or the social order is too deeply disturbed. Such defences signal that the text's individualist liberalism is occasionally curbed by moments of respect for the larger social stability. John attempts to operate outside the standards and structures of the community; however, as he transgresses these standards, he reveals his dependence on their existence, if only to illuminate his violations. Unable to escape the expectations that surround him, John is eventually drawn towards the increasingly dangerous and self-destructive behaviour of private drinking – which "wasn't happy" – and casual encounters with prostitutes, who infect him with "the dose" (BT, 255, 320). Any attempt to achieve a radical independence ends in despair, and John's rebellious pursuit of freedom eventually becomes too traumatic for the narrative to represent. The narrator rarely focalizes the text through John, and the one time it does attempt to see the world from his perspective it represents one of the youth's surreal nightmares in which he is surrounded by images of himself as an injured or dying man, "lips and chin dark grey" (BT, 263). The content of the dream reinforces the narrative's negative representations of radical independence and the style of the passage is so idiosyncratic that it appears symptomatic of the narration's struggle to represent his personality. John's search for liberty takes him not only beyond the boundaries of society and the limits of healthy behaviour, but almost beyond the limits of the realist narrative itself.

Richards resurrects John Delano in *Hope in the Desperate Hour* (1996), *The Bay of Love and Sorrows*, and *Mercy Among the Children*. At first Delano seems to have been transformed into a social conformist; he is a Sergeant in the RCMP, and he responsibly enforces the very rules he once flaunted. But if Richards has softened Delano's rebellious personality, he still suggests that John is an outsider who is viewed with suspicion by the larger community and is unable to maintain a stable relationship with any of his three former wives. Ultimately, the narrators of the novels seem to approve of this kinder and gentler version of Delano; he is one of the few figures who authentically cares for and protects the virtuous downtrodden in his hometown. In both *The Bay of Love and Sorrows* and *Mercy Among the Children*, he takes over criminal investigations that had previously been conducted by conformist and biased officers, and by daring to think independently he unravels the mysteries at the heart of each text. Indeed, he even seems to be a guiding figure in *Mercy Among the Children*, as he offers advice to Lyle that would have saved the troubled youth, if only he had followed it. In these later incarnations, Delano has returned to the fold of the acceptably free.

Liberal ideals drive the central plot of *Blood Ties* and underpin the development of the central characters, but they are not the only ideologies in play. In both the deterministic web surrounding the characters and the narration's own stylistic resistances to its most independent characters, there are signs that the novel is struggling to develop a vision of freedom within its Miramichi context. The textual ruptures that emerge as these ideological assumptions encounter each other become even more apparent when we consider the bleakest novel in Richards's oeuvre, *Road to the Stilt House*.

ROAD TO THE STILT HOUSE

David Adams Richards exhibits a degree of discomfort when discussing his fourth, and shortest, novel. In a 1985 interview with Linda-Ann Sturgeon, he called it a "nakedly horrifying book" and claimed it "was done as an exercise in anger, really I don't know how else to explain it, and that wasn't what I wanted" (1987, 239, 200).[3] In 1988 he remarked that "there's no doubt the book is a hard bargain" (Robb 1988, 25). That *Road to the Stilt House* should cause its author some anxiety is not surprising. In this exploration of the conditions that permit individual freedom, Richards asks whether it is possible for the very poor to function with the same liberty granted to the middle-class. In an attempt to reproduce the conditions of the region's economic and cultural underclass, Richards develops a naturalistic system of cause and effect to chronicle the destruction of a young man named Arnold. As the protagonist and his family disintegrate, this historicist methodology challenges Richards's liberal assumption that independence can be achieved through the confident and spontaneous exercise of one's free will. Although this novel attempts to protect its central assumptions through an interesting variety of narrative shifts, it is willing to confront and be overwhelmed by a powerful determinism.

Arnold, the central protagonist of *Road to the Stilt House*, has grown-up amidst severe emotional and economic impoverishment, which has diminished his sense of his own power and limited his ability to change his circumstances. While the text is clearly critical of the social and cultural forces that confine him, it holds out little hope that change is possible. Even the preface exposes the problems inherent in Arnold's inability to assert himself and resist authority figures. When the landlord throws Arnold's kitten outside and the dying pet "mews at the door all night long" (RSH, 11), Arnold's inability to react signals his sense of paralysis in the face of authority and anticipates his subsequent failure to establish and maintain a degree of freedom.

The individual subject is a construct that is articulated within and to some degree by social and cultural powers, and it cannot simply reshape itself; it must do so within or against the discourses of the larger community. Arnold recognizes that he and his family are viewed by their community as chronically failing members of the underclass, but he cannot find the means or courage to challenge that representation. Whatever avenue he pursues in order to establish his identity Arnold inevitably fails. When he attempts to speak his way into his community, he discovers that his impoverished language skills bar him from effectively communicating with others. Though Arnold is anxious about the external world and is particularly frightened by Jerry Bines, he is unable to express his anxiety to Juliet the social worker or Father Billy and concludes that there "is no-one to talk to about it" (RSH, 31). Using minimalist speech patterns, he asserts his name with a positivist bravado declaring, "I'm Arnold" (RSH, 74), "I am Arnold" (RSH, 87), "I'm Arnold" (RSH, 128); but the speech act does not register within the dominant power structure, and his pronouncements are dismissed as meaningless: "Arnold's got a dirty arse" (RSH, 128). Trapped in a culture of poverty, Arnold cannot speak or act within the vocabulary of the mainstream and "simply howl[s] in a low tone for an hour or more" (RSH, 87).

Barred from speech, he attempts to employ symbols of power to distinguish himself within his community, but the police quickly confiscate the "deadly" looking knife he begins to carry, and he is fired soon after he threatens his fellow road workers with a "rock over the side of their head" (RSH, 87). Arnold lacks the ability to locate himself in his alienating world and, feeling trapped, he begins to react violently against his family and himself: "I have hit my mother four times in the last month, just so I could feel sorry for her bruised mouth" (RSH, 101). Arnold almost seems to relish the role of victim he has been assigned by his community: in his despair, he inflicts pain upon himself. In the opening pages, he punishes himself in small ways; by the end of the novel, Arnold participates in his own predetermined destruction by eagerly escaping from prison with the people who will eventually murder him. In his poverty Arnold seems capable of making only those choices that lead to his own destruction. Though Arnold is initially constructed as a figure of protest, it becomes apparent that his naturalistic/historical context is so unavoidably complex that freedom ceases to be a possibility for him. In his other novels, Richards resolves similar tensions by including a kind of escape clause through which characters are able to transcend their immediate context and secure liberty without unduly disrupting the fabric of realism. Leah and Cathy escape down the highway to central Canada; Joe, of *Nights Below Station Street*, is inspired by sudden flashes of instinct or imagination; and even Sidney Henderson, in *Mercy Among The Children*, is comforted in the midst of his persecution by his conviction that he has aligned himself with the power of truth and love. Only in *Road to the Stilt House* does Richards refuse to provide his central protagonist with a way out and Arnold thus becomes his most extensive exploration of what happens to a character who is completely lost within the powerful, predetermining expectations of Miramichi society.

Just as Arnold is unable to free himself within his context, so his mother and brother are unable to stabilize or assert themselves. Mabel has so absorbed herself into the fantasy life of soap opera personalities and all things connected to the royal family that she is removed from her role as mother and is unable to "shed a tear over her children" (RSH, 48). The passivity that undermines her maternal instinct keeps her from expressing her health concerns to her doctor. She has several operations, at least one of which is mishandled, but Mabel's ignorance about the procedures and her sense of insecurity when faced with the medical profession prevent her from questioning the doctor's actions. Eventually she dies from post-operative complications. Randy is similarly so needy and incomplete that his desperate desire for acceptance undermines his own chance for success. When Randy finally puts on a Cub uniform to indicate he belongs to a respected group, his enthusiasm undercuts his own acceptability as he "wears his cub sweater until it smelled and had black wrists" (RSH, 66). His status as an outsider makes him a target for the abusive cubmaster, and his perpetual sense of failure only ends with his death while on a camping expedition. Richards protests against repressive social and cultural forces, but these characters are so carefully contextualized that eventually the reader wonders if any other course of action was conceivable. While the characters cannot establish alternate identities within their chaotic environments, these same social and familial contexts become the determining factors of their lives. The sense of determinism and nihilism – which is more forcefully expressed in The Road to the Stilt House than it has been before in any Maritime text, including the early fictions of Alden Nowlan – seems to make Richards uneasy, and this anxiety is manifested within the narrative itself.

As the possibility of freedom that glimmered briefly in The Road to the Stilt House is extinguished by the forces of social determinism, a series of complicated narrative shifts appear in order to draw the reader's attention away from Arnold's failures and to control the novel's ideological tensions. The first and eighth chapters make exclusive use of Arnold as a first-person narrator, and as he tells his own story he struggles to gain a measure of credibility. The second, sixth, and seventh chapters are related through an external, unidentified third-person narrator; and halfway through each of the third, fourth, and fifth chapters the text switches from external to internal narration. Richards works hard to include Arnold's perspective in the opening sections, and twenty-three of the first seventy pages (one third of the first half of "Part One") are related in the first person. As Arnold fails to emerge as a free character, his internal narration becomes chaotic, and his inner perspective is unable to account fully for the events he must endure. A sense of despair is produced by this internal lack of control, and, as the story continues, the novel shifts to the security of the external narrator. Arnold not only loses his voice in the community, but he also begins to lose his voice within the text. He is such a marginalized character that the narrative, like the local community itself, must exclude him in order to maintain its own dominant discourses. While short sections of chapters 13, 16, 20, and 21 still rely on internal narration, only eight of the last seventy pages of "Part One" reproduce Arnold's voice, and Arnold's most painful experiences are related through the relative security and stability of third-person narration. These narrative shifts away from Arnold lessen the impact of his despair on the reader, but they do not sufficiently soften the text's fatalistic edges. Eventually the desire to reassert the idea of free will forces the text to adopt a new narrator; then, the concluding thirty pages that constitute "Part Two" are related by Norman.

Norman is initially a narrator of convenience. With the death of Randy and Mabel, and Arnold's descent into incoherence following his decision to burn "the house to the ground" (*RSH*, 140), there are few sympathetic figures left to focalize the final events of Arnold's life. Norman is a relative and fellow road-dweller, and is thus able to narrate Arnold's final days without condemnation or condescension. As Norman's voice establishes itself, however, he ceases to be a mere observer and emerges as a man who is able to redefine his position as a subject in the very ways Arnold cannot. Indeed, Norman initially functions as a kind of tonic for the weary reader and his sudden dominance in the novel's closing pages seems to return us to the assertion that individuals are not always enslaved by their economic or cultural contexts. But if we are buoyed by Norman's independence, our elation is curtailed quickly as we realize that his freedom is costly.

From his earliest days, whether he is resisting his teachers or threatening Jerry Bines, Norman has the ability to assert his will in the public sphere. But as the tale unfolds, his powerful will crosses over into cold selfishness, and it becomes clear that Richards is not suggesting that his path to freedom is a viable alternative to Arnold's road to misery. Norman seems to work himself out of his impoverished condition and integrate into the cultural mainstream. As Arnold notes, he has the ability to "work all day in the woods [before] he goes to school. There is a scent of goodness about him, like sunlight upon a white tablecloth" (*RSH*, 138). This determination to assert himself comes at the expense of his relationships with others. Like his cousin, Norman suffers the loss of a loved one when his wife dies, but he recalls the period after her funeral with a forced sense of stoic understatement: "it wasn't a good time for me" (*RSH*, 160). When Arnold's only girlfriend flirts with Norman, he accepts her advances, and, even after her pregnancy makes public the fact that he has betrayed his cousin, his sense of guilt and shame do not prevent him from sitting "up nights waiting for her to come, praying that she would" (150). Norman is able to free himself from his past, but his freedom is possible only if he withdraws from his kin. Richards's reservations about his choices are apparent in Norman's lingering feelings of guilt and his sense that he has failed his family. By the end, Norman has established a new enduring relationship with a middle-class girl and found a place for himself within a wider social context, but he continues to be uncertain about his decision to leave the margins and enter society's centre. Norman's success thus underscores the grim vision initially conveyed by Arnold. Characters can either be crushed by their miserable circumstances, or they can harden themselves to their conditions and rise above them only by leaving their own better impulses behind.[4] Norman's victory after Arnold's long struggle, ultimately reinforces rather than relieves the grim naturalism of the novel. Despite the narration's efforts to soften the impact of Arnold's destruction, his empty life and meaningless death remain as the most powerful elements of the novel.

Road to the Stilt House is the only novel in which Richards has refused to veil the potentially destructive power of the region's fragmented culture. Having explored this grim world once, he has in subsequent novels attempted to place some critical distance between the narrator and the flailing heroes. Troubled by the nihilistic implications of Arnold's and Norman's experiences, Richards subsequently adopted a more removed style of narration that would allow him to "analyze at times and still be subjective" (Scherf 1990, 163). After 1985, his fiction reflects this "shift from a largely phenomenological realism … to a spare, analytical, discursive, narrative prose" (Armstrong 1997, 5). Indeed, the desire to prevent a similar sense of social chaos and individual disintegration often produces a strong and controlling narrator, and occasionally the "narrative discourse [is] marked by a defensive and polemical tone" (Armstrong 1997, 5). The novels following *Road to the Stilt House* have avoided the pessimism suggested by Arnold's disintegration by momentarily suspending the literary boundaries of naturalism, disrupting the patterns of causality, and allowing the protagonists to tap some transcendental or mythic power that permits them to achieve a secure and free sense of self.

FOR THOSE WHO HUNT THE WOUNDED DOWN

Some recent commentators have examined this shift in Richards's style and argued that his ideological perspective is moving towards the political right.[5] For example, in his article "Maritime Powerlessness: *Nights Below Station Street*," Frank Davey explores the levels of discourse represented in Richards's fifth novel and argues that, while the "dimly conscious characters" (1993, 76) struggle to become aware of their own determined condition and must ultimately accept that "it is useless for individuals to try and give shape to their lives" (1993, 77), the narrator emerges as elitist, part of a "knowing and patronizing discourse" and able to mysteriously think and write from outside the character's experience (1993, 70). Davey notes that the narrator's elevated and separate speaking position permits him to judge the various characters with a measure of condescension, and this disparity in the discursive levels confirms that the characters are powerless to shape their individual experience: "The characters who attempt to change their lives are mostly depicted as having merely the illusion that they are choosing to change; what is really happening to them is that they are being shaped, moulded, and scripted by large social forces beyond their understanding" (1993, 74). Arguing that Richards is adopting, if not endorsing, an elitist set of assumptions, Davey suggests that the novel is aligned with conservative values, an argument that is developed more fully by Christopher Armstrong and Herb Wyile, in their article "Firing the Regional Can(n)on."

Focusing on the second Miramichi trilogy – comprised of *Nights Below Station Street*, *Evening Snow Will Bring Such Peace*, and *For Those Who Hunt the Wounded Down* – Armstrong and Wyile conclude that Richards is "in danger of being lumped in with the contemporary neo-conservatives clamouring for the dismantling of the welfare state and generating a backlash against a demonized, progressive political correctness" (Armstrong and Wyile 1997, 15). They note that Richards criticizes "the reform identities of feminism and middle class progressivism" (1997, 13), celebrates the "dignity, self-reliance, self-sacrifice, and moral action" of the lone individual, and "reinvest[s] ... those keywords of conservative thought ... [in] an attempt to value the lives of the ostracized outside of the framework of a regionalized, pluralist state in non-voluntarist, unreflective, and essentialist terms" (1997, 15). Their assertion that Richards attacks liberal pluralism is accurate: as in his earlier fiction he consistently distances himself from the communitarian streams of liberalism. Their assertion that he is becoming increasingly aligned with the new wave of conservatism whose rhetoric is sweeping through American populist movements is more problematic, for their argument foregrounds a larger struggle having to do with the current use of such terms as liberal and conservative.

Since the late 1970s, political parties on the right have tried, with considerable success, to narrow the meanings of the term liberalism. Associating the term with left-wing ideologies and a range of narrow special-interest groups, the "conservatives" associated with Thatcher and Reagan in the late 1970s and early 1980s, redefined liberalism to signify only the more communitarian and leftist versions of the term. Though Britain's Conservative party and the American Republican party have since appropriated the term "conservative" to describe and defend their own policies of free-market capitalism and minimal state intervention, these positions are actually anchored in the individualist political philosophies that have descended from Locke, and have little in common with the traditional communal values that characterize conservatism. Thus, while Armstrong and Wyile correctly note that in "Richards' fictive world, voluntarist affirmations of social identity are the object of deep suspicion" and that he elevates instead the "un-self-conscious, independent action" of the individual, these qualities are in fact evidence of his ongoing, if newly sharpened, commitment to individualist liberalism, and not evidence of a flight towards a conservative position.

Richards's defence of the radically independent individual is articulated in *For Those Who Hunt the Wounded Down*. The most complex and important of the novels written after *Road to the Stilt House*, *For Those Who Hunt the Wounded Down* works hard to produce a fictional surface committed to the tenets of realism, but within the realist frame the figure of Jerry Bines reaches a heroic independence of near-mythic proportion. At first sight, *For Those Who Hunt the Wounded Down* fits within the realist and thematic frames employed in Richards's earlier texts. The central action of the text – from Jerry Bines's return to his Miramichi home town, to his eventual struggle and death at the hands of his old enemy Gary Percy Rils – is carefully constructed within a realist pattern of cause and effect so that each event seems completely probable when placed within its proper context. Similarly, many of the text's minor characters are constructed within the conventions of realism. As in Richards's other novels, the minor figures are knowable entities who react to and are shaped by their specific social and familial contexts. For example, Adele Walsh's distrust of Jerry Bines is deeply rooted in what she perceives to be her cousin's betrayal of her father, and Nevin White, who is plagued with guilt for betraying numerous women in his life, can restore his sense of self-worth only by healing some of the broken relationships of his past. Yet, if the action and characterization of the text fit within the discourses of realism, Richards's central protagonist, who certainly functions as a representative of independent subjectivity, seems to strain against these literary conventions.

Jerry Bines first surfaces in *Road to the Stilt House* as the grave-robbing petty criminal whose violent impulses identify him as a heartless villain. When he reappears as the central figure of *For Those Who Hunt the Wounded Down*, the five-page preface acknowledges that he is a man with a "terrible past," but it also ascribes to him a vulnerable sensitivity that suggests that Bines's character has been dramatically reworked. As the narrative unfolds, Jerry proves to be an independent and self-reliant person, the likes of whom has not appeared in Richards's fiction since John Delano was marginalized in *Blood Ties*. Unlike John, whose rebellion against community standards is suppressed by the narration, Bines is endorsed and celebrated by the text as a pure embodiment of individual liberty. Indeed, Bines's role as an admirable representation of independence and freedom begins to take precedence over his formal role as a realist character, and eventually he emerges as a romance hero – a saviour for the very community he does not need.

Unlike a conventional realist protagonist Jerry Bines is unconnected to his surrounding local community. Independent from the outset and blessed with a clear sense of who he is and what his power can accomplish, he does not need to expend energy attempting to confirm or assert his sense of identity. While other figures are linked to or obsessed with their family ties, Bines has emerged from an unusually fragmented personal life with little bitterness or sorrow. Though he is raised by a violent and abusive father, Jerry recognizes that in truth his father was a "frightened," "mentally unbalanced, melancholy man" who sought to protect and even love his "little boy" (*HWD*, 80–1). Jerry remains loyal to his father's memory long after the old man's death, but he is not preoccupied with family history and seems bemused by Vera's attempts to analyse his past. Just as he is only tentatively connected to society through kinship ties, so he is alienated from conventional institutions. Bines's years in the Kingsclear reformatory ensure that he is untouched by the traditional school system or religious institutions, and he emerges as a self-taught, distinctly powerful man.

In his attempt to create a character who embodies the values of independence and complete liberty, Richards isolates Jerry Bines from the communication and language practices of his community. He has little contact with the society's cultural assumptions as they are transmitted through the media, for he "hardly ever watched television and had never understood the fascination for it" (HWD, 97). Bine's use of language is also idiosyncratic. He avoids the more stable printed forms of language, claiming he "don't read so good" (HWD, 29), and communicates through a "peculiar way of expression [in which] almost everything seemed to be said slowly and in duplicate" (HWD, 7). Even the polyphonic narration of the text reinforces his status as an independent figure: numerous narrators produce tentative versions of Bines without assembling a single definitive picture of the character. Vera's methodological framework and the police reports misrepresent Jerry's personality and twist his intentions according to their own agendas: "Andrew's uncle [is a] ... cynical" observer who views Jerry with a judgmental eye; and the fatherless boy – who tends to view Bines as a heroic paternal figure – is overly "romantic" in his naive faith that Jerry was self-consciously "trying to save everyone" (HWD, 193). That each of the text's narrators presents a different version of Bines reinforces the initial impression that he operates outside the conventional reference points of the community.

The use of these multiple narrators does not indicate a shift on Richards's part into the style of postmodernism. While the narration admits it is impossible to recover a definitive representation of the central protagonist, it never self-referentially questions the nature of fictional representation itself, nor does it undercut the central assumption that there really is a "Jerry Bines" at the heart of the novel, however difficult it is to contain his character. Instead, the fragmented style of the text tends to position the reader as an member of the local community for the reader is forced "to read this novel (by fragment and innuendo, with prejudice and bias, moving roughly over the exposed seams of omniscient, intrusive, impersonal, and limited perspectives) [in] exactly the way the characters read and construct Jerry Bines" (Tremblay 1994, 119).

As Bines emerges from a variety of different perspectives, he becomes more than simply an unknowable character: he has characteristics of a Nietzschean "overman" who "in most ways in his life had willed himself to be, and made people conform to his will – not so much by physical strength as by a brutal nature" (HWD, 102). His appearance as an enigmatic figure with an "unfathomable sense of power" (HWD, 35), eventually moves him so far into the discourse of romance that he becomes a distinctly mythic, archetypal, and even redemptive romance figure. As Armstrong and Wyile point out, it is as if Richards has substituted the naturalism of material and historical causality for a "kind of naturalism grounded on religious and moral terms" (1997, 7). As romance conventions that substitute probability for certainty are called upon to reinforce the ideals of independence and liberty, Richards's work echoes similar shifts made by Hugh MacLennan and Frank Parker Day.

Initially, the impression that Bines has a near Christ-like potential to inspire adoration resides solely within the naive child narrator, whose own life is deeply infused with the teachings of the Catholic Church. However, as the narrative proceeds, the boy is not alone as he looks to Jerry with a sense of awe. In Bines's presence Lucy Savoie's face becomes "dazzling," and after his first meeting with Jerry, Ralphie feels "as if he had been filled with a kind of grace" (*HWD*, 19). Such emotional impressions are confirmed when, in the closing chapters, Bines sacrifices himself in order to keep Rils "from the Pillars – Ralphie and Vera" (*HWD*, 208). Francis MacDonald, in an otherwise overly general review of Richards's work, astutely notes that characters like Bines "renew our faith in the power of the human spirit to work out its own redemption" (1996, 20). Like a Christ figure self-consciously approaching his own Golgotha, Bines tells his son the parable/story of the wise old deer who sacrifices his own life in order to drown a determined hunter and save his young doe and fawn. The parable's conclusion that "you must either face your hunters or run from them" signals Bines's own heroic code and his determination to sacrifice himself for the sake of those he loves (*HWD*, 94).

Jerry is an independent individual whose self-sacrifice rejuvenates the community in ways the other characters can barely appreciate. When Nevin seeks Jerry's counsel, reveals a stash of pills, and obliquely refers to suicide, Bines hands him a book entitled *Sobriety Without End* and leaves the depressed man with the simple idea that if he wants to, he can change. The uncomplicated insight inspires the alienated Nevin White to return to his past, seek the forgiveness of his first wife, and then take a more courageously active part in his community. Similarly, Adele has long been tormented by the various absences in her life. The premature death of her father and her decision to give up her infant daughter – a decision Ralphie and she "had talked themselves into and regretted instantly and forever" (*HWD*, 25) – leave Adele with a sense of anger and bitterness that even her husband has difficulty confronting. After Jerry's death, however, Adele is called upon to replace him as the bone marrow donor for young William Bines's leukaemia treatments and this sacrificial act restores to Adele her sense that existence does have a purpose. During the spring following Jerry's death, Adele "plant[s] a garden," and "in early July, they adopt a child" (*HWD*, 224). In a very real sense, Bines's self-sacrifice sets off a whole sequence of events ending in a familial and communal renewal.

As in other earlier texts, this redemptive ending is a double-edged sword. On the one hand, the text is buoyed by this archetypal representation of a free and independent man who is able to transform, in life and in death, the troubled members of his community. At the same time, the implication remains that, were it not for an extraordinary character like Bines, the real conditions of the community would not have changed. Since such indescribably powerful, mythical, and independent figures are rarely produced within the community, it is apparent that when the next series of crises arise, life will not be lifted above the typically slow, bitter, and lonely grind that characterized Jerry's father's existence.

Indeed, even at the end there is evidence that, while single figures like Bines are able to attain freedom and independence, most of the other characters remain caught in the webs of social convention. This is certainly the case with each of the women in the text. In Richards's latest trilogy, there are no Cathys or Leahs who break from the repressive patriarchal system and venture out on their own. As if to reinforce the limiting nature of the community's patriarchy, each of the women in the text is carefully reinscribed within a narrow and typically maternal position. At the end Loretta is still a passive figure within her congregation, and the restoration of her son's health sets her at ease in a world that hardly deserves her trust. Adele's final sense of contentment is also framed within the discourse of maternity. While Ralphie must launch into a number of different occupational ventures before discovering that he can be content in his repair shop, Adele need only fulfill her biological absence by adopting a child, and the text is able to close with the sense that she lives happily ever after. Indeed, the predictability of the maternal role reaches the level of cliché when Nevin finds his first wife living a complete and satisfying life as a suburban housewife with three children. The "two peanut butter cookies ... still warm from the pan," which she sends to confirm her acceptance of Nevin's apologies, function as a reminder of how thoroughly – and in the narrator's eyes how unproblematically – the women are absorbed into the community's maternal roles (*HWD*, 153).The character of Vera Pillar also reinforces this trend: the text not only rejects her "rational coldness," it also denies her "much in the way of saving graces" (Lever 1994, 88). Indeed, if Vera's treatment of Jerry were not enough to cast her as a villain, her cold and rigid reactions towards her daughter Haley, who experiences "no happiness" as a child, are designed to convince the audience that she is wrong to attempt to redefine her gender/social role with the same confidence that inspires Jerry Bines (*HWD*, 77). The text's celebration and even deification of individual freedom does not extend to those persons tied to the patriarchal conventions at the heart of the society. The liberal ideals embodied by the romantic figure of Jerry Bines are not extended into other territories of the novel.

For Those Who Hunt the Wounded Down represents an interesting variation in Richards's work. As in the first trilogy, the novel focuses on a character who is seeking to retain and defend his sense of independence and personal integrity. Unlike *Blood Ties*, where the characters achieve their goals while largely remaining within a realist frame, complete liberty is only possible in the later texts by invoking the conventions of the romance. In the aftermath of *Road to the Stilt House*, Richards seems to have concluded that the hardships and disappointments experienced by marginalized individuals both within and without the Miramichi region – when combined with the literary tradition of realism, with its commitment to historicism – will inevitably produce a despairing sense of fatalism. While Nowlan responds to these pressures by foregrounding the image of the modernist, fragmented individual and MacLeod longs for the conservative and collective security of the clan, Richards increasingly revisits an even older tradition in Maritime literature. In the novels released after his second trilogy, Richards departs from his experiments in naturalism and protects his concept of free will by employing more fully the insights and secure structures offered by the conventions of romance.

RICHARDS'S MORAL ROMANCES

The Bay of Love and Sorrows, published in 1998, focuses on a little community on the edge of a small bay and examines a group of individuals – particularly the young Michael Skid and the beautiful Madonna Brassaurd – as they move beyond the help of caring characters like Tom Donneral and slip into the world of dangerous criminals like Everette Hutch. Drug deals go bad, murders are committed, and the novel employs a hint of melodrama as it systematically traces Michael's and Madonna's journey towards the redemption offered to those willing to risk radical independence. As in his earlier texts, Richards insists that his characters attain a sense of integrity only as they learn to stand alone; thus *The Bay of Love and Sorrows* is critical of any social institutions that attempt to bind the individual characters. In his analysis of Leo Tolstoy, a writer whom Richards has cited as an influence at various stages in his career, Ernst Simmons notes that the

Russian writer "seems determined to expose all the crassness, mean-ness, and criminal tendencies of representatives of several layers of society – peasants, workers, shopkeepers, policemen, jailors, clergy-men, magistrates, landowners, and government bureaucrats" (1968, 165). Simmons's comments could just as easily be applied to Rich-ards's later fiction. In an unvarying critique of powerful social agen-cies, Richards launches attacks on a series of targets. The university is again criticized for its role in reinforcing Michael Skid's sense of arrogance and fostering his ignorance of the ways in which authentic individuals interact. The judiciary, which unjustly condemns and sen-tences Tom Donnerel for a murder he did not commit, is represented as a self-serving system that is more concerned with the career paths of the lawyers than in ensuring fair and just trials. Similarly, the con-ventional media is criticized for pandering to a mob mentality, partic-ularly as they unjustly condemn innocent men like Donnerel. Even the influence of the Church is carefully curbed as Madonna disassoci-ates herself from the ecclesiastical hierarchy and affirms the value of individual commitment: "I don't believe in the church ... I don't be-lieve in the cardinals with their red hats and pomposity ... but I do believe in the faith. I believe in our virgin Mary – our immaculate conception, the body and blood of Jesus Christ" (*BLS*, 245). Richards not only maintains his attack on the conservative notion that the indi-vidual should attach themselves to a larger cultural system, he also narrows the ideological field of his text – in the way Armstrong and Wyile had predicted – by criticizing Michael Skid's self-indulgent be-haviour and launching a direct attack on liberal pluralism and its faith in the salutary actions of a beneficent government: "There were those young men and women who were liberal and believed in what had to be done to secure equality for everyone and there were those who still clung tenaciously to the repressive dogma of a former time, of community and church. Michael believed more than ever that he belonged to the former group, the best group, the more inclusive group" (*BLS*, 192). Instead of adhering to a collectivist ideology, Richards uses characters like Laura McNair's brother to reiterate his conviction that only the free and spontaneous act of an individual constitutes a virtuous response: "he died in simple unplanned heroism" (*BLS*, 43).

Richards's use of the romance form to defend his assumptions be-comes more evident when we examine the structure of *The Bay of Love and Sorrows*. Unlike the earlier novels, which attended to the subsur-face movement of history by tracing a careful line of cause and effect, the story of Madonna's journey towards martyrdom and Michael Skid's movement towards enlightenment is guided by a pattern that moves the characters towards predetermined ends. The text does not construct the internal casual logic typical of realism, instead it fore-grounds the moments of coincidence that remind the reader that the larger hand of destiny is at work. When Silver decides to break into Gail Hutch's cabin and murder anyone he finds inside, the text calls attention to the selfishness of his actions by contrasting him, at that exact moment, with the text's archetypal image of innocence and na-ivety: "Silver missed meeting them by twenty-eight seconds exactly. One second for every year of Vincent Donnerel's life" (*BLS*, 270). Laura McNair's self-centered behaviour is also contrasted with Vin-cent's selflessness when she throws her ring off the bridge, and the jewel "settle[s] hidden between a dark boulder and a fallen log, near Vincent Donnerel's pipe" (*BLS*, 261). Unlikely coincidences are thus used throughout the text to reinforce the dominant ethical concerns. Even the text's conclusion is carefully wrapped up. The final pages of *The Bay of Love and Sorrows* move "towards didacticism and closure [as] opposed to the more ambiguous endings of Richard's earlier fic-tions" (Doucet 1999, 29), and each of the characters' fates is revealed as appropriate amounts of joy and suffering are doled out to the re-deemed and damned respectively. Tom Donnerel is granted a happy marriage and a loving step-son, Everette Hutch descends into a con-dition of misery and pain, and, in a particularly unlikely twist, Michael Skid flees to Central America where he redeems himself by finally acting heroically and selflessly in the face of terror and violence.

Just as the plot is indebted to the conventions of the romance, so the characters are moulded into sharply defined and sometimes even formulaic figures. While only Jerry Bines seemed capable of tran-scending his contexts in *For Those Who Hunt the Wounded Down*, the narrator of *The Bay of Love and Sorrows* asserts that each of the mem-bers of the community are responsible for their condition and blames or celebrates each of the figures according to their ability to tap into an instinctual, transcendental source of power in order to assert their integrity. Instead of developing the characters into the multidimen-sional figures typical of realism, the community members along the bay tend to be either sacrificial or selfish, honourable or corrupt, vic-tims or predators. While numerous traits were fused within the char-acter of Jerry Bines, these traits have been isolated and linked to separate individuals in the Bay community. Madonna Brassaurd emerges as the Christ figure who admonishes characters to live by faith, stares at the villain with "the simplicity of truth and justice and determination" (*BLS*, 231), and receives a vision commanding her to "pick up your cross and follow me" before she sacrifices her life in order to keep the violence of Everette Hutch from breaking upon the others in her community (*BLS*, 215). Silver Brassaurd, Madonna's brother, plays the role of Judas as he betrays his sister and murders the immature and naive Karrie, only to hang himself with nothing but "thirty-five dollars in his pocket" (*BLS*, 296). Everette is a concentrated form of Bines's blunt and conscienceless power, and he too suffers for refusing to take responsibility for his disastrous life and accepting the consequences of his selfish decisions. Each of the characters face a moment in which they could freely choose to do the right thing, and each is thus rewarded or punished in the course of the novel according to their final decisions. Those, like Madonna, who accept the challenge of transforming themselves, reach a state of full personhood. Those who refuse to embrace the opportunities to become free and responsible selves descend into conditions of illness and decay and, like Dora and Everette, end up "bitter," "feeble," "invalid[s]" (*BLS*, 300–1). Richards has, more forcefully than before, defended his particular version of liberalism, but occasionally his emphatic tone has limited the text's ability to engage and compel his audience. It is particularly interesting that Richards should dedicate *The Bay of Love and Sorrows* to Alistair MacLeod, given that both writers have, in the process of maturing as novelists, produced the occasional didactic moment within their texts, as they struggle to defend their central ideological assumptions.

Of course, I do not want to leave the impression that Richards is engaged in creating some kind of morality fiction in which the good are inevitably rewarded and the villains are consistently damned. In *Mercy Among the Children*, Richards demonstrates, through the figure of Sidney Henderson, that the determination to stand apart for simple truths and values, may destroy the individuals who dare to distinguish themselves. Sidney sets the benchmark of virtuous behaviour by keeping his vow to "never raise his hand or his voice to another soul" (*MAC*, 22), and the novel becomes a detailed illustration of his assertion that "no one can do an injury to you without doing an injury to themselves" (*MAC*, 35). But if Sidney is a remarkable man in his determination to never harm a fellow human being, his acts of selflessness and passive nonresistance ostracize him from the community to such a degree that he is masochistically loaded down with a world of troubles. Sidney, his wife Elly, and youngest son Percy are lauded for their spontaneity and goodness, but the text is also a relentless chronicle of their deaths. The path to a position of independence is not always smooth.

If the highly patterned nature of Richards's most recent novels is, at moments, less engaging than the ambiguity of his previous fictions, there is certainly no reason to diminish his broader accomplishments or downplay his importance to the region. Now in his fifties, David Adams Richards holds a unique place in Maritime letters. He has not only won a long list of literary prizes and held a variety of writer-in-residence positions across the country, but he is one of only three people in the history of the Governor General's Award to win in both the fiction and nonfiction categories. He is also one of only a few writers who has managed to produce an evolving and ever-growing body of work. Unlike Bruce and Buckler – who each produced one thoroughly engaging work and then a number of less impressive texts – Richards has assembled a wide and varied cast of characters and set them in a number of distinctive literary worlds. Much of this consistency and continuity may lie in two qualities that characterize most of his fiction. First, his confident decision to break from the region's traditional idealization of its own past has freed him from the tendency, exhibited by both Buckler and Bruce, to articulate only a narrow spectrum of the rural experience. His conviction that all classes and generations of the Miramichi struggle with conflict and anxiety has yielded a variety of marginalized characters and intriguing situations within his fiction.[6] Second, Richards's distinctive blend of Lockean liberalism and naturalism, in his earlier novels, has been equally important in maintaining his remarkable level of productivity. His sense that independence is difficult but not impossible – his conviction that freedom and self-determination are viable ideological assumptions – has given him an evolving perspective, which helps focus each text without prescribing particular narrative or discursive structures. In the face of Richards's reputation as a grim or dreary pessimist, the voice of affirmation that echoes through much of the fiction has continued to fuel his investigation into how characters grapple with issues of selfhood and independence in even the most unusual circumstances.

7 Breaking Silence: Smyth, Bauer, Wilson, Corey, Coady, Bruneau, MacDonald

> I stole a look into Ma's attic room. There were library books on the table, material in the sewing machine, paper piled on the floor for her letters to me and to the boys. I respected her privacy and did not go in. But the room, even in that chilly winter attic, looked like an inviting place.
>
> Budge Wilson, "The Leaving"

A variety of writers have emerged from the Maritime region. Some have sprung from abject poverty, while others have emerged from comparatively comfortable backgrounds; some have worked within the protective enclave of academia, while others toiled in less profitable or secure professions such as farming and freelance journalism. However, we cannot help but notice that Maritime realist writers, regardless of class and background, who published fiction between the late 1920s and the late 1970s were, in at least two ways, a rather uniform and even homogenous group. First, we must note that, without exception, each of the writers examined thus far comes from an Anglo-Saxon heritage. While people of colour were active in a number of literary fields including journalism, and while archivists are beginning to recover a rich body of poetry, essay, memoir, and fiction that has thus far gone unexamined or unpublished, there have been few writers from the region's aboriginal and multicultural communities who have published works of realist fiction. The absence of their voices in the literary history of the region should remind us that through much of the twentieth century, the Maritimes was a racially divided and deeply biased society. Few educational, economic, political, or literary resources were available to minority writers in the region, and if it was hard for writers in the dominant culture to establish themselves, the circumstances were much more difficult for artists who had to labour under the additional burdens imposed by systemic discrimination. While we cannot examine realist fictions that were never published, neither should we ignore the gap or the conditions that produced this vacuum.

While factors of race and ethnicity played a role in the production of the region's realist fiction, we must also recognize that gender also influenced the development of Maritime texts. By the time Richards and MacLeod had established their careers in the late 1970s, virtually no woman writing in and about the region had elected to work within the realist tradition in order create her texts. Women were not completely silent during this period, but many of the region's texts written by women tended to explore avenues and genres other than realism. Writers such as Lucy Maud Montgomery, Margaret Marshall Saunders, Carrie Jenkins Harris, Alice Jones, Susan Carleton Jones, Evelyn Eaton, and more recently Evelyn May Fox, all won significant reading audiences – at least in their own day – through their use of the romance. Writers such as Anne Copeland and Beth Harvor adopted realism, but decided to set their most recent fictions in the United States or Central Ontario. Other works, including the poetic novels of Susan Kerslake and the later texts of Nancy Bauer, have ventured towards more experimental forms, using multivoiced narratives, fluid and decentered plots, and large mythic patterns to develop their vision of women's experiences in the Maritimes. Yet if women were productive and expressive, we still might ask why they did not adopt the literary genre that dominated the work of women writers elsewhere in the country. The reasons for this lacuna in Maritime literature are not easily determined.

The first reason why Maritime women may not have adopted realism, may be the same reason why women in the Maritimes in general were less inclined to enter the field of the expressive arts: the roles assigned to females by the larger patriarchal culture did not include artist, novelist, or short-story writer. Though general cultural trends are sometimes difficult to document, some critics have argued that women writers in the Maritimes felt a "constant pressure ... to keep silent, or at least, to use as few and as simple words as possible in their daily living" (Kulyk Keefer 1987, 241). Thus the culture in general tended to discourage women from publishing fiction, and presumably those who did break the barriers and become writers, like Montgomery and Marshall, did so in part by directing their work towards the gendered and therefore acceptable children's and women's markets.

If the region itself was patriarchal in character it would be hard to argue that it was more masculinist than other parts of the country. Perhaps this broader patriarchal character was more potent in the Maritimes when it was combined with the region's persistent sense of nostalgia. As was noted in the opening chapter, the region experienced an authentic as well as a manufactured sense of longing for its misremembered past, and this tendency to idealize previous conditions – and the conservative politics that are often associated with that impulse – would not be conducive to a transformation of women's roles. Writers like Buckler celebrate the traditional family unit as a part of their hymn to a fading heritage, and thus a strong regional sense of nostalgia might further compel women to remain within their traditional stations.

Finally, some genre critics have argued that realism itself may be antagonistic towards feminist experience. Patricia Smart asserts that realism's intense interest in a unified, integral self is inherently phallogocentric. Smart argues that the emphasis on the individual subject and the use of authoritative/authoritarian narrators in realist fiction reproduces a "masculine epistemology" that "dominates the multiplicity of the real and reduces it ... to the smooth fabric of a unified vision" (Smart 1991, 11). Some aspects of realism may be insensitive to a feminine experience, but the genre's use of internal perspectives, as well as the emergence of unreliable and even ironic narrators help make the genre available to multiple ideologies. Such writers as Gabrielle Roy, Mavis Gallant, Ethel Wilson, Adele Wiseman, Margaret Laurence, and Alice Munro have all employed realism and still managed to produce feminist perspectives. Eventually Maritime women began to follow in their footsteps.

By the late 1970s, the conditions for the production of women's realist fiction were in place. Engaged in the same set of struggles that swept North America, Maritime women struggled successfully for higher wages, greater access to educational resources, more opportunity in nontraditional workplaces, more resources dedicated to childcare, and a host of other legal, political, and economic advances. Even within the fields of literature, such writers as Nowlan and Richards began to curtail the nostalgic impulse in their fiction, and little by little it became possible to view the traditional culture through critical eyes. The second wave of feminism combined with the cultural shift to change the literary landscape in a dramatic way. Inspired by the politics of liberation, writers emerged to challenge the traditional power structures. In the last two decades a surprising number of women writers have represented versions of women's experiences in both short fictions and novels. In the 1980s, such writers as Donna Smyth, Nancy Bauer, and Budge Wilson addressed directly the issue of gender imbalances in the region and developed a clear and focused feminist analysis of the problem. Their groundbreaking fictions reveal the intensity of women's struggles against cultural restrictions. Each of their texts point with surprising confidence towards the possibility of transformation. In the years that have followed, writers have built on this foundation, though the texts produced by Deborah Joy Corey, Carol Bruneau, Lynn Coady, and Ann-Marie MacDonald have tended to explore the issue of gender in greater detail and have been less confident that women can emerge from these power structures unscathed. If the first women realists focused on characters who were determined to break their silence, subsequent writers have suggested that some women continue to break beneath that silence.

DONNA SMYTH

Donna Smyth's *Quilt*, published in 1982, confronts an ideologically engaged situation as the older women in a rural community attempt to protect and comfort Myrt, a young woman who is in flight from her abusive husband. As the older women contemplate their own sometimes difficult marriages and attempt to help Myrt overcome her passivity, they form a community that reverses many of the assumptions produced by earlier patriarchal Maritime texts. Smyth's depiction of the little rural backwater of Dayspring functions as a mirror image of Buckler's Entremont, as the characters give voice to the many experiences that were silenced in *The Mountain and the Valley* and unveil the grim aspects of the region's patriarchal family structure. Kulyk Keefer argues that *Quilt* functions as a "regional idyll or rather, a cracked mirror of that genre," and she suggests that Smyth's Dayspring is a kind of literary response to Buckler's intensely patriarchal representation of Norstead in *Oxbells and Fireflies* (1987, 208).

As a feminist, Smyth places the issue of gender and the imbalance of power within a patriarchy at the heart of the novel, not to preach about the problem but to make visible the conditions through which those imbalances are maintained. Smyth makes the masculine hegemony visible by shifting back and forth between a series of characters, both male and female, as they contemplate their different versions of reality within their community. The male characters are not flat or demonized, but the female characters are the focal points of the narrative and thus the reader is predisposed to sympathize with their experiences. Three characters form the heart of the novel: Sam, the recently widowed older woman who is still recovering from the loss of her husband; Hazel, who has made her marriage work despite her husband's predisposition towards selfishness; and Myrt, who is in the process of escaping – but is uncertain about the prospect of ending – her relationship with her abusive husband. The external narrator focalizes through each woman, and the text reveals that the mechanisms that regulate the distribution of power are anchored in cultural norms, not natural hierarchies. Smyth thus opens up the distinction between culture and nature that was conflated in earlier Maritime fictions. Throughout *Quilt*, Smyth examines and resists the ways in which gender imbalances are reinforced by the valley's sexist traditions.

If the text has a wise or authoritative voice, it would belong to Sam, a complex figure who "seemingly walks right off the pages into life [as a] testimony to Smyth's considerable abilities at characterization" (Godard 1984, 89). Sam is a strong figure, but she has been shaken by her decision to help her ailing and suffering husband end his own life. Walt was a good husband for Sam, not because he was weak or dying – though that irony could be available to the critic who attempts to read against the grain of the novel – but because he recognized that he and Sam formed a mutually supportive and cooperative union. Sam retains and even grows in personal strength through her relationship with Walt, but it would be a mistake to think that she is in any way defined by her role as wife. Walt was not an ideal mate: he was so integrated into the patriarchal system as to be unaware of its potential injustices and abuses. For example, he trusts his unworthy nephew Ed and wrongly assumes that his family will care for Sam and protect her interests after his death. Far from naive, Sam understands that the culture's assumptions make her vulnerable, and she uses the legal mechanisms available within the system to frustrate any potential abuses of power. Her ability to work within the system to achieve ends that the system opposes is evident when she has Walt draw up a will that protects her title to the farm, and then reveals that she herself will grant the land away from the patriarchal, hereditary line by willing the land to the deserving young man, Jack.

Sam's canny resistance to the patriarchy is matched by her determination to restore a feminine network through her insistence that the local women gather to sew a quilt, an image that is used "as a metaphor for women's creations,"which are"collective, material, for private consumption, [and] fragmented" (Godard 1984, 88). Sam sees the self as an entity that requires community in order to flourish: thus, to stave off the "silence and aloneness" that "filled up" the house after Walt's death, she fosters the quilting group that draws people "together talking and laughing" (*Q*, 48). The group of women constitute an alternative to the dominant masculine culture as they "told each other these stories, all the time working and stitching" (*Q*, 49). As one of the text's central voices, Sam articulates Smyth's perspective and echoes the feminist communitarian liberalism developed by Carol Gould, who argues that "the concern that individuals have for each other is defined by their participation in a common activity oriented to shared ends, or to what they take to be a common good. The care in this case is therefore aimed at the achievement of this good that in turn requires their concern for each other's participation in this common activity and concern about their own responsibility for the joint undertaking" (1994, 351). It is an ideological position that is supported by other key characters.

Compared to Sam, the character of Hazel is a more troubled figure. Less able than her friend to suspend the dominant ideology, she must endure her husband's demand that she abandon her quilting activities and spend her time preserving the summer's harvest. Driven by economic motives that simply reinforce his own desire to control his spouse, Herb is not overtly abusive, but neither will he recognize the mutual nature of his interdependence with his wife. In the end, Hazel is only able to stage small resistances, taking pleasure in her kitchen work as a way of connecting back to her mother, and finally abandoning the kitchen to seek solace at Sam's house, where her friends will listen to her troubles and "understand on account of … being women too, they would know a woman's life and what she has to put up with" (Q, 33). The text is thus critical of the way in which economic interests are wedded to patriarchal assumptions to form an oppressive system, but not immediately hopeful that this entrenched system can be reformed. Herb asserts that "the man had to run the place," and, although Hazel cannot reverse the demands of this system, she can stage a series of minor rebellions and join an alternate community that give her an opportunity to grow: "I'll wave from Sam's place" (Q, 66).

Of all the women in the community, Myrt is certainly the most vulnerable, and through her character Smyth develops a careful critique of the larger social mechanisms that subtly encourage women to accept their own powerlessness as natural. As Myrt contemplates her situation and remembers her past, the reader is granted a snapshot of her childhood, through which it becomes clear that she has been conditioned to her role as victim, so much so that she is "helplessly inert [and] ready, in her confusion and boredom to leave the shelter a social worker has found her" (Kulyk Keefer 1987, 208). Encouraged to "dress smart" as a child, but not necessarily to act smart, Myrt is willing to construct herself an object for the perception of others: she cites as one of her greatest disappointments the fact that her "stupid" decision to marry prevented her from being "Apple Blossom Queen in Hanover" (Q, 13). Her inability to perceive herself apart from the images developed by the consumer culture and the expectations of her patriarchal heritage acclimatize her to accept Ralphie's abusive behaviour. Her journey towards a more complete understanding of her self in relation to a large community of women is difficult, and the narrator grants no assurances that she will be able to free herself from her self-destructive patterns.

Smyth's vision of Ralphie is similarly ambiguous. Initially he is represented as a violent, self-involved man who is the product of the worst aspects of his culture. As a construct of his society he is responsible for his choices, and the text seems initially to suggest that if he has learned to be violent, he could choose to unlearn those behaviours. Midway through the text, however, Smyth links Ralphie to the image of a tomcat that prowls around Sam's property, and threatens the litter of kittens nestled within the barn's stores of hay. The "wild" Tom is a "mean one" and "up to no good," and it eventually kills all six kittens as a symbolic reminder that some males are essentially and irredeemably violent and dangerous. Smyth is careful to present the women in the text as flexible and changeable figures, but she implies that Ralphie is naturally aggressive, perhaps in order to justify the text's final move to solve the problem of patriarchal violence by having Ralphie kill himself. The shift away from the discourse of freedom to that of determinism makes the ending seem more logically necessary, but it does produce a shadow over Smyth's otherwise convincing defence of communitarian liberalism. But for Ralphie's natural propensity towards violence, all the other characters are viewed as subjects who are shaped within and capable of responding to the larger community that articulates their sense of self. Smyth's faith in the self's ability to interact with the community is threatened only by the realization that Ralphie would be violent regardless of whatever community pressures were marshalled against him.

NANCY BAUER

Smyth examines the collective identity of the society, the impact of patriarchy, and the necessity of feminism at the level of the self/community. Nancy Bauer examines these issues at the micro level and reproduces an individualist liberalism as she traces the search of a single character to find an identity apart from the conventional patriarchy. Born Nancy Luke in Massachusetts in 1934, she grew up in Chemlsford and received a Bachelor of Arts from Mount Holyoke College. Between 1956 and 1965, she moved throughout the United States with her husband, William Bauer, before the couple settled in Fredericton, New Brunswick. Nancy Bauer joined the "Tuesday Night Group" – an all male circle of writers that included Bob Gibbs, Kent Thompson, Bill Bauer, Joe Sherman, Dave Richards, Michael

Pacey, Dale Estey, Brian Barlett, Andrew Bartlett, and Ted Colson – and began to write fiction (Bauer, interview).[1] While her later novels move stylistically away from psychological realism towards a kind of futuristic magic realism, her first novel, *Flora, Write this Down*, published in 1982, is very much within the conventions of realism as Flora, a middle-aged woman, is suddenly unsure of her identity and must renegotiate her place within her larger family. Her sense of disruption and alienation eases only as she experiments with forms of storytelling in order to recover her own voice.

Flora, Write This Down was the first book printed by Goose Lane Editions and the initial small run has long been sold out. One of Bauer's strongest texts, *Flora, Write This Down* revolves around the title character, Flora, who accompanies her young son to the United States, where he is to have a delicate operation on his hand. Flora's own family is stable, but, as she visits with her maternal relations, Flora feels increasingly uncertain about herself and her role. Overwhelmed by family memories, Flora embarks on a near Oedipal struggle in order to reinscribe herself in the shadow of her powerful mother: "God know's I'm no Doc. A pale imitation perhaps" (*F*, 12).

Nicknamed "Doc" for her "gentle manner in looking after the young ones when they were ill" (*F*, 7), Flora's mother has been elevated to mythic stature by the family. Aged thirteen when her own mother died, Doc "took on the responsibility of raising five children" (*F*, 9). She soon becomes the authority within the family and even watches over her father, whom she occasionally reprimands in the name of her absent mother:

"Pa," Doc said, "you can't go out like that. It isn't right. Change and put on your good clothes."

"These look all right and I'll miss the cars."

"They don't look all right. Ma would not have liked your going to the library in your working clothes." (*F*, 9)

Doc accumulates the full power of the matriarchal line and her strengths are legendary. It is Doc who insists that the family will raise Winkie's illegitimate boy without a sense of difference or shame (*F*, 27–8), and when the picnicking family is attacked by a hobo, it is Doc who wounds him as they escape (*F*, 62). Flora and Doc's niece both name their daughters after her, and, although she has been dead for eight years, stories of her determination and insight are touchstones for the family. The text's celebration of powerful women echoes Bauer's own sense of history: "I grew up with very strong women. My mother really was a very saintly person. She died in

1969. Her funeral was immense. The church was totally filled and the church yard was full of people who just wanted to be there. My grandmother was strong. She was a midwife and had a hospital and my aunt was saying that she never had one case of infection in all those years. She boiled everything. And all my Aunts on my father's side were strong dynamic women. So I grew up with them all around me" (Bauer, interview).

But *Flora, Write This Down* is not an idealistic text, and despite the family's desire to mythologize their own past, Doc is not a stereotypical matriarch. Though she is remembered as being complete and self-sufficient, Doc does not escape paying a price for her heroism, and she develops "several secret eccentricities and one that was well known. She wrote everything down" (*F*, 104). When the family grows up and moves out, Doc feels a void and the lists that she once made to keep a sense of order become obsessive. She generates lists of "things to do today, things that need to be done tomorrow ... clothing to buy, grocery lists for the week, grocery lists for the winter, flowers I've planted, plants I've given away" (*F*, 104). The lists are not emotional records, but they form a curiously intimate chronicle of Doc's daily life as she supplements her emptiness with text. Her elaborately decorated account books become symptomatic of her essential strengths: determination, drive, and foresight. They also testify to her deepest wounds: her longing for love and security.

In a masculinist text – for example, Thomas Raddall's *His Majesty's Yankees* – the son must often resort to violence in order to clear a space for himself within his father's world.[2] Flora's struggle is less direct. Doc was a formidable character while alive, and the trace of her memory remains influential long after her death, but Flora finds it difficult to define herself against the shifting stories and the enigmatic account books that are her mother's only remaining presence. The family is a unit without a tangible centre to challenge, and thus Flora remains a daughter without a clear sense of her abilities: "the house is the centre of the family. While Doc lived, she was the centre, but no one now has the same authority. They look to me, but I live in another land and am not a natural born leader" (*F*, 26). Flora's sense of dislocation is addressed only as she exercises her own voice and begins to compile her own family history.

In the second section of the novel, "Family," Flora retells stories of her own youth and is able to demythologize her mother. She recalls her mother's strengths and records Doc's heroic attentions to her dying father, but she also reconstructs her weaknesses. She recalls how Doc's unyielding sense of discipline was unable to accommodate the needs of Marion, a minor who briefly lives with the family until she

flees from Doc's rigidity and returns to a prior destructive relationship. As Doc is returned to a stature that her daughter can embrace,
the narrative increasingly signals that Flora is able to reproduce many
of her mother's strengths. Just as Doc's resistance to the threatening
hobo is part of family folklore, so Flora's attack on Paul Pelletiers, a
boy who had cut her cousin with a rock-filled snowball, attains the
status of legend:

Remember the fight we had with the Pelletiers that time? You almost beat the
shit out of Paul you were so mad. He never knew what hit him ... He said
he'd never dared tangle with a woman since. (F, 29)
My God, Flora, you kneed him in the balls, and I thought he was going to
croak ... (F, 52)

Flora's storytelling, her own supplement to the absence of her
mother, is a successful response to her insecurity. In the final section
of the novel she begins to link her past and present. She recognizes
her mother's influence, saying, "In a family where there has been a
Doc, there will always be a Doc. The founder of a family is the one
who raises the family to such a level that it can never fall permanently below that level again" (F, 114). Flora then immediately turns
to consider how Doc's powers echo in her own daughter, Priscilla,
whose strengths are so evident that a neighbour remarks that she
would "rather leave Priscilla with the children when they were sick
than with her husband" (F, 114).

The novel retells the traditional liberal narrative of a protagonist's
search for her identity, but it does not reconstruct old hierarchies or
teleologies. The "God" invoked in the text is not the phallocentric
source of all meaning, but a being at whom Doc can shout threats and
to whom Flora can successfully pray "that Marion have her period"
(F, 75). Here, writing is not an attempt to confine the world within a
perfect order of words, but an experimental process by which Flora
evokes a series of images that generate individual meanings but resists systematic closure. The stories of Mr Johnson, whom Winkie
found "dead for several days, covered with flies" (F, 18), or the
strange home of Bozo Talty whose floors were covered with pots
filled with "custard" (F, 36), remain unresolved enigmas of sexuality
and mortality. In the final scenes of the novel, Flora is comfortable
with the uncertainties of her life and is able to retreat by herself to a
cabin in the woods. Her final decision to work out her issues by herself confirms that, while Bauer recognizes the importance of community, a woman's identity as an individual must be formed or
confirmed apart from the larger society. She does not attempt to find

permanent answers and is simply glad, "I stuck it out. The whole exercise was probably silly, but at least I did what I said I was going to do" (F, 133).

BUDGE WILSON

Like Donna Smyth and Nancy Bauer, Budge Wilson attends closely to the struggles of the individual who attempts to define herself in relation to or apart from a larger community. And like Smyth and Bauer before her, she addresses directly the ways in which female characters confront issues of gender and particularly the ways in which they react to the constraints inherent within the traditional patriarchal society. Wilson's individuals are inevitably constrained by their cultural contexts, but within particular boundaries a degree of freedom is often possible. Born in Halifax in 1927, and educated at Dalhousie University, before moving to Ontario for thirty-three years, Wilson began to publish fiction relatively late in life. In 1990, a year after returning to Halifax to live, she published her first collection of short stories; since then her level of productivity has been astonishingly high. Besides the numerous children's books that have won Wilson both critical acclaim and a wide readership among young people, she has also published two more volumes of short fiction. Two of her three collections have been marketed to younger readers, though all three can also be viewed as appropriate fare for adults. Wilson's fiction has been examined by a few critics, and her tendency to affirm the independence of her characters has been noted by reviewers. Thus far only Janice Kulyk Keefer has produced a lengthy analysis of Wilson's first collection *The Leaving*. Focusing on Wilson's recurring attention to women's engagement with language Kulyk Keefer argues convincingly that the stories "underscore the regrettable fact that few women ever speak for themselves and to their daughters of their most intimate and important experiences ... These stories show us that to become agents rather than receivers of language helps us to retrieve the repressed experiences vital to understanding ourselves as subjects instead of objects and to survive in a brutalizing environment" (1997, 198, 201). Wilson's determination to celebrate women's linguistic empowerment transfers as well to her larger project: exploring the ways in which individuals must struggle to achieve a tentative sense of identity while dealing with the sometimes harsh pressures of the larger society. "A self-confessed optimist," Wilson encodes within her texts the sense of hesitation and anxiety that is familiar to readers of Maritime fiction, but ultimately she affirms that her characters can "gain some measure of self knowledge, whether modest or revolutionary, which helps free them in varying degrees from paralyzing unhappiness" (Garvie 1994, 20). This balanced liberal defence of the individual is evident if the title stories from her three collections of short fiction are examined.

The story "The Leaving" is narrated by a young woman who recalls a crucial moment in her life, when her mother left the family for a few days in order to think about her marriage and her station in life. The text is related in the past tense, and, because the narrator focalizes the tale through her own eyes as a thirteen-year-old, the reader is given an intimate yet sometimes fragmented set of impressions, which must be assembled in order to appreciate the difficult conditions under which the mother exists. Like the early fiction of Alistair MacLeod, Wilson's story explores the harsh, impoverished conditions of a family trapped in rural Nova Scotia. The family's poverty is apparent in their sparsely finished house, the building's unpainted exterior, and the yard, which "was a confusion of junk of all kinds" (L, 91). The mother, Elizabeth, struggles with economic constraints, but is oppressed more directly by her harsh and cruel husband, who greets her return after a three-day absence with the command, "Shut your mouth, woman, and git my supper" (L, 92). Trapped in a life-denying situation, the mother bears a considerable burden, but unlike MacLeod's early stories, the characters of Wilson's fictions are granted a considerable degree of agency. A year earlier the mother received a copy of *The Feminine Mystique*, hidden in a box of books delivered by the Salvation Army. The modern world has a significant impact on Elizabeth, and, though she tells her daughter that Friedan's feminist classic "was a real troublin' book," she treasures it because she "found out I weren't alone" (L, 90).

Most of the stories in Wilson's first collection suggest that choice is possible; though complete liberation is not an option for the protagonists, greater liberty for the self is. The mother demands and is eventually granted a measure of respect from her husband and sons, and, more importantly, opportunities are opened for the daughter who goes to university. Drawing from Rita Felski, Janice Kulyk Keefer argues that Wilson's writing "can be a liberating step for [Maritime] women, which uncovers the political dimensions of personal experience, confronts the contradictions of existing gender roles, and inspires an important sense of female identification and solidarity" (1987, 198). Wilson's commitment to the concept of liberalism is more fully explored by Diana Austin who observes that the mother "gradually brings about enough small changes to feel some satisfaction with her lot. In these examples, as in the entire collection, there is a quiet recognition that life is a continued engagement with the still smouldering brushfires of earlier desires and anxieties; control can never be absolute, perhaps, whether over oneself or others, but at least the struggle is worth attempting for it serves as a shaping force in the chaos of experience" (1991, 113). The characters in Wilson's first collection affirm that individual creative and personal impulses can help release the average woman from some of the burdens that oppress her.

The stories in *The Leaving* are tightly constructed, exploring a wide variety of protagonists and narrators as they recall or record the crucial moments when they "come of age." Wilson's next collection, *Cordelia Clark* (1994) is a more uneven volume. Most of its stories explore characters, many of whom are entering their later years, though there are a few odd tales, including "The Happy Pill," which combines didacticism and parable to produce a uncompelling narrative. More often the stories examine the way in which the self is constructed through language, and the frequently tentative nature of that process. In the title story, Trudy, an older woman, recalls her experiences as a twelve-year-old in the "sleepy little town" of Wolfville, Nova Scotia, and reflects on her sense of anxiety as she remembers the way in which a child from Halifax terrorized her for the better part of a year. As she remembers her nemesis Cordelia, she recounts how her sense of self – a construct that could emerge only in conjunction with her community – was fragmented and shattered by Cordelia's persistent and nasty gossip: "I was not always blessed with this ability to disregard the opinions of others. And I will have to admit, Charlie, if I'm totally honest, that I'm still more vulnerable in this area than I like to think" (*cc*, 16). Because the individual's identity is tied to the perceptions of the community, the process of forming a self is subject to manipulation and abuse by those who can shape the public's response. Cordelia proves adept at playing one girl off another, and she uses the established codes of the society – codes that determine "correct behaviour" for young girls – to gossip about Trudy, fabricate imaginary violations of the public norms, and thus alienate her from the community. Cordelia is able to "Divide and conquer. Destroy and possess" (*cc*, 41). As an outsider who is not touched or shaped by the community norms she manipulates, she forfeits her opportunity to have a stable identity, but wins in return a kind of ruthless power. Indeed, the entire Clark family lays bare the problems inherent in the wider community because it is bound by these limiting roles. Mrs Clark's supposed sexual adventures make the married women in the community nervous, and the formerly staid housewives begin to follow their husbands at night and adopt innovative ways to tempt their husbands back to the marriage bed. The wry humour and irony of the story reinforce the point that the Clarks, both junior and senior, are able to prey on the townspeople only because the town is already divided and vulnerable. When individuals begin to assert themselves, they are able to defend against the chaotic influence of the urbanites, but in the end only blind chance saves the town from self-destruction: the Clarks move on to a new town. Time will not bring about complete healing, but it is possible for former friends to reestablish ties and restore their sense of identity. In Wilson's second collection, freedom for the self is a possible, but nonetheless tentative business.

Released the same year as *Cordelia Clark* (but from a different publisher), Wilson's third collection of stories, *The Courtship*, continues to examine the nature of individual freedom and the ways in which community and cultural norms impinge on personal choice. In the story "The Courtship" the central figure, Mrs Knickle, has been a widow and has enjoyed her sense of personal independence, but has recently decided that "ten years was long enough to be free" (*TC*, 16). Longing for a permanent relationship and the limitations that accompany it, she contemplates giving up aspects of her freedom in order to reenter the conventions of the society that still regulate relationships between men and women. As she admires her handsome neighbour, the retired professor Mr Vanbusbirk, Mrs Knickle's is aware that the conventions governing romance are highly constructed, and thus she is able to control and use those customs in a sophisticated fashion. She literally tabulates the strengths and weaknesses the retired professor could bring to a relationship before she develops her strategic plan to "Lead from strength" (*TC*, 23). Recognizing that she was partly responsible for the unsatisfactory elements of her first marriage, she vows to be more forward and direct in her courtship behaviours, and thus Wilson seems to be arguing that the malleability of human conventions grant each individual a considerable degree of freedom as they set out their own path. Individual agency is possible not despite social conventions, but because of them. In a sense then, Wilson's final collection fuses the different versions of liberalism apparent in the texts of Bauer and Smyth, as she both attends to the individual's need to realize a form of selfhood, while insisting that this process is one which necessarily happens in conjunction with the larger community.

A MORE SOMBRE TONE

Smyth, Bauer, and Wilson were some of the first women writers to bring realism to bear on their Maritime experience. All three writers have produced confident expressions of their diverse forms of liberalism and have argued that their female characters are capable of resisting the region's confining patriarchal assumptions in order to find a more complete sense of self. As the first volumes of realist feminist fictions emerged in the region, the writers were uniformly clear that progress was possible, if difficult.

In the texts of subsequent writers, we discover a grimmer depiction of the individual's dilemma, and fewer solutions are being proposed. The tragic oppression embedded in the region's alienated condition, depressed economy, and patriarchal systems is examined, but the writers no longer feel compelled to ease the sense of tragedy by freeing their central characters. Thus a more sombre tone begins to emerge in the fictions of Deborah Joy Corey, Lynn Coady, Carol Bruneau, and Ann-Marie MacDonald. Corey traces an individual's struggles during childhood, and each subsequent writer addresses a later stage in the subject's journey towards old age.

DEBORAH JOY COREY

Deborah Joy Corey's novel, *Losing Eddie*, was published in 1993 and won the SmithBooks / Books in Canada First Novel Award. Printed in an unusually large type, the two-hundred-page novel is, in reality, a fairly short text, characterized by its clipped sentences, evocative imagery, immediate dialogue, and unlaboured symbolism. Set in rural New Brunswick, Corey's text focuses on Laura, a preadolescent girl who is the narrator and central character and whose dysfunctional family and community are wracked by a series of tragedies. Corey's fiction follows the long regional tradition of relying on realism to examine, or in this case disassemble, the traditional family while attempting to explore the maturation of the young heroine.

The conditions that threaten the young narrator are multiple, and indeed in her family and community there are few opportunities for her to escape. Family members are prey to the violent aspects of the patriarchal order, which are manifested most clearly within the marriage of the oldest sister. The text opens with a description of the sister being beaten by her husband, and his desire to control her eventually touches the entire family as he later drives into the front yard and threatens the household with a rifle. The sister eventually returns to her mate, arguing that "he's gone on the wagon and when he doesn't drink, he doesn't hit me," but neither the family nor the reader believe that she is safe (LE, 34). The family's economic constraints also limit the options of the various characters, and Corey insists that individual freedom is difficult in the midst of chronic underdevelopment. Money is so tight that they are unable to bail

Eddie, their troubled eldest son, out of jail, and, when the sister asks to move back home, her mother's first response is "You know we have nothing extra" (*LE*, 6). The family and community show signs of strain even when things are going comparatively well. The father is a kind and well-intentioned individual, but he is incapable of protecting his children and in times of difficulty he retreats to his bottle in the wellhouse. Laura is obviously a bright, thoughtful, and intelligent girl, but Theresia Quigley has noted her gifts may work to her disadvantage as she is forced to relinquish her childhood innocence too quickly and like a "miniature adult" she becomes the caregiver of her parents (1995, 82–3). Given the conditions that surround and shape her, she will not be able to transcend her environment.

As *Losing Eddie* unfolds these difficult conditions deteriorate further. The eldest brother returns from reform school only to be killed when the car he is driving hits a grader and bursts into flames. Overwhelmed by her grief after Eddie's death, the narrator's mother slips into madness and must be twice hospitalized. The sense of instability spreads through the neighbourhood: next door the mother of Laura's best friend dies of cancer and an acquaintance from a fundamentalist Christian family down the road endures her own brother's sexual assaults: "'I can't keep him out.' She turns her back to me and cries way down deep inside of her, little tiny cries that echo off one another" (*LE*, 130). Though a summary of the plot makes *Losing Eddie* sound like a soap opera, the narrator's even, immediate, and sensitive observations prevent the novel from slipping into melodrama. Given the traumatic losses she has experienced in the course of her summer, it is not surprising that the narrator is both anxious about her future and longing for a way to retreat to a safe past. "The child is, of course, not capable of assuming a parental role indefinitely" (Quigley 1995, 83), and three quarters of the way through the novel the main character reveals that she sometimes dreams that she is back in her mother's womb, where "you sway back and forth, but you feel happy, and the very very best part is that it's just the two of you and you are safe in there with her"(*LE*, 156). Laura and her friends long to escape to a space where the protective power of a mother is paramount, but even they recognize that these fantasies are impossible in this rather barren neighbourhood.

For all the grim moments in *Losing Eddie*, Corey's novel is not unremittingly bleak, for she "offers her characters a kind of stubborn hope of redemption" (Homel 1994, 9). By the conclusion, the mother returns from the sanatorium, and her younger bother is resuscitated after nearly drowning; a fragment of the family survives and faces the coming year with determination. Neither maudlin nor sentimental, the narrator is surprisingly resilient, and her ability to endure harsh conditions in the hope of finding something better comforts both the character herself and the reader. Granted, these hopeful moments are as much the product of the narrator's naivety as they are credible responses to their immediate circumstances. In the final pages, as the young girl defiantly names herself before her classmates and teacher, she proceeds to adopt a lyrical tone as she finds and takes to school a wounded bird, only to return after lunch to learn that the bird has disappeared. Hints are provided that the teacher has dumped the bird and folded the pink towel in the bottom of the box, and the text does not endorse Laura's hope that "the sparrow with its wing healed [is] flying … straight without wobbling up to the sun" (*LE*, 222). Brief comfort might be found in her idealism, but Corey stops short of arguing that Laura's is a credible response to the oppressive conditions that bind her. Unlike the confident vision developed by Bauer and Wilson, Corey's text is politically ambivalent. The reader is called to sympathize with the individual, but the narrative does not construct a clear framework that guarantees that her identity will be secured either within or apart from her community.

LYNN COADY

Six years after Corey published her account of a preadolescent's experiences in the region, Lynn Coady released her acclaimed novel *Strange Heaven*, which explores the life and times of a young adult. Coady's first novel attracted a wide audience when it was nominated for the 1998 Governor General's Award and won both the Canadian Author's Association Award for best writer under thirty and the Dartmouth Book and Writing Award for Fiction. *Strange Heaven* is a compelling novel that examines a season in the life of Bridget Murphy. Only eighteen years old, Bridget gives birth to a child and then falls into a depression so severe that she enters the psychiatric ward of a children's hospital. The first half of the novel chronicles her experiences in the ward, and the second half depicts her return home over the Christmas holidays. Given the two settings through which the central character moves, the title is deeply ironic, for both environments promise to provide a kind of emotional shelter for the distraught girl, and both deliver only a sustained chaos, which is matched in turn by the character's own sense of turmoil. Not since Nowlan's early stories, or Richard's *Road to the Stilt House* – a writer for whom Coady has expressed strong admiration – has a text moved so determinedly towards a nihilistic position only to pull back at the last moment.

Bridget Murphy is represented through a third-person narration, but the text is closely focalized through her identity and, thus, dominated by her sense of confusion. Coady completely dispels any nostalgic impulse that might have entered the text and promised to anchor the young woman to her past or heritage. Whether she is in the hospital or back in the family home, there is little of value or comfort to be attained through the attempt to reconnect to the society's traditional structures. Even more than the grandmothers who populated Richards's texts, Bridget's gran, Margaret P, proves to be a symbol of the family's disconnection from its past. At her most lucid, she declares that "she senses darkness on all sides," and more frequently she rants about demons and destruction as she curses her family. If the elderly are fully engaged in the painful and turbulent process of dying, little comfort can be found in family, friends, or other community institutions.

Bridget's family may mean well, but it is dysfunctional at the best of times. The father's domineering manner silences rather than encourages Bridget, and his desire to control rather than support his daughter is evident in moments preceding the Christmas dinner: "Bridget came down in her pyjamas and her father sent her back up to change. Her father was finding his footing with her again, slowly. With every edict to wrap Christmas presents or change her clothes or pick up her own goddamn tea cups he regained the old confidence … He was a man who attributed deviation from the normal mode of behaviour to just stubbornness … Stubbornness was eminently curable when Robert Michael Murphy was present to take it in hand. You kick their shitty arses into gear is what you do" (*SH*, 128). Nothing in Coady's fiction echoes Buckler's idealized portrait of the patriarchal family. In *Strange Heaven*, and in the short stories recently published in *Play the Monster Blind*, the father figure is more likely to be an emotionally warped figure whose influence is felt only as his legacy of miscommunication launches the family on a path towards self-destruction. This tendency to carefully critique the father figure for his damaging influence is particularly evident in the title story of *Play the Monster Blind*, in which a young woman accompanies her fiancé to his home, and discovers that the father bears an eerie resemblance to the Boris Karloff's version of the monster in the movie *Frankenstein*. The incoherent old man has so conditioned his family into a cycle of violence that even the young woman feels like a member of the clan only after she has been struck by the erratic sister.

Bridget's family, as a whole, is more likely to espouse an exhausted proverb or platitude than attempt to address the problems engulfing them. Bridget's friends are similarly unhelpful as they tempt her to return to her previously empty cycle of drunken parties and painful recoveries. Even conventional institutions like the Church are unable to offer much comfort. The local priest comes over for a game of cards, but the closest the family comes to a sense of religious experience would be the sculptures that Bridget's mentally challenged brother produces, which the father astutely markets as his number-one seller, by advertising them as "Religious Wooden Statues. Done by Retarded Man. Twenty-Five dollars a piece" (*SH*, 78). Through this litany of social chaos, the novel insists that the meaning of life cannot be found beyond the immediate experience of the individual self.

For a long time, even the possibility of a privately constructed sense of significance seems to be beyond Bridget's powers. Most of the time, she is curiously detached from her surroundings. In the hospital she is disengaged and removed from all around her. "Things" she says "were happening without reason or point," and even the news of a friend's violent death "is like a thing on a screen ... it didn't concern her any more" (*SH*, 9–10). Though she does care for the anorexic Mona and enjoys her time with the rather superficial and inauthentic Alan, she ultimately understands that Mona is obsessed only with her own pain and Alan will inevitably betray her when he returns to his girlfriend Deanna. Even after she is released from the hospital, she seems distant from family and friends. This may be a useful tactic as she attempts to ward off the unhealthy aspects of her home life, but she passively slips into the behaviours that produced her unwanted pregnancy in the first place. Even her family doctor seems resigned to the futility of her life, as he advises her to simply abort her next accidental pregnancy: "Next time, however," said Dr Bransk, "you will know to come to me" (*SH*, 182).

Only in the closing pages does Bridget finally articulate the agony of her experience, and as she claims a place for her own voice we can hope, for the first time, that she may be able to confront and overcome the bleak circumstances that have thus far defined her. In the closing pages, Bridget manifests a new sense of self, and, if the transformation is as sudden as the narrative shift in *Road to the Stilt House*, it is executed with a greater degree of subtlety, as Coady weaves together several key concerns within a single outburst. When her former boyfriend attempts to win pity for himself by claiming that he regrets losing his son, Bridget exclaims furiously, " 'Eat your own shit.' She said. She said that because Margaret P had been saying it to everybody of late ... 'See a round mouth opening and closing toward your tit and live after that,' she said. 'Live and live and live after that' " (*SH*, 105). Though Bridget has few connections to her family, she quotes her dying grandmother and thus finds, in the old lady's abusive speech, a kind of ground on which she can securely stand and defend her interests. Moreover, Bridget focuses on her lost connection to her child and identifies herself within the discourses of the feminine and the maternal; as she uses her words to express the love, longing, and sense of grief surrounding the birth of her child, the narrative suggests that she really will be able to refashion her life. The closing scene, in which she refutes the selfishness of the all the various masculine and paternal realms and claims her own individuality, works as a wonderful reply to the opening scene in which she learns that Archie Shearer has killed his girlfriend Jennifer MacDonald. Bridget is determined that she will not be silenced, either literally or symbolically: the last pages pull us back from the abyss of meaninglessness. Coady argues gracefully, in this last scene, that an identity is possible, though it is available only when the protagonist freely produces it from her own painful, emotional experience. Through its rather perilous journey towards its tentative conclusion, *Strange Heaven* reproduces a constrained individualist liberalism and affirms a woman's right to determine her own identity.

CAROL BRUNEAU

The individualism envisioned by Coady is, in some ways, appropriate within a text that explores an adolescent's attempt to take control of her own life. Carol Bruneau's series of linked short stories, collected in *After the Angel Mill*, attends to a set of older characters who are more tightly bound to their community. The mosaic, made up of eleven stories and an epilogue, traces the "matriarchal line of a family through four generations in the coal mining town of Blackett" (Dewar 1996, 124). The eldest mother, Sarah, is featured in the title story: she is a courageous woman who leaves her own mother – a cloth-worker in an English textile plant called Angel Mill – to emigrate to the new world with her husband James. Her youngest daughter Hattie then emerges as one of the collection's recurring narrators, though we also watch her daughter Gracie attempt to escape from Blackett, and finally Gracie's daughter Nancy who returns, or more accurately is returned, to the troubled town. Along the way a selection of sisters and aunts help round out the representation of the larger community of women. Given that the eleven stories are narrated in the first person, and that the narrators vary from the barely literate grandmother to the educated schoolteacher Mary Beth, it initially seems odd that each of these women sound eerily alike. The common tone in each voice might first seem to be a mark of Bruneau's own uncertainties as a writer, but it would be more accurate to

read the recurring voice as a reminder that all the women have
emerged from a similar community and context, and each has been
shaped by similar crises and struggles. The problems that confront
these women, generation after generation, arise from the troubled
economic and cultural assumptions that have persisted in the Maritimes for nearly a century. In order to understand the responses
of these women, the persistent struggles that they face must be
examined.

An admirer of the work of Ian McKay – whom she cites as a "tremendous influence" in his efforts to revive "our industrial history, or
real history, the history of the real people who built the region" – Bruneau insists throughout the text, that problems at the interpersonal
level of the family, have their roots in, or at the very least are influenced by, the economic struggles that plague the region as a whole
(Minard 1995, 9). Bruneau critiques the exploitative practices of the
Cape Breton mine owners: she traces the series of deadly accidents
that kill or maim dozens of workers at a time and documents the limited options available to the average worker, she paints a grim and almost deterministic portrait of the region. A fatalistic and funereal
tone is established early; the collection opens and closes with two
completely black pages, as if to warn the reader of the despairing contents to be found within. Even the name of the town – Blackett – becomes a reminder of the despair running through the book.

Difficult as life is for the average people who are at the mercy of the
whims that sway the mining industry, the problems are, in Bruneau's
mind, clearly more difficult for some than for others. The economic
structures of this society dictate that the middle class will suffer less
than the working class and that the men earning a working wage will
have greater power and opportunity than the dependent women who
wait at home. Gender and economics are thus intertwined. Life is no
doubt difficult for the men who toil and suffer throughout the stories,
but if the men become silent, taciturn figures, life is even harder for
their wives, whom they are likely to either strike or abandon. In each
story, the women are ultimately left to deal with the social and economic hardships, and not all the ways in which they choose to cope
are equally effective.

Some women in Bruneau's stories simply try to escape from the region and its troubled history. Gracie attempts to find a way "out of
Blackett" and hopes that John Alec MacNeil will be her means of
flight to the city of Halifax. But just as he exploits her sexually, so he
manipulates her financially and exhausts "the five hundred dollars
[she'd] saved up for Miss Murphy's Business College" before he
finds a job as a stevedore (AM, 92). Gracie tries to abandon her

familial roots, in the hopes of escaping the poverty that attended her childhood and discovers instead that she has abandoned the only system that could help buffer the deeper hardships of poverty: "life can go sour when the requirements of love are left unattended" (Minard 1995, 9). Other women remain in the community, but attempt to protect themselves from the cycles of misery that afflicted their mothers by remaining partly isolated from others. Hattie's sister Mary Beth removes herself from her community by pursuing her education and elevating herself to the station of a teacher. Hattie's sister-in-law, Irene, simply distances herself from others by adopting an elitist and superior attitude towards the relatives who might have been willing to forge a bond with her: "those MacCallums are well known for their breeding, And I do not mean pedigree" (AM, 138). In both cases, the women do win a degree of financial security, but both prove to be lonely figures, whose economic independence is not matched by a similar level of personal fulfillment.

The only way in which the women in *After the Angel Mill* survive the double disadvantages of economic and sexual disenfranchisement is to return to the family unit and the larger community and build a protective layer of co-operative defences. For Bruneau, then, feminism leads to a communitarian liberalism that argues that the individual is inevitably linked to the larger community and must accept the responsibilities and opportunities offered by this social reality. As some women take up their social and familial roles and spend their days supporting others, it seems as if the stories reinscribe the traditional patriarchal emblems associated with the feminine. Sarah is illiterate and underconfident, but the text presents her work as a supportive wife and loving mother as honourable: "What did reading and writing have to do with birthing babies and cooking and cleaning and cutting down clothes to dress them all? A mother's love?" (AM, 45). Hattie is very similar to her mother, as she devotes herself to her husband Thomas and her many children and becomes selfless, compliant, and emotional rather than rational. But the real values for which these women are celebrated are not these stereotypically feminine virtues. Hattie and Sarah are redeemed because they are authentic, true to themselves, willing to encourage rather than oppress others, and ultimately respectful and patient with the wills of others regardless of the social expectations of the traditional, conservative society. This strength of character allows Hattie to maintain a relationship with her son Archie despite the admonitions from the community that she should kick him out. Similarly, she accepts the responsibility of raising her granddaughter Nancy. She has strengthened rather than exploited others and thus she sets up a kind of cooperative economy that offers a viable alternative to the self-oriented, capitalist position developed by the patriarchal order. In this context, the epilogue is affirmative, for the granddaughter Nancy has absorbed the essential message of the stories and vowed not to flee Blackett like her mother; instead, she will be "staying with Arch until I decide" (*AM*, 168). Despite the final black page, the communitarian vision has been successfully communicated to at least one member of the next generation.

ANN-MARIE MACDONALD

Corey, Coady, and Bruneau have taken up the issues and concerns first articulated by Smyth, Wilson, and Bauer and continued to employ the formal traditions of realism as they explore and develop their feminist vision. It is worth noting, however, that some writers have started to blend these realist traditions with other literary forms in order to critique more fully the reach and impact of the region's patriarchal structures. Published in 1996, Ann-Marie MacDonald's debut novel, *Fall On Your Knees*, immediately climbed both national and international bestseller lists. The popularity of the novel is due in large part to the compelling nature of the central characters and the effectiveness of the strong omniscient narrator. It is not due to optimism in the overall vision of the text; quite the contrary, compared to the other recent writers discussed above, MacDonald's novel is a grim chronicle. *Fall On Your Knees* focuses on the figure of James Piper and his wife Materia and examines the impact of his possessive and harsh patriarchal desire to control the lives of his daughters: Kathleen, Mercedes, Frances, and Lily. The novel employs many of the standard conventions of realism as it develops its critique of the region's patriarchal structures, but then veers towards other literary forms in order to represent the experiences of the few figures who dare challenge those dominant powers.

From the opening sections, MacDonald carefully reproduces "the most pressing social, political, economic, and racial issues faced by" the residents of New Waterford and Sydney, in order to situate her characters and create the illusion that we are peering through a window into the complexities of life in Cape Breton (Andrews 1999, 10). The novel is alert to the general historical changes sweeping the multicultural communities of New Waterford and Sydney as they emerge from their late Victorian sense of security and experience the trauma of the First World War, the difficulties of the depressions, the hardships and opportunities of the coal mine strikes, the realities of outmigration, and the general conditions of instability that characterize life in the middle of the century. As she attends to the ebb and flow of historical forces, MacDonald erases completely any lingering nostalgia for the past and explores instead the specific racial codes of segregation, the tightly constructed gender roles, and the rigid religious assumptions that structure Maritime society and shape each of the characters, empowering some and reducing others to the status of victim. She does not simply document and attack the vicious patriarchal assumptions that lead the men in this novel to their despicable acts, rather she places each of the men, particularly each of the fathers, in a specific context so that we understand that even though each is personally responsible for the miseries they cause, they are enmeshed in a whole web of cultural, social, and economic factors, which are, in turn, critiqued for the destructive behaviours they support. In short, MacDonald uses one of the central impulses of the realist tradition – the sensitivity to historicist assumptions – to develop her feminist critique of the patriarchy.

Most of the fathers in *Fall On Your Knees* are overbearing dictatorial figures who sacrifice the interests of their children, particularly the interests of their daughters, to their own impulses or desires. The text documents the legacy of misery generated by Mahmoud as he forces Materia to marry James, compels a second daughter to marry the brutal Jameel, and arbitrarily dismisses Teresa from his household, but MacDonald also carefully notes that his actions are not an aberration, but the logical product of his religious beliefs, ethnic heritage, economic status, and historical identity. James Piper is even more carefully contextualized. His incestuous desire for his eldest daughter Kathleen and his subsequent sexual and physical abuse of Frances are seen as revolting by all who learn of them, but his legal, economic, and social status as a man and father either allow him to hide his actions or prevent those in the know from challenging him or defending his daughters. The only fathers in *Fall On Your Knees* who do not behave badly are men who are themselves alienated from the dominant patriarchal power structures. Ginger Taylor is a gentle and loving father, and the text suggests that his compassion is, in part, the product of his own sensitivity to his marginal status as black man in a racist society.

If MacDonald reproduces the social and historical contexts in a fashion typical of realism as she explores and critiques the patriarchal males of the text, she also attends to the line of cause and effect as she traces the lives of each of Piper's daughters and untangles the many ways in which they are shaped and scarred by the tragedies that unfold within their family. She is particularly careful to employ realist techniques as she demonstrates that there is no safe or wholesome

way for a woman to comply with the role set out for her by the patriarchal culture. Materia is literally a child when she marries James,
and in her inexperience she is unable to imagine a response other
then compliance as she is transferred from her father to her husband.
Unfortunately for her, submission to the patriarchy proves to be fatal;
as she attempts to negotiate her role as wife and mother, she increasingly loses her sense of identity. James forces Materia to leave her
Lebanese heritage behind and commands that she "speak English" to
her baby; he then attacks her for gaining weight and dismisses her
depression with the conclusion that she has "gone slack in her mind"
(FYK, 35,37). When she channels her resistance to the forces that oppress her into her job as a vaudeville pianist – she subversively plays
"The Wedding March" while "villains struggled with virgins" – her
last effort to establish a sense of herself is crushed when James declares "I want you to quit your job now, missus ... and don't be
traipsing around town on your own" (FYK, 54–5). Convinced by her
Catholic sensibility that all her sins and "badness [have] rolled back
in and enveloped her," she lets "her mind ebb away" (FYK, 55–6).
When she falls asleep in front of her gas oven, her death seems like a
suicide though MacDonald has constructed such a clean plotline that
the reader understands that in fact she has been murdered by the
gender code that demanded her compliance and then extinguished
her identity.

If compliance is lethal, complicity is no less problematic. Mercedes,
James's second daughter, willingly steps into Materia's place, declaring "I'm the mother now," in no small part because she longs for the
approval and power she receives as she works within her father's
system. Complicity is more damaging than compliance, for Mercedes
not only loses any opportunity she might have to define herself, she
eventually hurts and nearly destroys those she claims to protect. As
she actively embeds herself in the rigid moral, spiritual, racial, and
sexual binaries that structure the dominant culture, she willingly betrays the individuals she loves in the vain hope that her actions will
elevate and restore the name of the family in the public's eyes. Not
only is she an abusive authoritarian teacher whom "everyone fears,"
but MacDonald carefully traces how her desire to establish herself
within the patriarchy leads her first to betray both Frances, to whom
she lies about Anthony's death, and Lily, who she attempts to force
into the role of saint. She is willing to deny the individuality and
unique gifts of her sisters, and as she realizes that she is "damned"
for her complicity, she, like her mother, contemplates suicide before
finally recognizing that she can only restore herself if she admits her
family's torturous past and makes reparations for her selfishness.

MacDonald successfully embeds her characters within complex environments and then carefully, even systematically, documents the negative impact those patriarchal traditions have on each figure.

While MacDonald wants to document the negative effects that a masculinist, heterosexual, and racist culture has on the individual, she also longs to explore the opportunities available to those few individuals who dare to resist the dominant system. But as she turns to explore the personalities of Kathleen, Frances, and Lily, it is interesting to note that she seems to doubt that their search for freedom can succeed within the thoroughly contextualized world she has imagined. Indeed, in an attempt to uphold the characters who resist or rebel against the established system, MacDonald is willing to suspend the conventions of realism and employ a variety of other narrative techniques.

In her study of *Fall On Your Knees*, Jennifer Andrews notes that MacDonald blends together a number of formal traditions. For example, throughout the text, MacDonald is willing to draw on the conventions of the gothic novel in order to trace Frances's resistance to her father's world. From her midnight baptism of Kathleen's twins to Ambrose's subsequent burial beneath the scarecrow, from her descent into the hell of the burlesque night-club scene to her mythic seduction of Ginger in the abandoned cave, MacDonald regularly employs gothic motifs in order to express both the difficulty and the extent of Frances's resistance. Frances certainly launches one of text's most persistent attempts to operate apart from the patriarchy, and, though she does manage to nurture and sustain others, she cannot finally save herself. She resists the gender and racial binaries of her society by transgressing the norms governing sexual purity and actively seeking a black lover in the hopes of creating a child of mixed race; such a child would force a permanent rupture in the ordered world constructed by James and Mercedes. Just as she succeeds is bringing such a child into her world, so she is able to help many lost souls. Through her melodramatic act of forgiveness, she heals some of the bitterness that infects Teresa, who has suffered at the hands of a racist society. Through her stash of money, saved from her years of work in the sex industry, she is able to send Lily to New York, where she is reunited with her mother's lover, Doc Rose. And through her brutal commitment to the truth, she is finally able to force Mercedes to admit the tragic secret of Lily's parentage. But Frances is not able to completely free herself. When she thinks she has lost her son, Anthony, she loses much of her rebellious spark and becomes an emblem of maternity; she slows down, sits beside her suffering father, and cooks massive meals that are picked up and consumed by some of the institutions that had previously oppressed her, "the hospital, the rectory, the convent" (*FYK*, 555).

Just as a series of gothic transgressions are unable to fully liberate Frances, so MacDonald is unable to liberate Kathleen, even after switching to the techniques of magic realism. James and Materia's eldest daughter first seems to be the epitome of the patriarchal system: her physical beauty and lovely voice combine with her economic and racial status to make her the golden child of her society. But, as Andrews notes, her determination to follow her heart and pursue her love for Rose, her black accompanist, transforms her into the text's most transgressive character, as she "problematizes patriarchal and heterosexual constructions of what femaleness is all about" (1999, 13). While Andrews traces the influence of magic-realist techniques throughout the novel, she notes that MacDonald draws from that tradition in particular near the end of the novel, when Kathleen's diary moves to the foreground. Magic realist techniques suspend the normal causal logic of realism and contest

"the notion of history as a linear and logical phenomenon from a wide variety of perspectives by including superstition, folklore, and the voices of the otherwise neglected members of the population ... Magic realism pays particular attention to places and communities that have been marginalized. Magic, in this context, becomes a tools for challenging power structures and may facilitate that metamorphoses of characters and communities." (Andrews 1999, 4)

MacDonald draws on these formal conventions as Kathleen's lyrical, poetic, and sometimes nonlinear entries chronicle her desire for Rose and their mutual discovery of their own complicated heritage. They transgress the conventional gender roles, and, by "communing with ghosts, both women experience a dimension of themselves that momentarily transcends the realities of time and space" (Andrews 1999, 14). But while these ventures into magic realism help MacDonald document the richness of the experiences that await those who dare to venture beyond the boundaries established by the patriarchy, she does not suggest that these dominant forces can be escaped. James assaults Kathleen, and her resulting pregnancy and subsequent death remind the reader, in brutal terms, that the destructive reach of the patriarchal arm is long. MacDonald values freedom, self-expression, tolerance, and individuality enough to suspend the realist conventions that structure her text and employs a series of other literary devices in order to explore these ideals, but in the end she retains serious reservations that the patriarchal systems she carefully reproduces can be overturned. The maternal and feminist impulse is celebrated as the source of life, authenticity, and hope, but in this text most loving figures – particularly loving mothers, including Mrs Mahmoud, Materia, Kathleen, and Frances – end up as corpses, leaving only fragments behind to comfort the children who never really got to know them. Certainly, the reunion of Lily, Rose, and Anthony in the final pages confirms that the people who have been marginalized can find truth and a sense of identity through their interdependence, but as they come together and have a final "cuppa tea," we remember that there are a horrifying number of broken bodies lying just off in the wings. Those who resist the patriarchy emerge as more engaged characters than those who comply or submit, but the grim opening resonates throughout the text, and we are always aware that, "They're all dead now." MacDonald has articulated one of the most intricate, and certainly the most widely read, exploration of gender in the Maritimes.

PATRIARCHY'S WAKE

There is always a danger, when exploring a group of writers who address similar issues and concerns, that the very act of critiquing their work as a unit could produce a reductive version of a complex field. While this chapter runs the risk of ghettoizing these women writers by bringing them into the foreground as a group, that risk is worth taking if it demonstrates the powerful and productive relationship that has developed in the Maritimes between realism and feminism. The fiction that has emerged from this conversation between form and ideology has given voice to the most important shift to occur in the final decades of the twentieth century. The political positions themselves are not entirely new, for the texts of each of these recent writers has been exploring the efficacy of various forms of liberalism. But the central cultural issues that form the ground on which the political issues are negotiated are fresh: in the wake of a long period of patriarchal fictions, these recent texts are exploring a different set of assumptions. Recent realist feminist fictions have helped complicate and advance the region's literature, and although women writers have been engaged in their work for two decades, there are still many stories waiting to be recovered.

8 Diverging Streams: Fiction at the End of the Century

NOSTALGIA IN THE LATE TWENTIETH CENTURY

Nicole stared at the letter, trying to recall the early days when she was a child. But the pictures she remembered most clearly were the more recent ones: her father alone in his chair, the invisible wall that surrounded him, the disappointment, the anger, the failure. And yet, somewhere, behind all that, there had once been this … He had had a life before them.

Simone Poirier-Bures, *Candyman*

Since the 1940s, realism has been the genre most often employed by Maritime writers to explore a multitude of themes and to reproduce a variety of political perspectives, and yet beneath this diversity lies a persistent and coherent sense of regional identity. Maritime fiction writers have shaped their ideological concerns around the region's deeper cultural tensions; tensions that have arisen as the region has struggled through its uneasy transformation from an intensely communal traditional economy, towards its fragmented and incomplete existence within a modern industrial state. While the region's authors have reacted differently to these place-shaped concerns – the shared memories of a past security and the collective fear of an unpromising future – these cultural tensions have remained at the core of their various texts. Thus, as it has been pulled between the two dominant cultural tensions of nostalgia and hesitation, Maritime realist fiction has attained a distinctive character that sets its apart from the literatures produced in the other regions of Canada. None of the fictions written in the final decade of the century have completely fused these two cultural impulses, and perhaps we are now past that unique moment inhabited by Buckler, when the two strands of longing and anxiety can be tightly bound in a single work. (MacLeod may be the exception to this rule, in that *No Great Mischief* draws on both of these cultural impulses, though they are not as smoothly interconnected as they could be.) Buckler produced his fiction at a time when he could tap into a personal and living memory of the cultures embedded in the traditional primary economies, while still being able to clearly identify the full impact of modernism. By century's end, that traditional economy and culture has largely been erased from the experience of contemporary writers, and thus the sense of memory and nostalgia within recent texts tends to be of a more local and personal nature. Similarly, the sense of uncertainty that Buckler anticipates in his best fiction, has hardened into a deeper sense of despair as multiple generations have lived with the seemingly unsolvable problem of underdevelopment. Thus, the final chapter will examine the ways in which recent fictions follow one stream or another, and either reproduce a nostalgic sensibility or a more fatalistic sense of despair as they contemplate the past and future of the region. Of these two currents, nostalgia is the more popular.

The nostalgic impulse is a complex force within Maritime culture. Though nostalgia has sometimes been carefully manufactured, manipulated, shaped, and marketed as a part of the tourist industry's desire to promote the region as a retreat from the modern world – a haven from the rush of industrial life – there is a more persistent and less commodified "memory of a shared community" that has also played a role in Maritime culture throughout the twentieth century. Writers in recent years have continued to explore this realm of memory – or reconstructed memory – and have produced texts that look to the past, in order to recall some aspect or experience that will enrich a diminished present. For as long as nostalgia has been used by writers as a way of creating a version of the world that differs from their own unsatisfying contemporary condition, the genre has tempted writers to produce sentimental or overly idyllic texts. Nostalgia need not produce an overly sweet tone, however, and, in a number of recent texts, versions of the region can be found that span the lyrical, the elegiac, and the tragic. Such writers as Linda McNutt, Alan Wilson, and Simone Poirier-Bures have avoided producing sentimental or sanitized versions of the past; instead, they have found personal moments of remembered continuity. Indeed, a number of these recent writers have turned to the genre of the fictional memoir as a means of reconnecting with the past and relocating a coherent sense of self and community.

Drawing in part on her own youth in New Brunswick, Linda McNutt taps into a nostalgic vein as her central narrator/protagonist remembers the childhood summers she spent at her family's cottage. Published in 1997, *Summer Point* is a record of comparative serenity. The first-person narrator is a young adult named Sarah. She has recently inherited the family cottage on the Northumberland Strait, where, as a child, she spent her summer holidays. As she reflects on her new responsibilities as an owner, she remembers one particular year when she spent the entire summer with her Aunt Maud, while her father recovered from a heart attack and her mother cared for her newborn brother. Though the narrator does not diminish the fear, anxiety, and loneliness she felt as a child, the adult Sarah recognizes that her summer of relative independence was formative, in that she gradually experienced a complex social environment and began to recognize her own role within that broader community.

The style of the prose is lyrical but not self-consciously poetic, and the text is clearly framed within the discourses of realism as the narrative maintains a stable community of characters whom Sarah gradually meets and considers. At the beginning of the novel, young Sarah is a self-involved child who "ostentatiously" leaves her copy of *Othello* "lying around" in the hope that it will be noticed by the adults whose attention she craves (*SP*, 22). After her father collapses, her concern is primarily for herself: "I sat at the table, kicking my feet against the rungs of my wooden chair. My throat was tight. My parents had left me here with The Aunts" (*SP*, 29). In the course of the summer, however, she meets a diverse and, one might even argue, unlikely group of individuals, and as she begins to appreciate the diverse foibles and needs of those around her, she begins the gradual process of maturation.

In terms of Sarah's own experience, the summer place is home for two populations of people, each of which have a distinct impact on her. There are the elderly relatives to whom she is directly responsible, and there are the local children whose backgrounds and outlooks are different from her own. The elderly crew prove to be an eccentric lot. Sarah's Aunt Maud, her father's elder sister, is a tender individual who is able to transgress the gender norms of her society, abandon her dirty kitchen for others to clean, and retreat with a book for hours at end. She is a removed, enigmatic figure, whom "no one ever touched ... I don't know why. I never asked why" (*SP*, 82). But if she is carefully controlled, Aunt Maud is also compassionate, as she and her niece establish a ritual of searching for wrapped library books before they settle down together for a long afternoon of reading. From her aunt, Sarah learns that emotions are a complex web, and that patience and care is required of those who seek to decode the behaviours of another.

If Maud is a quiet and contained soul, Uncle K is a more overtly odd man. Shell-shocked in the First World War, an experience about which "he could never be made to talk," he returns to New Brunswick with a stutter, a drinking problem, an aversion to regular work, and deep empathy for all beings. Unconcerned with the conventional norms of society, Uncle K skips church, goes to the town tavern, befriends the local pariahs, the Whittakers, and is periodically escorted off to jail for drunkenly "taking off his clothes and rolling on the carefully sculpted lawn" (*SP*, 136). Yet for all his foibles, Uncle K is one of the community's more authentic and caring figures, and the text conveys his tale with a considerable sense of longing as Sarah recognizes that such eccentric yet real identities are difficult to craft in the conformist world of the modern urban setting. Apart from these two central figures, Sarah is also alert to the other idiosyncratic characters on the Strait including Aunt Wynd who cheats at bridge, Aunt Byrd who compulsively bosses all around her, and the middle-age lesbian couple, Margaret and Lavinia, whose sexuality cause a mild stir in the conventional community. Each of these figures provide living examples of the wide variety and potential of the human personality. In a sense, the memories of these figures become guiding points for the older narrator, who can justify her own unique artistic choices by citing the picturesque characters who preceded her.

But if the older characters demonstrate that some social conventions should be transgressed in the search for a stable identity, other limits are only to be violated at considerable risk to the individual. *Summer Point* records Sarah's adventures with a variety of other children and occasionally they traverse borders and enter a more troubled territory. With the Ontario boy named Chester, Sarah experiences her first kiss. Through this innocent and enlightening encounter, she discovers that although she "is supposed to feel overpowered, vulnerable, pressured, bashful," she actually feels "intrigued, powerful, [and] compassionate towards this shaking boy" (*SP*, 50). Other events that summer are of a more disturbing nature, as she meets the troubled local girl, Eli Whittaker, and confronts her new friend's anger and bitterness at her impoverished home life. Eli has been raised in a rough and uncaring environment, and when she falls and breaks her ankle, her selfish family barely recognize her pain and fear. Clearly, if an individual is to have a complete identity she needs the support and protection of a larger community. Without those forces, McNutt argues, Eli is a doomed character. Eager to express her anger, Eli takes Sarah out "to break into cottages" and encourages her apprentice to steal "stuff ... that means a lot to those people" who could "afford to spend their summers at the sea" (*SP*, 62). If the summer cottage is in part a repository for positive memories of eccentric personalities, Eli's presence in the novel demonstrates that the past also harbours pain and fear, and these too broaden Sarah's understanding. By the conclusion, all these aspects of the larger society have been deeply integrated into the older narrator's personality. As the adult Sarah proceeds to close up the cottage, she watches her new boyfriend carefully and judges his reactions to the summer rituals as a way of gauging his reactions to the essential components of her own personality. In this lyrical form of nostalgia it is possible to integrate the past into the present; it is possible to leave the place of childhood and plan to return in the spring.

For other writers, returning to the past proves to be a more difficult affair, and sometimes the nostalgic impulse is wedded to a more elegiac sensibility in order to convey the notion that some conditions can never be reproduced. In the first volume of a projected trilogy, Alan Wilson draws from autobiographical materials to construct a narrative that examines the forces of change and longs to resist those powers. Published in 1999, *Before the Flood* brings together two narrative forms as Wilson both chronicles the adolescence of Samuel MacFarlane and documents the life of the small town of Woodstock before it is transformed by the flood waters of the Mactaquac dam. As might be expected in a text that examines both the development of the individual and the life of the town, Wilson's *Before the Flood* reproduces a communitarian liberalism that defends the notion that identity must be forged or refined in the immediate context of a solid community.

Before the Flood is first of all a bildungsroman; the novel's thirteen chapters follow Samuel MacFarlane through his fifteenth and sixteenth years. Like McNutt, Wilson employs Samuel as both narrator and central character, and the adolescent who emerges from the text is intelligent, articulate, a bit bookish, and occasionally annoying in his self-interested and myopic perceptions. Given his youth, he is a bit limited in his experience, but he is aware of his foibles and his progress towards a sense of independence is clearly marked. In the early chapters, Samuel is more child than adult, as he bows to his father's demand that he "get a haircut" and allows himself to become entirely obsessed with "a table hockey game that preoccupies [him and his friends] for a whole winter" (Compton 1999, 110). As the tale unfolds, his initial compliance turns inevitably towards youthful defiance, and eventually he moves beyond the realm of parental authority. When his mother "advanc[es] on him with a wooden spoon" intending to enforce her demand that he stay home, Samuel "grab[s] her wrist ... and yank[s] away the spoon and thr[ows] it across the waxed floor" (*BF*, 161). The boy is slowly transforming into a man, and even the mother must admit that "those days are over" (*BF*, 161).

If Wilson has employed the standard elements of the novel of education, some aspects of that form are recast to meet the writer's needs. Unlike some of the regional bildungsromans by such writers as Bruce, Buckler, and Nowlan, Wilson tends to underrepresent Samuel's relationships with his parents and immediate family. The autobiographical roots of the narrative may make this territory difficult to represent or critique, but, with the exception of a few incidents, like that involving the spoon, the family's identity is not fully developed. In lieu of a complete family, the protagonist develops in relation to his broader community of friends and the collection of "wise oddities" that make up the village's population (Compton 1999, 111). If the parents are rather thinly drawn, Samuel's peers emerge as a more complex and intriguing set of characters. By constructing such diverse figures as the oddly intellectual and self-confident Andrew and the bawdy, rowdy Virgil, Wilson creates a set of friends who allow Samuel to discover and contemplate the competing impulses in his own personality. He pursues his own love of astronomy and learns to read the skies, at the same time as he scours his house in search of safe hiding places for his diary and his risqué pencil drawings of cheerleaders. When the three lads take an epic canoe trip down the Saint John River just before it is sealed by the new dam, Samuel has clearly integrated some of his friend's strengths into his own personality. The voyage is shaded with a sense of irony; Samuel sleeps most the way downstream. With a comic touch untainted by a hint of condescension, Wilson brings to life the victories of self-discovery and the minor traumas of adolescence through which Samuel learns to accept his own idiosyncrasies.

But exploring Samuel's gradual maturation is only part of Wilson's project in this novel. *Before the Flood* is also a memoir, not of Wilson's own childhood but of the town of Woodstock, which in the late 1960s was about to be transformed and reshaped by the "technological wonder" of the Mactaquac dam. Wilson contributes to a long tradition in Maritime fiction, as he produces an elegiac tone and records the richness of life in a small town before it is swamped, in this case literally, by twentieth-century technology. Many Maritime writers from Ernest Buckler to Alistair MacLeod have celebrated the humane values of the rural world and lamented the encroachments of urban and modern sensibilities. Wilson is usually subtle, and at times even poetic, as he remembers and reconstructs his small town. He represents it as a close-knit community in which eccentric individuals are gossiped about, tolerated, and protected. The cat-loving albino owner of the Nighthawk Café, who prefers to serve customers at midnight, the Alzheimer's afflicted Miss Baird, who emerges as a subtle symbol as she searches for her childhood home, and the young lonely Arthur, who celebrates his birthday with a marsh-mellow roast in the graveyard, are memorable characters. They are sharply drawn and interesting figures who evoke our sense of compassion not just for their individual plights, but for the town they inhabit. Indeed, the reader and the narrator/character gradually appreciate that identity can only be formed and supported within a larger community. As Samuel recognizes that his town is about to be reshaped by the forces of "progress," he and the readers understand that the question of identity itself is being challenged by technology. Wilson is thus able to fuse his bildungsroman with its assertion of communitarian values and his more nostalgic celebration of the not-so-distant past.

The nostalgic impulse – the desire to fondly remember the things that never were – is a difficult force to control, but as Wilson memorializes his "once upon a time" town, he includes numerous portraits of troubled or lost characters who remind us that not all aspects of the past were idyllic. A chapter about an old eccentric butterfly collector remind us that a few of the townspeople have a deep understanding of time and its relentless pressures. Yet even as Templeman expands his collection of insects, the reader cannot help but recognize that the past can be captured and retained only if it is first killed. The half-crazed United Church minister who is tormented by his fundamentalist past also acts as a handy emblem of the valley's emotionally difficult religious heritage. And the cruel English teacher who mocks her students and employs her "hair trigger venom" to enforce her style of "brutalized learning" reminds the reader not to yearn for all aspects of the past (BF, 124, 140). Wilson's generally balanced memories of a bygone era more then compensate for the occasionally didactic moments when the text is marred by a palpable regret that the old-fashioned town was swept away by time and flood waters. The mysterious character of old Noah, the fisherman who casts his line throughout the text, becomes an overly obvious symbol of the river's heritage and a strained lament for the death of the river. Fortunately, such didactic moments temper but do not endanger the complex sense of nostalgia to be found in the novel.

If the impulse to look back inspires sometimes lyrical, sometimes elegiac fictions, the desire to record the losses of the past can also produce a tragic sensibility. Some texts – for example, Alistair MacLeod's *No Great Mischief* – look back in order to examine the tragic demise of a passing way of life. The same potent sense of regret is evident in Simone Poirier-Bures's first novel. Poirier-Bures notes that she began *Candyman* when, on the anniversary of her father's death she "got to remembering what [he] was like," "began writing things down," "realised that my random recollections didn't add up to much of a story," and subsequently "invented the life that I imagined my parents must have experienced" (Poirier-Bures, "A Few Words," 1). Having started to write through memory and having completed the text through imagination, *Candyman* reproduces the Maritime sensibility in the second half of the twentieth century. It is a rare text in Maritime literature; a novel that is set in the suburbs of Halifax in the decades following the Second World War. In a tiny house, on a small plot of land, Charles and Claire LeBlanc play out their postwar family drama. As Poirier-Bures constructs a record of the past and chronicles the demise of her small Acadian family, she blends the nostalgic with the tragic and sometimes the pathetic.

Charles LeBlanc is a kind of everyman, an emblem of the postwar Maritimes. In the opening scene he is fifty-seven, and, though he is past his prime and newly unemployed, he initially possesses a kind of confident certainty. Forced to become a small business man selling candy to corner stores, despite his years of experience as an engineer, economist, manager, columnist, salesman, and farmer, Charles is initially a vibrant father, reminiscent of Buckler's Joseph Canaan. He is "the big hubby" ("Le Gros Mari") who longs to care for his young wife, Claire, and their four children, as he mops the floor and does the "heavy work" (c, 7). The opening pages establish that love and domestic peace are possible, but these brief moments of plentitude cannot withstand the harsh environment. After a debilitating heart attack, Charles begins the slow decline into illness and old-age that will claim his spirit. Poirier-Bures is careful to create moments of contentment early in her novel, but, unlike McNutt, she does not pretend that these brief moments can be reclaimed or recovered. As the tale unfolds, Charles struggles to maintain his family. His candy business furnishes a meagre living, but overtaxed and underemployed, Charles's spirit and body are exhausted and eventually defeated as he is forced out of business by the highly competitive big industry wholesalers. As he enters a period of decline – like the region itself – the narrative ceases to be focalized through his perspective, turning instead to the mother, and then the second daughter in an effort to relay the story through a position that is not wedded to a sense of despair. By the end of the novel the many creditors of his bankrupt business threaten the security of the family, but Charles, paralysed and confused by a world he no longer understands, retreats and sits "in his chair like a lump of dough" (c, 142). He passes control of his family and his life over to his wife and retires in humiliation and disgrace. Poirier-Bures traces the inadequacies of the patriarchal system that placed the economic reins in Charles's hands, but at the same time even the daughter cannot help but long for the time when her father tried to steer and aid his family.

With Charles in retreat, Claire, his young wife, emerges as the breadwinner for the family and the next central focalizer in the text. Claire is less passive than Charles, though no happier. Her life also acts as a representation in miniature of the region's transformation in the postwar era as she makes the unhappy transition from her childhood on a rural farm to her existence as an astute urban teacher. The text reproduces her longing to return to the village of her childhood "along Saint Mary's bay, where everyone knew everyone," but Poirier-Bures subverts her sentimentality when, at the end of a summer family vacation to her rural home, her son contracts typhoid. She cannot "go home" again. Claire eventually reshapes her identity, loses her homespun character, returns to her career as a teacher, and draws her family back from the brink of financial ruin. It is not a heroic story, however, for her string of boyfriends and her alienation from her daughters confirm that Claire's spirit, as much as Charles's, has been exhausted by urban life. This husband and wife – these parental figures from the 1950s and 1960s – have been recast within the writer's late twentieth-century sensibility, and, while both try desperately to achieve their dreams, they are able only to acknowledge their own gradual diminishment.

As Claire begins her descent into despair, the narration once again shifts in order to focalize the text through the eyes of the next character who is going through a moment of transformation. When the parents settle into their shabby urban perspectives, the narrator focalizes through Nicole the second daughter. She becomes the postwar poster child, whose intelligence will allow her to enter the new economy. Thoughtful and highly disciplined, she excels in school, wins a scholarship, and leaves her region to study in New York. Yet even as she modernizes herself, the narrator records with a sense of regret and irony that she chooses to abandon her "country French," her Acadian dialect and heritage, in order to adopt the "Parisian pronunciation. She could trill her Rs like a real French girl" (C, 144). Nicole escapes from the suburban trap that had closed around her parents, but she cannot help but feel a sense of longing for the family life she never experienced. The reader empathizes with her sense of sorrow when she realizes her father is going to die before she gets a chance to really know him, and her mourning for her father echoes the late twentieth century's cultural experience that a previous era is almost beyond memory. Nicole's mind will not stretch back far enough to recover that hopeful past, but, as she reflects on the circumstances that destroyed her father, she feels the full force of the tragedy of his life, and closes the text with a speech that echoes Cordelia's longing for her own misunderstood and willful king: "Nicole stared at [the love letter her father had written her mother before they were married], trying to recall the early days when she was a child. But the pictures she remembered most clearly were the most recent ones: her father alone in his chair, the invisible wall that surrounded him, the disappoint-ment, the anger, the failure. And yet, somewhere, behind all that, there had once been this. He had noticed things. He had felt things. He had had a life before them. And she had thrown him away, like a shabby old box, not knowing what was hidden inside" (*c*, 154). Like many citizens of the modern world, she remains haunted by his memory, but she is haunted somewhere outside the Maritimes.

The nostalgic impulse that has long been a part of the Maritime ex-perience, has also been a significant force within the region's litera-ture. But as these recent novels demonstrate, this desire to look back, this longing for a now distant security or wholeness, is not simple. Each writer combines this nostalgic sensibility with their own lyric or tragic perspective to produce a wide variety of fictions. But Maritime culture is not always absorbed by the backward glance. Some writers attend to the immediate present and these have often produced fic-tions that view the world with a sense hesitation that has bordered on the edge of despair.

CHRONICLES OF DESPAIR

> I'm tired … Tired of everything … Tired of me. Tired of you.
> Tired of us." You pressed your thumbs into your temples and
> made circles. "I feel like putting a bullet into my head."
>
> Leo McKay Jr, "Oil"

Since the initial emergence of realism, some Maritime writers have used the form to explore the bleaker aspects of the region's culture. Nowlan, MacLeod, and Richards started their careers chronicling the sense of despair and even nihilism that has plagued some communi-ties in the region. And while Smyth, Bruneau, and Coady have at-tempted to conclude their texts by focusing on the salutary effects of the community, they too have documented the violence and resigna-tion that moves within aspects of the region's culture. Indeed, given the ongoing uncertainties and the persistent economic hardships that have plagued the Maritimes throughout the twentieth century, it is not surprising that at least a few writers would emerge to explore that sense of hesitation, anxiety, and ennui that is endemic to the re-gion's heritage. Less plentiful than those who adopt a nostalgic tone, these authors need to be considered in any examination of recent literature.

Sheldon Currie, an English professor at St FX in Antigonish, Nova Scotia, has produced two collections of short fiction – *The Glace Bay Miners' Museum* (1979) and *The Story So Far* (1997) – and a novel, *The*

Company Store (1988). But Currie is probably best known for his book-length revision of "The Glace Bay Miners' Museum," released in 1995, after a film based on the story won national attention. The novella focuses on the narrator/heroine Margaret MacNeil and her relationship with Neil Currie, a piper turned miner in Glace Bay, Cape Breton. From the opening scene, in which the lovers begin their courtship by declaring that the other is the biggest and smallest "son of a bitch I ever saw," it is clear that Currie is deconstructing the form of the romance in order to unveil not only the frailty of those romance conventions, but to develop a critique of the larger society that systematically extinguishes vibrant individuals.

Currie unabashedly plays with the formula of the romance in the early sections of *The Glace Bay Miners' Museum*. Given that both Margaret and Neil are outsiders in the community, it is immediately evident that destiny has brought these two together, an impression that Currie reinforces by having Neil come over to her house each night to serenade his beloved – with his bagpipes. Functioning as an emotional replacement for the father and brother whom Margaret has already lost in mining accidents, Neil brings to the troubled young woman a sense of happiness. But Neil is not just a knight errant for Margaret, he is representative of a whole alternate culture to the raw industrial capitalism that plagues the city. Currie is the embodiment of the older Gaelic culture. He speaks the language that others have forgotten, if only to tease Margaret by calling her his little "groyach," that is, his "little pain in the arse" (*mm*, 34). Similarly, Neil functions as a kind of repository for Celtic history and music, which was in danger of being lost, given that only Margaret's grandfather, a voiceless and breathless old man, knew the old ways.

Neil thus represents the traditional culture, but Currie insists that he is not a representation of the Folk as Innocent, the cultural production that Ian McKay argues is a tool by which class conflicts and economic injustices are veiled. In contrast, Neil and Margaret are rough-edged manifestations of their culture. Neil is troubled by the historical inequities that have plagued his community; he stands on the beaches, staring across the Atlantic, becoming "crosser and crosser" about the injustices visited upon his ancestors. He then channels this anger, first into music and later into labour activities. He and Margaret's brother Ian lead the workers in a strike against the company that exploits them. Though the strike does not accomplish their goals, Currie has clearly demonstrated that Neil's energy constitutes a vibrant reply to the modern, capitalist economy.

But the real power of the text emerges not as Neil galvanizes the workers in the attempt to improve their condition – indeed, Margaret passes over the strike itself with surprisingly few words – but in Margaret's reaction after Neil and Ian die in the mines. In a single accident, the labour leaders and the cultural heritage of the region are eliminated. In some ways the deaths are hardly a surprise. A tragic figure-in-waiting from the outset, Margaret has alluded to Neil's death in earlier sections. But if Neil's death is expected, Margaret's reactions are not. Refusing to simply mourn her husband's passing or to slip off into a passive madness like some Cape-Breton-Ophelia, Margaret closets herself with the bodies and disassembles them. She dissects the corpses and places Neil's lungs, his fingers, his tongue, Ian's "dick," and her grandfather's lungs in pickle jars full of formaldehyde. Though her community thinks she has gone insane with grief, Margaret herself insists that she wants those particular body parts as a physical reminder of the men and their essential identities. Her private memories are then reshaped into public artifacts, and, as an act of personal resistance and political agency, Margaret sets up her own "Glace Bay Miners' Museum." Bypassing the conventional artifacts of the industrial collections, she displays the fragments from her loved ones as a replacement and supplement for the vibrant culture that the modern industrial economy has murdered. As the text closes and we realize that the first-person narrator is addressing her first visitor to the museum, we recognize that Margaret herself has become a repository and living memory of the region. In order to fully mourn the failure of the modern society to uphold the communitarian perspective, the conventional romance formula has been subverted by the forces of melodrama and the casual logic dictated by the traditions of realism. Currie's narrator has slipped into a powerful sense of despair that borders on the edge of madness.

While Currie explores the life and struggles of the larger Glace Bay community, Leo McKay's collection of minimalist short stories, *Like This*, published in 1995, produces more intimate portraits that are so firmly anchored in the discourse of naturalism that both nostalgia and optimism are discredited as options. McKay's short stories stand in stark contrast to the fiction produced by Alistair MacLeod in the late 1960s and in the 1970s. MacLeod's characters move through a deterministic world but are afforded, within the confines of the rigid culture, desperate economy, or harsh environment, the opportunity to make small choices. Indeed, in his later fiction MacLeod produces a nostalgic tone, by invoking the romance and folk conventions of the Gaelic past. McKay's characters seem disconnected from their cultural heritage and are immersed in the immediate, insurmountable problems of the present.

McKay's stories explore the small moments in the lives of society's poorest and least powerful members. His texts carve out very small territories, and his first-person narrators do not usually have the ability or the background to provide informative overviews of their own lives. The story ironically titled "A New Start" depicts the grim lives of an impoverished family as they eat a Kraft Dinner meal, after which "Daddy" takes the two children on a collection round of the local dumpsters in a search for bottles to supplement the family's welfare cheque. The trio of searchers are guided by an admirable middle-class work ethic as they scavenge with determination and skill, but, when the father must momentarily trap the kids in a mall dumpster in order to avoid being detected by the police, McKay provides a jarring image of how the underclass are becoming a disposable commodity in the contemporary world. Indeed, these fictions echo a strong left-wing perspective as protagonists are continuously aware of their class position and their inability to change it.

The small band of recyclers hit pay dirt when they go to a local university and visit a local men's dorm, where they are literally showered with bottles. But it is clear that they are being mocked, not helped, by the students who toss their empties out their windows: "Hey mister bottle man. Let's see you dance for a bottle" (LT, 75). The immediate daily lives of the poor are difficult, and given that the university is training the next generation of business and social leaders, it is obvious that the lives of the disenfranchised will not be getting better in the future. Though the family has moved to the new town and avoided contact with Children's Welfare in order to escape from their past problems, the story ends with the father taking their night's earnings and heading off to the liquor store across the street. The penniless drunks, who existed only on the margins of mid-century Maritime novels like *The Channel Shore*, have become the central figures at the end of the century.

McKay's brief story "Like This" is a similarly grim response to the region's earlier depictions of the idyllic nuclear family. In the opening scene, a teenage son, who is watching television with his mother, awaits the return of his drunken father. Unlike any of the fathers represented in other Maritime fictions, including those produced by Bruneau and Coady, McKay's patriarch is only "two weeks out of the detox" when he "comes home ... drunk" (LT, 19). After he hits his wife across the face, the son decides to take matters into his own hands and goes "to the drawer under the counter and [pulls] out the butcher knife," before demanding that the old man "Turn around that door and get out" [sic] (LT, 21). After a fight in which both men are wounded, the father is finally knocked unconscious and "that's the end of him. For this night" (*LT*, 23). Refusing to reinscribe any of the conventional myths of the family, McKay does not attempt to resolve the conflict between the generations by having the father reform or leave. Knowing that "he done something bad, but he can't remember what," the best the father can offer his son is his own example as a failure. When the father hears the narrator declare "I ain't going back" to school, he "gets up from his chair and stands in the centre of the floor," presenting his wounded and broken body as material evidence of what will happen to the youth if he abandons his education. His subsequent speech is full of self-loathing, for both father and son know that he can offer little to his family: "tell me if you want to end up like this" (*LT*, 25). McKay represents the people living on the margins as lost souls; characters who are – despite their best intentions – trapped in very difficult situations. Throughout the collection, the author captures the sense of alienation and despair that moves through the region. When they choose to lift the veil of nostalgia, such writers as McKay and Currie are able to focus on the cycles of recession and enduring poverty that are undermining the social structures of the past. Indeed, although prophecy is often little more than blind speculation, given the persistent nature of the problems that have plagued the region and given that the Maritimes is unlikely to soon lose its status as a have-not region, we will likely see an increasing number of writers combine realism with these hesitant and despairing tones. It would not be surprising if more and even grimmer texts emerged in the future.

Realism's Wake: A Conclusion

wake: v. to stop sleeping, to rouse from sleep, to become alive
      or active
wake: n. a watch held over the body of a dead person before
      burial, sometimes accompanied by festivities
wake: n. the track left behind a moving ship; the track left
      by anything.

Gage Canadian Dictionary

In the course of the twentieth century, Maritime writers have consistently produced a wealth of fiction that has emerged as a complex and diverse body of literature. As each writer responded imaginatively to his or her particular time and place, drawing from the traditions of realism but blending this genre with other influences ranging from romance to magic realism, a wide variety of texts have been produced. Frank Parker Day's confident use of mythic patterns to restore David to a heroic position might seem unconnected to the grim naturalistic depiction David Adams Richards develops in the figure of Arnold. And the longing nostalgia and sense of regret that flows through so much of Ernest Buckler's fiction differs from the anti-nostalgia evident in the world of Lynn Coady and Ann-Marie MacDonald. And yet, in their different ways each of the writers considered here has returned to, reproduced, and reexamined the larger cultural experiences of the region. Though each of the texts could stand by itself within the wider fields of Canadian and international literatures, we gain even greater insight into them if we are also willing to see them as productions from a distinct cultural context. These texts are diverse, but they return to the same territory of nostalgia and hesitation as they create their vision of the world, and such similar impulses begin to connect these disparate parts into a larger literary whole. And, if we are willing to attend to these fictions as a larger body of work, they inform us about the distinct patterns of a larger culture: they tell us about the East Coast's particular sense of a past and its uniquely troubled relationship with the future. In the twentieth century, the Maritimes evolved into a culture of memory unleavened by dream, and realism has been an effective tool for writers who have attempted to articulate the vexed assumptions of their home.

And so this study has been about several kinds of wakes. Texts have been examined in which the writers, and through them the readers, awaken to a new, modern, and sometimes distressed version of the Maritimes. MacLennan's central character in *Barometer Rising*, Angus Murrey, wakes up on the morning of the explosion and recognizes that he is going to be able to face the difficult modern world which is emerging before him, and he immediately is granted an opportunity to test his resolution as Halifax is laid low by the explosion. In Bruce's *The Channel Shore*, Alan Marshall/Gordon awakes to a new identity as he asserts his independence in the defence of his community and his family. And in Budge Wilson's "The Leaving," young Elizabeth wakes to find that her mother has not only been transformed by her contact with the modern ideals of feminism, but that her own world will soon be reshaped by their fateful trip to the city. While some writers reproduce their region's awaking to the troubled conditions of modernism, others have sounded notes of nostalgia and sorrow, and sometimes their realist texts have seemed to function as literary wakes for a passing era. Raddall rescues his central characters in *The Nymph and the Lamp* and removes them to an island setting where they are safe from the ravages of a modern world, a chaotic twentieth-century society that he writes off as bankrupt. Buckler's sense of mourning is even stronger, as seen in his celebration the traditional agrarian social order and simultaneous documentation of its passing forever out of reach. And MacLeod's *No Great Mischief* is a compelling elegy to the demise of Calum MacDonald, the last true representative and symbolic embodiment of the traditional clan structure. Whether Maritime writers address the misremembered past or anticipate the future, realism has been the dominant tradition that has shaped and communicated the region's experience the twentieth century. Realism has been the vehicle of choice for many of the best writers of the twentieth century, and we cannot account for the literary identity of the Maritimes without recognizing the centrality of its role. Indeed, to spin the pun in one final direction, the genre is still so powerful that we have yet to determine what literary traditions may follow in its wake. Tracing the "track left behind," the legacy of this literary heritage, is a critical task that is still just beginning.

Certainly this study is but a small venture into a territory that remains largely unmapped. Since the renaissance of Canadian studies began in the mid-1960s, relatively little attention has been paid to the literatures of the Maritimes. There seem to be a number of forces that continually draw the eye away from the Maritime region, and these need to be brought into focus if they are to be overcome. First, in *Under Eastern Eyes*, the only full-length study of Maritime fiction, Janice Kulyk Keefer suggests that part of that lack of attention from "most Canadians outside the region, can perhaps be related to the Maritimes' general economic and political decline after 1867" (1987, 20). Since the region itself did not share in the economic prosperity that buoyed the central and western provinces, it is not surprising that there is much in Maritime realist fiction that does not fit into the various models and assumptions that have governed the fictions created in other parts of the country. The Maritimes have cast a small shadow within the national economic and cultural consciousness, and it should not startle us that, with a few exceptions, the region's realist texts have not attracted widespread critical interest.

Another reason for the lack of attention paid to Maritime realist texts may lie in the fact that, across Canada, realism itself has been attracting less critical attention. Long treated as the highest of literary genres, classic realism has more recently been viewed as passé, and critics have turned to neglected marginal texts or towards currently challenging and vigorous fields such as magic realism and postmodernism. Whether the sense of tentativeness and uncertainty that has affected the Maritimes for generations has stilled those voices that might otherwise have produced the types of literary experiments that would be attractive to this new wave of critics, or whether individual writers have simply not been interested in developing the intense parody and self-reflexivity that characterizes postmodernism, few recent East Coast writers have ventured beyond the discourses of realism, and thus few Maritime texts have benefited from the recent shifts in critical interest. Critics who are interested in the currents of postmodernism still turn their eye towards realist texts, but sometimes do so with a measure of condescension. Witness the patronizing opening paragraph from Donna Pennee's review of Richards's fifth novel, in which she declares, "Readers accustomed to some degree of self-consciousness in fiction will find little, if anything, to interest them in *Nights Below Station Street* … unless of course, the deja vu effect of reading a regional fictive documentary, still constitutes the apex of Canadian literary experience" (1990, 41). Fortunately, if the shifts in literary fashion have tended to bypass Maritime realist fiction, the emergence of new critical frameworks, particularly from poststructuralist theorists, have breathed new life into texts whose critical possibilities may seem to have been exhausted. Some critics have begun to reassess the realist texts of the Maritimes using new paradigms, and such ventures are particularly promising.

Whether or not Maritime texts win wide critical attention, realism will remain the dominant genre within this region. This study has certainly not provided an encyclopedic analysis of its subject, and the overview of recent Maritime writing is particularly incomplete, given that I have not examined – solely for the reason of limited space – the engaging work of numerous writers whose feminist, nostalgic, or despairing perspectives would have warranted their inclusion. For example, Elin Elgaard, Wayne Curtis, Leslie Choyce, Herb Curtis, and Rita Donovan could all have been included within this study. Nevertheless, this exploration has hopefully opened up territories and methodologies that could be extended to other writers. Many particular communities and subgroups inhabit the Maritimes, and their literary diversity warrants future exploration. It would be unfortunate if the rich collection of texts from the Maritimes should escape the appreciation of either readers or critics. The region's fictions will hopefully not echo the fate of Ivan Basterache – the protagonist of Richards's *Evening Snow Will Bring Such Peace* – whose headstone was "famous for a while, and then overgrown and forgotten altogether" (1990, 226).

Notes

CHAPTER ONE

1 While 15 percent of postwar prairie farms operated at the subsistence level, 54 percent and 67 percent of farms in Nova Scotia and New Brunswick were subsistence or part-time operations (Brym, 65).
2 In popular usage, The term "alienation" signifies a sense of being cut off from one's roots – a sense of feeling out of place in what should be "home." This more general meaning of alienation as dislocation is as applicable to the experience of Maritimers as is the more specific Marxist use of the term above.
3 A note of thanks to Darin Barney, a political scientist at the University of Ottawa, who helped me to define and clarify the terms conservatism, communitarianism, and liberalism. While reviewing this section, he suggested several valuable modifications and additions. All quotations attributed to him are taken from personal correspondence.

CHAPTER TWO

1 Short stories by Alice Jones and Susan (Morrow) Jones have been reprinted in *New Women: Short Stories by Canadian Women 1900–1920*, edited by Sandra Campbell and Lorraine McMullen. Basil King's novel, *In the Garden of Charity*, was reprinted by Tecumseh Press in 1996, with an introduction by John Coldwell Adams. Though some of the earlier Maritime books have tended to fall out of print, students of Maritime fiction have

been fortunate, by and large, in that the books of many of the region's most interesting authors are still in print. Throughout this study, I have tended to use, as primary texts, the editions that are most readily and reliably available. In many cases, this means the McClelland and Stewart *New Canadian Library* edition.

2 For a full discussion of Day's unpublished novels found in Frank Parker Day Papers at Dalhousie University Archives, see Andrew Seaman's "Heroes, Heroines and the Lost Kingdom in the Unpublished Novels of Frank Parker Day" (1993).

3 Day's correspondence with Broddy as well as the draft versions of his novel can be found among the Frank Parker Day papers that are housed at the Dalhousie University Archives under the heading MS 2, 288.

4 In his first two unpublished novels, MacLennan experimented with the styles of the preeminent modernist novelists of his day. Because Hemingway's narrative style focused too exclusively on the individual at the expense of the larger society, MacLennan rejected him as a model (Woodcock 1989, 16).

5 For an analysis of how Raddall's conservative ideology is reproduced in his early historical fictions, see David Creelman's "Conservative Solutions: The Early Historical Fiction of Thomas Raddall" (1995).

CHAPTER THREE

1 Since the novel's reappearance, critic John Moss has explored the "patterns of moral complexity" within the narrative by tracing the way individuals touch the whole community (1974, 178), Andrew Seaman has focused on the "unity and salvation rooted in the ongzing process of community living" as it is experienced by the people on the shore (1976, 30), and Andrew Wainwright has argued that Bruce "creates a timeless country" in which "time past" fuses with the present and future to generate a process of growth and fulfillment (1983, 242).

2 A more complete bibliographic history of when each story was written and published can be found in the discussion of the *Township* stories in Andrew Wainwright's "Hearsay History" in *World Enough and Time: Charles Bruce, a Literary Biography* (1988:).

CHAPTER FOUR

1 The links between Buckler's short stories and his first novel have been carefully traced by Alan Young in his article, "The Genesis of Ernest Buckler's *The Mountain and the Valley*" (1976b). The best of Buckler's short fiction was collected and published in 1975, under the title *The Rebellion of Young David and Other Stories*, by McClelland and Stewart. The most com-

plete overview of reviewer responses to Buckler's fictions can be found in Dvorak's *Ernest Buckler: Rediscovery and Reassessment* (2001).

2 Any reader interested in the philosophical underpinnings of Buckler's work would be well advised to examine Marta Dvorak's study *Ernest Buckler: Rediscovery and Reassessment* (2001). While Dvorak does not address the impact of local and regional experience on Buckler's fiction, she undertakes the most complete study to date of the complex intellectual and philosophical traditions with which Buckler was familiar and on which he anchored the ideas of his fictions.

3 The diaries of Rebecca Chase Kinsman Ells and Laura Kaulback Slaunenwhite – collected in *No Place Like Home, Diaries and Letters of Nova Scotia Women 1771–1938*, ed. by Margaret Conrad, Toni Laidlaw, and Donna Smyth (1988) – record the rigorous and exhausting work habits of two rural women who seem to have less leisure time to change their clothes and visit friends than the women of Buckler's Entremont.

CHAPTER FIVE

1 The editor of *The Wanton Troopers*, who oversaw the publication of the novel by Goose Lane Editions in 1988, misidentifies the year of the Canada Council grant and the completion date of the novel as 1960.

2 The use of the term "mosaic" to describe "a book made up of interrelated short stories, either with or without the use of interstitial material to join them together" (Lalumière, 2000) comes from science-fiction and fantasy criticism. As it vividly articulates the nature of those book-length works of fiction that neither "novel" nor "collection" can adequately describe, I have decided to extend its use to this study.

3 Nowlan first met Hatfield in Hartland before the young lawyer became the leader of the provincial Progressive Conservative party and the long serving premier of the province. Nowlan worked for Hatfield as a speech writer and benefited directly from the government's long-term commitment to the University of New Brunswick's writer-in-residence program.

4 In his 1998 article, "Various Persons Named Kevin O'Brien: Nowlan's Novel Response to the Critics," Milton notes that "in naming Kevin's antagonist Bob D'Entremont, Nowlan alludes to another Maritime *Kunstlerroman*, Ernest Buckler's *The Mountain and the Valley* ... Kevin's punch seems to respond in comic fashion to some anxiety of influence harboured to by his creator, Alden Nowlan; the stronger man, D'Entremont, stands in for the strong author-father Buckler, who needs to be conquered in order that the younger writer might be freed."

5 He obtained his Teacher's Certificate from the Nova Scotia Teacher's College, before taking his BA and B.Ed. from St Francis Xavier University and his MA from the University of New Brunswick in 1961.

6 All subsequent references to MacLeod's short stories are from *Island: The Collected Stories.*

7 For a more complete analysis of critics' attempts to view MacLeod as a postmodern writer, see Andrew Hiscock's article, " 'The Inherited Life': Alistair MacLeod and the Ends of History" (2000).

8 "The Boat" first was written in 1968, "The Vastness of the Dark" was published in 1971, and "In the Fall" was first published in 1973. "The Closing Down of Summer" first appeared in 1976, "The Tuning of Perfection" was first published in 1984, and "Vision" first appeared when *As Birds Bring Forth the Sun* was published in 1986.

9 Tony Tremblay noted, in his review of *No Great Mischief*, that the unusual circumstances leading to the novel's publication will enter the realm of legend: "the handwritten manuscript carried for ten years in the truck of his car; the summer trips to Cape Breton to shape its form and broaden its canvas, coax it along by little more than twenty pages a year in a rustic cabin without electricity or telephone; the coercion, then harassment, then hijacking by his publisher in a Toronto train station; and finally McClelland and Stewart's self-admitted bungling of its release date, disqualifying the novel for the Giller Prize and the Governor General's Award" (1999b, 271–2). In his article "Alligators in the Sewers: Publishing Alistair MacLeod" (2001), Douglas Gibson, a publisher for McClelland and Stewart, provides a more meticulous record of his firm's long anticipation of the novel and the editing decisions that helped polish the book.

10 In her article "Loved Labour Lost: Alistair MacLeod's Elegiac Ethos," Janice Kulyk Keefer argues that Calum's death represents the demise of a particular set of labour practices. She notes that the description of Calum's passing functions as an elegy "for a form of labour, an ethic and aesthetic of work which has vanished, and with it, the values and meanings that formed that very identity of the *Clann Chalum Ruaidh* and others like it in the Maritimes" (2001, 79).

11 The notion that MacLeod is a writer who reproduces the assumptions of the Celtic Diaspora is implied in Uwe Zagratzki's article "Neil Gunn and Alistair MacLeod: Across the Sea in 'Scotland,' " in which he compares MacLeod's short fiction to the work of the pre-eminent Scottish novelist Neil Gunn. The idea was articulated more forcefully in spring 2000 by Gwen Davies, in the course of conversations about MacLeod's work.

CHAPTER SIX

1 In his interviews and essays, Richards often sounds confident that complete freedom is possible. In his essay entitled "Power Games," Richards describes social power as a matrix of authority and force that operates completely apart from individual subjects, who can – if they have the

strength of will – conduct their lives free from its seductive charms. Though he presents power as something to which people are drawn – in which they "become enmeshed" – he finally declares that it is a force from which individuals can, should, and would divorce themselves, if only they understood that "power destroys us" (1994, 58, 61). It is, of course, too easy to hope that "power" can simply be avoided through an ideological "Just say no" program, and Richards's novels confirm that negotiating with power structures is a far more complex process than his essays and interviews suggest.

2 Given the size of his oeuvre, only these five novels will be examined in detail.

3 Four long interviews that examine Richards's early texts can be found in the appendices of Linda-Ann Sturgeon's MA thesis, *David Adams Richards: Loving Against the Odds* (1987).

4 This reading of Norman's character is deeply indebted the anonymous reader for McGill-Queens University Press whose comments shaped the revision of this section.

5 Criticism of David Adams Richards's texts falls into three categories: traditional, ideological, and celebratory. Of the substantive articles focusing on Richards, most critics have tended to examine his novels from traditional critical perspectives and have produced solid explorations of the writer's stylistic techniques, central moral concerns, and dominant themes. Philip Milner explores Richards's structural and stylistic complexities. The writer's technique has been of interest to both Susan Lever and Sheldon Currie, who examine Richards's evolution as an artist and trace the shift between the subjective mode of early work and the more analytic quality of the later fiction. William Connor has produced solid thematic readings tracing Richards's first novel's elegiac spirit and his first trilogy's interest in "escape and entrapment" (1986, 269), and a similar thematic perspective has been employed by George Byrne and Frances MacDonald, who have attempted to read Richards's fiction as moral allegory. In a similar vein, more recently, J. Russell Perkin has examined how Richards uses the "paradigms and imagery of Christianity in the name of a humanism which overlaps with religion" in order to oppose "a dogmatic social-scientific world view" (1998, 55). Janice Kulyk Keefer addresses issues of regional representation and argues that Richards creates literary texts out of a "sub or post literary world" (1987, 171). Kathleen Scherf was the first critic to engage in a more confrontational ideological approach: she argues that *Blood Ties* constructs essentialist yet "deeply feminist" representations of women (1991, 30). Her early work on the ideological implications of Richard's fiction has been extended by Frank Davey, Christopher Armstrong, and Herb Wyile, who have turned a critical eye towards Richards's recurring interest in individual freedom and

problems of determinism in contemporary society. A third critical camp
has emerged as scholars have taken up the task of celebrating Richards
and attacking those writers who have, in their eyes, failed to appreciate
the novelist's ideals. Richards has long felt a strong distrust for academ-
ics, and he has carefully examined the ways in which the systems of priv-
ilege tied to universities have further marginalized the vulnerable sectors
of society. But a number of critics have adopted Richards's skepticism and
have championed his work as if to defend it against the academy. Such
celebratory pieces have been produced by Tony Tremblay, who suggests
that "Richards is the most admired and berated and misunderstood Canadian writer of the century" (1999a, 3), that he is "one of the literary giants
of the twentieth century" (1998, 7), and that he is "our great moralist"
(1998, 7). Such absolute claims may be true, but the tendency to deify the
writer, instead of examining the texts, tends to focus attention on the eval-
uative impulse of criticism, which can preclude rather than facilitate a
deeper analysis of the work itself. A more disturbing example of this celebratory school is found in Lawrence Mathews's article, "Richards Demonized: The Academy as Greenpeace," which implies that those critics who
have examined Richards from a poststructuralist position are "patronizing," arrogant, and "superior," and bent on "demonizing" Richards
(1998, 60, 62). The celebratory critics who sarcastically attack positions
that differ from their own, ultimately do a disservice to Richards, for if
these writers increasingly place themselves in the position of being guard-
ians of his texts, it will become difficult to appreciate the complexity – the
strengths and the weaknesses – of his work.

6 While some critics have argued that Richards focuses on working-class
characters, the author himself has argued that in, for example, *Lives of
Short Duration* he is equally attentive to the middle and even upper
classes: "It's so bloody silly to assume that I'm writing about the working
class as a class of oppressed people. Half the characters in my novels earn
more than the critics that are criticizing them for being poor. It doesn't
matter how much you earn but it's what you do" (Scherf 1990, 166–7).

CHAPTER SEVEN

1 All biographical information was obtained during an interview with
Nancy Bauer recorded at her studio in Fredericton on 12 August 1992.
2 For a more detailed psychoanalytic reading of Raddall's *His Majesty's
Yankees*, see Donna Smyth, "Raddall's Desiring Machine: Narrative Strate-
gies in the Historical Fiction" (1991) and David Creelman, "Conservative
Solutions: The Early Historical Fiction of Thomas Raddall" (1995).

Bibliography

PRIMARY SOURCES: MARITIME FICTION

Bauer, Nancy. *Flora, Write this Down*. Fredericton: Goose Lane Editions, 1982.
Bruce, Charles. *The Channel Shore*. Toronto: McClelland and Stewart, 1984 reprint (1954).
– *The Township of Time*. Toronto: McClelland and Stewart, 1986 reprint (1959).
Bruneau, Carol. *After the Angel Mill*. Dunvegan: Cormorant Books, 1995.
Buckler, Ernest. *The Mountain and the Valley*. Toronto: McClelland and Stewart, 1989 reprint (1952).
– *The Cruelest Month*. Toronto: McClelland and Stewart, 1977 reprint (1963).
– *Oxbells and Fireflies*. Toronto: McClelland and Stewart, 1983 reprint (1968).
Coady, Lynn. *Strange Heaven*. Fredericton: Goose Lane Editions, 1998.
– *Play the Monster Blind*. Toronto: Doubleday Canada, 2000.
Corey, Deborah Joy. *Losing Eddie*. Chapel Hill: Algonquin Books of Chapel Hill, 1993.
Currie, Sheldon. *The Glace Bay Miners' Museum*. Wreck Cove: Breton Books, 1995.
Day, Frank Parker. *The Autobiography of a Fisherman*. Garden City: Doubleday, Page, and Co., 1927.
– *Rockbound*. Toronto: University of Toronto Press, 1989 reprint (1928).
– MS 2, 288. (Papers housed at the Dalhousie University Archives.)
MacDonald, Ann-Marie. *Fall On Your Knees*. Toronto: Knopf Canada: 1996.
MacLennan, Hugh. *Barometer Rising*. Toronto: McClelland and Stewart, 1989 reprint (1941).
MacLeod, Alistair. *The Lost Salt Gift of Blood*. Toronto: McClelland and Stewart, 1976.

– *As Birds Bring Forth the Sun*. Toronto: McClelland and Stewart, 1986.
– *No Great Mischief*. Toronto: McClelland and Stewart, 1999.
– *Island*. Toronto: McClelland and Stewart, 2000.
McKay, Leo. *Like This Stories*. Toronto: House of Anansi Press, 1995.
McNutt, Linda. *Summer Point*. Dunvegan: Cormorant Books Inc., 1997.
Nowlan, Alden. *Miracle at Indian River*. Toronto: Clarke, Irwin, and Co. ltd., 1982 reprint (1968).
– *Various Persons Named Kevin O'Brien*. Toronto: Clarke, Irwin, and Co. ltd., 1973.
– *Will Ye Let the Mummers In?* Toronto: Irwin Publishing, 1984.
– *Wanton Troopers*. Fredericton: Goose Lane Editions, 1988.
Poirier-Bures, Simone. *Candyman*. Ottawa: Oberon Press, 1997.
Raddall, Thomas. *His Majesty's Yankees*. Toronto: McClelland and Stewart, 1977 reprint (1942).
– *Roger Sudden*. Toronto: McClelland and Stewart, 1972 reprint (1944).
– *The Nymph and the Lamp*. Toronto: McClelland and Stewart, 1968 reprint (1950).
– *Tidefall*. Toronto: McClelland and Stewart, 1953.
– *In My Time: A Memoir*. Toronto: McClelland and Stewart, 1976.
Richards, David Adams. *The Coming of Winter*. Toronto: McClelland and Stewart, 1982 reprint (1974).
– *Blood Ties*. Ottawa: Oberon, 1976.
– *Lives of Short Duration*. Ottawa: Oberon, 1981.
– *Road to the Stilt House*. Ottawa: Oberon, 1985.
– *Nights Below Station Street*. Toronto: McClelland and Stewart, 1988.
– *Evening Snow Will Bring Such Peace*. Toronto: McClelland and Stewart, 1990.
– *For Those Who Hunt the Wounded Down*. Toronto: McClelland and Stewart, 1993.
– *A Lad From Brampton and other Essays*. Fredericton: Broken Jaw Press, 1994.
– *Hope in A Desperate Hour*. Toronto: McClelland and Stewart, 1996.
– *The Bay of Love and Sorrows*. Toronto: McClelland and Stewart, 1998.
Smyth, Donna. *Quilt*. Brampton: Women's Educational Press, 1982.
Wilson, Alan. *Before the Flood*. Dunvegan: Cormorant Books Inc., 1999.
Wilson, Budge. *The Leaving*. Toronto: Stoddart Pub. Co. ltd., 1990.
– *Cordelia Clark*. Toronto: Stoddart Pub. Co. ltd., 1994.
– *The Courtship*. Toronto: House of Anansi Press ltd., 1994.

SECONDARY SOURCES: REFERENCES, HISTORY, THEORY, AND CRITICISM

Acheson, T.W. "The Maritimes and Empire Canada." *Canada and the Burden of Unity*. David Jay Bercuson, ed. Toronto: Macmillan of Canada, 1977: 87–114.
Alexander, David G. *Atlantic Canada and Confederation: Essays in Canadian Political Economy*. Toronto: University of Toronto Press, 1983.

Althusser, Louis. "Ideology and Ideological State Apparatus." *Lenin and Philosophy and Other Essays*. London: New Left Books, 1971.

Andrews, Jennifer. "Rethinking the Relevance of Magic Realism for English-Canadian Literature: Reading Ann-Marie MacDonald's *Fall On Your Knees*." *Studies in Canadian Literature*, vol. 24, no. 1 (1999): 1–19.

Armstrong, Christopher and Herb Wyile. "Firing the Regional Can(n)on: Liberal Puralism, Social Agency, and David Adams Richards' Miramichi Trilogy." *Studies in Canadian Literature*, vol. 22, no. 1 (1997): 1–18.

Arnason, David. "Canadian Nationalism in Search of a Form: Hugh MacLennan's *Barometer Rising*." *Journal of Canadian Fiction*, vol. 1, no. 4 (1972): 68–71.

Atkinson, Ian A. "*The Mountain and the Valley*: A Study in Canadian Fiction." Masters Thesis, Guelph, 1969.

Auerbach, Erich. *Mimesis*. Willard Trask, trans. New York: Doubleday Anchor Books, 1957 reprint (1946; trans. 1953).

Austin, Diana. "Helping to Turn the Tide: An Interview with Thomas H. Raddall." *Studies in Canadian Literature*, vol. 11, no. 1 (Spring 1986): 109–39.

– "What do Women Want?" *Fiddlehead*, no. 167 (1991): 110–4.

Bains, Y.S. "The Poor and Dispossessed in David Adams Richards' *Nights Below Station Street*." *New Weekly Magazine*, vol. 3, no. 24 (28 June 1989): 17–22.

Bal, Mieke. *Narratology: Introduction to the Theory of Narrative*. Toronto: University of Toronto Press, 1985.

Barbour, Douglas. "David Canaan: The Failing Heart." *Studies in Canadian Literature*, no. 1 (Winter 1976): 64–75.

Barthes, Roland. "The Reality Effect" (1968). Reprinted in *The Rustle of Language*. New York: Hill and Wang, 1986.

Barrett, L. Gene. "Underdevelopment and Social Movements in the Nova Scotia Fishing Industry to 1938." *Underdevelopment and Social Movements in Atlantic Canada*. Robert Brym and James Sacouman, eds. Toronto: New Hogtown Press, 1979: 127- 60.

Becker, George J. *Documents of Modern Literary Realism*. Princeton: Princeton University Press, 1963.

– *Realism in Modern Literature*. New York: Frederick Ungar Pub. Co., 1980.

Berces, Francis. "Existential Maritimer: Alistair MacLeod's *The Lost Salt Gift of Blood*." *Studies in Canadian Literature*, vol. 16, no. 1 (1991): 114–28.

Bevan, Allan. "Rockbound Revisited: A Reappraisal of Frank Parker Day's Novel." *Dalhousie Review*, no. 38 (Autumn 1958): 336–47.

– Introduction to *Rockbound*, by Frank Parker Day. Toronto: University of Toronto Press, 1973, vii–xxvii.

Bickerton, James P. *Nova Scotia, Ottawa, and the Politics of Regional Development*. Toronto: University of Toronto Press, 1990.

Bissell, Claude. Introduction to *The Mountain and the Valley*, by Ernest Buckler. Toronto: McClelland and Stewart, 1961.

– *Ernest Buckler Remembered*. Toronto: University of Toronto Press, 1989.

Bisztray, George. *Marxist Models of Literary Realism*. New York: Columbia University Press, 1978.

Boone, Laurel. "*Each Man's Son*: Romance in Disguise." *Journal of Canadian Fiction*, no. 28/29 (1980): 147–56.

Bruce, Archibald. "Atlantic Regional Underdevelopment and Socialism." *Essays on the Left: Essays in Honor of T.C. Douglas*. Laurier LaPierre, ed. Toronto: 1971: 103–20.

Bruce, Harry. *Down Home: Notes of a Maritime Son*. Toronto: Key Porter Books Ltd., 1988.

Brym, Robert J. "Political Conservatism in Atlantic Canada." *Underdevelopment and Social Movements in Atlantic Canada*. Robert Brym and James Sacouman, eds. Toronto: New Hogtown Press, 1979: 59–79.

Buitenhuis, Peter. *Hugh MacLennan*. Toronto: Forum House Pub. Co., 1969.

Butler, Judith. *Gender Trouble: Feminism and the Subversion of Identity*. New York: Routledge, 1990.

Byrne, George. "Blood Hardened and the Blood Running: The Character of Orville in *Blood Ties*." *Studies in Canadian Literature*, vol. 7, no. 1 (1982): 55–62.

Cameron, Donald. "Thomas Raddall: The Art of Historical Fiction." *Dalhousie Review*, no. 49 (Winter 1969–70): 540–8.

Cameron, Elspeth. *Hugh MacLennan: A Writer's Life*. Toronto: University of Toronto Press, 1981.

– "Will the Real Hugh MacLennan Please Stand Up: A Reassessment." *Hugh MacLennan*. Frank Tierney, ed. Ottawa: University of Ottawa Press, 1994: 23–36.

Chambers, Robert Douglas. *Sinclair Ross and Ernest Buckler*. Vancouver: Copp Clark, 1975.

– "Notes on Regionalism in Modern Canadian Fiction." *Journal of Canadian Studies*, vol. 11, no. 2 (May 1976): 27–34.

Chapman, Marilyn. "The Progress of David's Imagination." *Studies in Canadian Literature*, no. 3 (Summer 1978): 186–98.

Cockburn, Robert. "Nova Scotia is my Dweelin Plas': The Life and Work of Thomas Raddall." *Acadiensis*, vol. 7, no. 2 (Spring 1978): 135–41.

Cogswell, Fred. "Alden Nowlan As Regional Atavist." *Studies in Canadian Literature*, vol. 11, no. 2 (1986): 206–25.

Cohen, M. "Notes on Realism in Modern English-Canadian Fiction." *Canadian Literature*, no. 100 (Spring 1984): 65–71.

Compton, Anne. "Seeing Things." *Fiddlehead*, no. 201 (Autumn, 1999): 109–12.

Connor, H.W. "Reply to G. Byrne." *Studies in Canadian Literature*, vol. 8, no. 1 (1983): 142–8.

– "Coming of Winter, Coming of Age: The Autumnal Vision of David Adams Richards' First Novel." *Studies in Canadian Literature*, vol. 9, no. 1 (1984): 31–40.

- "The River in the Blood: Escape and Entrapment in the Fiction of David Adams Richards." *World Literature Written in English*, vol. 26, no. 2 (Autumn 1986): 269–77.
Conrad, Margaret. *Recording Angels, The Private Chronicles of Women from the Maritime Provinces, 1750–1950*. Ottawa: Canadian Research Institute for the Advancement of Women, 1982.
Conrad, Margaret, Toni Laidlaw, and Donna Smyth. *No Place Like Home: Diaries and Letters of Nova Scotia Women 1771–1938*. Halifax: Formac Publishing Co., 1988.
Cook, Greg. "Ernest Buckler: His Creed and His Craft." Masters Thesis, Acadia, 1967.
- *Ernest Buckler*. Toronto: McGraw-Hill Ryerson, 1972.
Creelman, David. "Conservative Solutions: The Early Historical Fiction of Thomas Raddall." *Studies in Canadian Literature*, vol. 20, no. 1 (1995): 127–49.
Currie, Sheldon. "David Adams Richards: The People of the Roadway." *Critical Essays on Contemporary Maritime Canadian Literature*. Wolfgang Hochbruck and James O. Taylor, eds. Trier: WVT Wissenschaftlicher Verlag Trier, 1996: 133–42.
Daly, Markate. *Communitarianism: A New Public Ethics*. Belmont: Wadsworth Pub. Co., 1994.
Davidson, Arnold E. "As Birds Bring Forth the Story: The Elusive Art of Alistair MacLeod." *Canadian Literature*, no. 119 (Winter 1988): 32–42.
Davey, Frank. *Post National Arguments: The Politics of the Anglo-Canadian Novel Since 1967*. Toronto: University of Toronto Press, 1993.
Davies, Gwendolyn. "Ernest Redmond Buckler Remembered (1908–1984)." *Canadian Literature*, no. 103 (Winter 1984): 87–9.
- Afterword to *Rockbound*, by Frank Parker Day. Toronto: University of Toronto Press, 1989: 295–328.
- *Studies in Maritime Literary History*. Fredericton, Acadiensis Press, 1991.
- ed. *Myth and Milieu: Atlantic Literature and Culture 1918–1935*. Fredericton: Acadiensis Press, 1993.
Davis, R.C. "Tradition and the Individual Talent of Charles Bruce." *Dalhousie Review*, no. 34 (autumn 1954): 319–21.
Dermert, Elroy. "Canadian Voices from the Region: W.O. Mitchell, Buckler, MacLeod, and Vanderhaege." PhD Dissertation, University of Alberta, 1994.
Dewar, Christine. "Secret Rituals." *Event*, vol. 25, no. 2 (Summer 1996): 122–8.
Ditsky, John. "'Such Meticulous Brightness': The Fictions of Alistair MacLeod." *The Hollin's Critic*, vol. 25, no. 1 (February 1988): 1–9.
Dixon, Michael. review of *As Birds Bring Forth the Sun*, by Alistair MacLeod. "Letters in Canada, 1986, Fiction." *University of Toronto Quarterly*, vol. 57, no. 1 (1986): 11.

Doerksen, Leana M. "*The Mountain and the Valley*: An Evaluation." *World Literature Written in English*, vol. 19, no. 1 (Spring 1980): 45–56.

– "Ernest Buckler's Holy Family." *New Quarterly*, vol. 7, no. 1–2 (Spring-Summer 1987): 232–9.

Dooley, D.J. "Style and Communication in *The Mountain and the Valley.*" *Dalhousie Review*, vol. 57 (Winter 1977–78): 671–83.

– "*The Mountain and the Valley*: The Uncreated Word." *Moral Vision in the Canadian Novel*. Toronto: Clarke Irwin, 1979: 49–59.

Doucet, Robbie. "The Trajectory of David Adams Richards' Fiction." Honours Thesis. University of New Brunswick, 1999.

Drabble, Margaret. "Mimesis: The Representation of Reality in the Post-war British Novel." *Mosaic*, vol. 20, no. 1 (Winter 1987): 1–14.

Duren, Stephen L. "Bruce's Living Past." *Journal of Canadian Fiction*, vol. 4, no. 3 (1974): 153–7.

Dvorak, Marta. "Ernest Buckler's *The Mountain and the Valley*: Broader than Space, Faster than Time." *Etudes canadiennes/Canadian Studies*, no. 36 (June 1994): 25–36.

– *Ernest Buckler: Rediscovery and Reassessment*. Waterloo: Wilfrid Laurier University Press, 2001.

Dyck, Rand. *Provincial Politics in Canada*. Scarborough: Prentice Hall Canada Inc., 1986.

Eagleton, Terry. *Literary Theory*. Minneapolis: University of Minnesota Press, 1983.

Ennals, Peter and Deryck Holdsworth. "Vernacular Architecture and the Cultural Landscape of the Maritime Provinces." *People, Places, Patterns, Processes*. Graeme Wynn, ed. Toronto: Copp Clark Pitman ltd., 1990: 177–95.

Ermath, Elizabeth. "Realism, Perspective and the Novel." *Critical Inquiry*, vol. 7, no. 3 (Spring 1981): 499–520.

Fee, Margery. "Ernest Buckler's *The Mountain and the Valley*, and 'That Dangerous Supplement.'" *Ariel*, no. 19 (Jan. 1988): 71–80.

Forbes, Ernest R. *The Maritimes Rights Movement, 1919–1927*. Montreal: McGill-Queen's University Press, 1979.

– *Aspects of Maritime Regionalism, 1986–1927*. Ottawa: Canadian Historical Association, 1983.

– *Challenging the Regional Stereotype*. Fredericton: Acadiensis Press, 1989.

Forbes, Ernest R. and D.A. Muise. *The Atlantic Provinces in Confederation*. Toronto: University of Toronto Press, 1993.

Fraser, N.W. "Development of Realism in Canadian Literature During the 1920s." *Dalhousie Review*, no. 57 (Summer 1977): 287–99.

Friesen, Peter. "Jane Eyre's Conservative Canadian Cousin: *The Nymph and the Lamp.*" *Studies in Canadian Literature*, vol. 15, no. 2 (1990): 160–73.

Frye, Northrop. *Anatomy of Criticism*. Princeton: Princeton University Press, 1957.

- *The Secular Scripture: A Study of the Structure of Romance*. Cambridge Massachusetts: Harvard University Press, 1976.

Fussell, Paul. *The Great War and Modern Memory*. New York: Oxford University Press, 1975.

Garvie, Maureen. Review of *The Courtship*, by Budge Wilson. *Quill and Quire*, vol. 60, no. 7 (July 1994): 20.

Genette, Gerard. *Narrative Discourse*. Jane Lewin, trans. Ithica: Cornell University Press, 1980.

Gibbs, Robert. Afterword to *The Mountain and the Valley*, by Ernest Buckler. Toronto: McClelland and Stewart, 1989: 297–302.

- "Various Persons Named Alden Nowlan." *The Alden Nowlan Papers: An Inventory of the Archive at the University of Calgary Library*. Comp. Jean M. Moore. Calgary: The University of Calgary Press, 1992.

Gibson, Douglas. "Alligators in the Sewers: Publishing Alistair MacLeod." *Alistair MacLeod: Essays on His Works*. Irene Guilford, ed. Toronto: Guernica Editions Inc., 2001: 112–24.

Gittings, Christopher. "Sounds in the Empty Spaces of History: The Highland Clearances in Neil Gunn's *Highland River* and Alistair MacLeod's *The Road to Rankin Point*." *Studies in Canadian Literature*, vol. 17, no. 1 (1992): 93–105.

Glover, Douglas. "Violent River: David Adams Richards, Novelist, Poet, Playwright and Screenwriter." *Books in Canada*, vol. 17, no. 4 (May 1988): 9–12.

Godard, Barbara, "Crazy Quilt." *Fiddlehead*, no. 141 (Autumn 1984): 83–9.

Gould, Carol C. "Feminist Theory and the Democratic Community." *Communitarianism: A New Public Ethics*. Markate Daly, ed. Belmont: Wadsworth Pub. Co., 1994: 344–53.

Grant, George. *Lament for a Nation*. Toronto: McClelland and Stewart, 1965.

- *Technology and Empire*. Toronto: House of Anansi, 1969.

Gray, James. Introduction to *His Majesty's Yankees*, by Thomas Raddall. Toronto: McClelland and Stewart, 1977: xi–xviii.

Greenwald, Elissa. *Realism and the Romance*. Ann Arbor, Michigan: UMI Research Press, 1989.

Grimes, Alan P. *Liberalism*. New York: Oxford University Press, 1964.

Guilford, Irene, ed. *Alistair MacLeod: Essays on His Works*. Toronto: Guernica Editions Inc., 2001.

Hawkins, Walter John. "The Life and Fiction of Thomas H. Raddall." Masters Thesis, New Brunswick, 1965.

- "Thomas H. Raddall: The Man and His Work." *Queen's Quarterly*, no. 75 (Spring 1968): 137–46.

Hinchcliffe, Peter. "Sketches and Jokes." *Canadian Literature*, no. 105 (1985): 167–8.

Hiscock, Andrew. "'The Inherited Life': Alistair MacLeod and the Ends of History." *Journal of Commonwealth Literature*, vol. 35, no. 2 (2000): 51–70.

Homel, David. "Absolutely Luminous." *Books in Canada*, vol. 23, no. 3 (April 1994): 7–11.

Horowitz, G. "Conservatism, Liberalism, and Socialism in Canada: An Interpretation." *The Canadian Journal of Economics and Political Science*, vol. 32, no. 2 (May 1966): 143–71.

Hoy, Helen. "Hugh MacLennan and his Works." *Canadian Writers and Their Works*, vol. 5. Robert Lecker, Jack David, and Ellen Quigley, eds. Toronto: ECW Press, 1990: 149–212.

Hyman, Roger Leslie. "Hugh MacLennan: His Art, His Society, and His Critics." *Queens Quarterly*, no. 82 (1975): 515–27.

Jakobson, Roman. "The Metaphoric and Metonymic Poles." *Fundamentals of Language*, by Roman Jocobson and Morris Halle. 1965.

Jameson, Fredric. "Postmodernism, or The Cultural Logic of Late Capitalism." *Postmodernism: A Reader*. Thomas Docherty, ed.. New York: Columbia University Press, 1993: 62–92.

Jirgens, Karl. "Lighthouse, Ring and Fountain: The Never Ending Circle in *No Great Mischief*." *Alistair MacLeod: Essays on His Works*. Irene Guilford, ed. Toronto: Guernica Editions Inc., 2001: 84–94.

Kamboureli, Smora. *On the Edge of Genre: The Contemporary Canadian Long Poem*. Toronto: University of Toronto Press, 1991.

Kaminsky, Alice R. "On Literary Realism." *The Theory of the Novel: New Essays*. John Halperin, ed. New York: Oxford University Press, 1974: 213–32.

Kavanagh, James H. "Marxism's Althusser: Towards a Politics of Literary Theory." *Diacritics*, no. 12 (Spring 1982): 25–45.

Kertzer, J.M. "Past Recaptured." *Canadian Literature*, no. 65 (Summer 1975): 66–9.

Kristiansen, Erik. "Time, Memory and Rural Transformation: Rereading History in the Fiction of Charles Bruce and Ernest Buckler." *Contested Countryside: Rural Workers and Modern Society in Atlantic Canada, 1800–1950*. Daniel Samson, ed. Fredericton: Acadiensis Press, 1994: 225–56.

Kulyk Keefer, Janice. *Under Eastern Eyes*. Toronto: University of Toronto Press, 1987.

– "'Brightly, aggressively golden': Verbal Agency in Budge Wilson's *The Leaving*." *Atlantis*, vol. 20, no. 1 (Fall/Winter 1995): 195–201.

– "Loved Labour Lost: Alistair MacLeod's Elegiac Ethos." *Alistair MacLeod: Essays on His Works*. Irene Guilford, ed. Toronto: Guernica Editions Inc., 2001: 72–83.

Kymlicka, Will. "Liberalism and Communitarianism." *Canadian Journal of Philosophy*, vol. 18, no. 2 (June 1988): 181–203.

LaBonte, R. "Social Realism and the Future of Fiction." *Canadian Fiction Magazine*, no. 27 (1977): 123–36.

Lalumière, Claude. "The Essential Science Fiction Library." *January Magazine*, January 2000. http://www.januarymagazine.com/features/essentialSF.html

Lamont-Stewart, Linda. "From the Romance of Innocence to the Romance of Experience: Metaphor and Metonymy in the English Canadian Novel in the 1920s." Diss. York University, 1986.

Leahy, David. "Engendering Wo/men and 'Other' Anxieties in Hugh MacLennan's Novels." *Hugh MacLennan*. Frank Tierney, ed. Ottawa: University of Ottawa Press, 1994: 157–70.

Lee, Philip. "Overcoming Personal Demons." *Telegraph Journal*, 14 August 1993. Sec. D, p. 1, col. 2.

Leitold, John Ronald. Introduction to *Roger Sudden*, by Thomas Raddall. Toronto: McClelland and Stewart, 1972: iv–viii.

Lever, Susan. "Against the Stream: The Fiction of David Adams Richards." *Australian-Canadian Studies*, vol. 12, no. 1 (1994): 81–9.

Levine, George. "Realism Reconsidered." *The Theory of the Novel: New Essays*. John Halperin, ed. New York: Oxford University Press, 1974: 233–57.

Light, Beth and Joy Parr. *Canadian Women on the Move: 1867–1920*. Toronto: New Hogtown Press and the Ontario Institute for Studies in Education, 1983.

Lucente, Gregory. *The Narrative of Realism and Myth*. Baltimore: The John Hopkins University Press, 1979.

Lukacs, Georg. *The Historical Novel*. Hannah Stanley Mitchell, trans. Harmondsworth: Penguin Books Ltd., 1962.

– *The Meaning of Contemporary Realism*. London: Merlin Press, 1963.

Lyon, John E. "The Challenge of Nihilism: Problems in the Works of Ernest Buckler." Masters Thesis, Waterloo, 1975.

MacDonald, Bruce F. "Word Shapes, Time, and the Theme of Isolation in *The Mountain and the Valley*." *Studies in Canadian Literature*, no. 1 (Summer 1976): 194–209.

MacDonald, Frances. "War of the Worlds: David Adams Richards and Modern Times." *Antigonish Review*, no. 104 (1996): 17–24.

Macherey, Pierre. *A Theory of Literary Production*. London: Routledge, 1978.

MacLulich. T.D. *Hugh MacLennan*. Boston: Twayne Pub., 1983.

MacMillan, Carrie. "Seaward Vision and Sense of Place: The Maritime Novel 1880–1920." *People and Place: Studies of Small Town Life in the Maritimes*. Larry McCann, ed. Fredericton: Acadiensis Press, 1987: 79–97.

Marx, Leo. *The Machine in the Garden: Technology and the Pastoral Ideal in America*. New York: Oxford University Press, 1964.

Mathews, Robin. "Hugh MacLennan: The Nationalist Dilemma in Canada." *Studies in Canadian Literature*, no. 1 (1976): 49–63.

Matthews, John. Introduction to *The Nymph and the Lamp*, by Thomas H. Raddall. Toronto: McClelland and Stewart, 1964: v–ix.

Matthews, Lawrence. "Hacking at the Parsnips: *The Mountain and the Valley* and the Critics." *The Bumper Book*. John Metcalf, ed. Toronto: ECW, 1986: 188–201.

– "Calgary, Canonization, and Class: Deciphering List B." *Canadian Canon: Essays in Literary Value*. Robert Lecker, ed. Toronto: University of Toronto Press, 1991: 150–66.

– "Richard's Demonized: The Academy as Greenpeace." *Pottersfield Portfolio*, vol. 19, no. 1 (Fall 1998): 59–63.

McCann, L.D. "Metropolitanism and Branch Business in the Maritimes, 1881–1931." *People, Places, Patterns, Processes*. Graeme Wynn, ed. Toronto: Copp Clark Pitman ltd., 1990: 233–46.

McKay, Ian. *The Quest of the Folk: Antimodernism and Cultural Selection in Twentieth Century Nova Scotia*. Kingston: McGill-Queens, 1994.

McKay, Janet Holmgren. *Narration and Discourse in American Realistic Fiction*. Philadelphia: University of Pennsylvania Press, 1982.

Mill, John Stuart. "On Liberty." *Communitarianism: A New Public Ethics*. Markate Daly, ed. Belmont: Wadsworth Pub. Co., 1994: 11–21.

Milner, Philip. "Structure in David Adams Richards' Unfinished Miramichi Saga." *Essays on Canadian Writing*, vol. 31 (1985): 201–10.

Milton, Paul. "The Psalmist and the Sawmill: Alden Nowlan's Kevin O'Brian Stories." *Children's Voices in Atlantic Literature and Criticism*. Hilary Thompson, ed. Guelph: Canadian Children's Press, 1995: 60–7.

– "*Various Persons Named Kevin O'Brien*: Nowlan's Novel Response to the Critics." *Studies in Canadian Literature*, vol. 23, no. 2 (1998): 36–48.

Minard, Nancy. "Beauty Hides a Blade." *Atlantic Books Today*, no. 11 (Fall 1995): 9–10.

Minogue, Kenneth. *The Liberal Mind*. New York: Random House, 1963.

– "Conservatism." *Encyclopedia of Philosophy*. Paul Edwards, ed. New York: The Macmillian Co. and The Free Press, 1967: 195–8.

Moss, John. *Patterns of Isolation in English Canadian Fiction*. Toronto: McClelland and Stewart, 1974.

New. W.H. "The Storm and After: Imagery and Symbolism in Hugh MacLennan's *Barometer Rising*." *Queen's Quarterly*, no. 74 (1967): 302–13.

– "Maritime Cadences." *Canadian Literature*, no. 68–69 (Spring-Summer 1976): 3–6.

Nicholson, Colin. "Signatures of Time: Alistair MacLeod and his Short Stories." *Canadian Literature*, no. 107 (Winter 1985): 90–101.

– "Alistair MacLeod." *The Journal of Commonwealth Literature*, vol. 21, no. 1 (1986): 188–200.

– "'The Turning of Memory:' Alistair MacLeod's Short Stories." *Recherches Anglaises et Nord-Americaines* (*RANAM*), no. 20 (1987): 85–93.

Noonan, Gerald. "Egoism and Style in *The Mountain and the Valley*." *The Marco Polo Papers One: Atlantic Provinces Literature Colloquium*. Kenneth MacKinnon, ed. Saint John: Atlantic Canada Institute, 1977: 68–78.

O'Donnell, Kathleen. "The Wanderer in *Barometer Rising*." *University of Windsor Review*, vol. 3, no. 2 (1968): 12–18.

Oliver, Michael. "Dread of the Self: Escape and Reconciliation in the Poetry of Alden Nowlan." *Essays on Canadian Writing*, vol. 5 (1976): 50–66.

– "Alden Nowlan and His Works." *Canadian Writers and Their Works*. Robert Lecker, Jack David, and Ellen Quigley, eds. Oakville: ECW Press, 1990.

Orange, John C. "Ernest Buckler: The Masks of the Artist." Phil.M. Thesis, Toronto, 1970.

– "Ernest Buckler (1908–1984)." *Canadian Writers and Their Works*. Robert Lecker, Jack David, and Ellen Quigley, eds. Oakville: ECW Press, 1990.

Pell, Barbara. *A Portrait of the Artist: Ernest Buckler's The Mountain and the Valley.* Toronto: ECW Press, 1995.

Pennee, Donna. "Still More Social Realism." *Essays on Canadian Writing*, no. 41 (Summer 1990): 41–5.

Perkin, J. Russell. "Learning about the Crucifixion: The Religious Vision of *For Those Who Hunt the Wounded Down.*" *Pottersfield Portfolio*, vol. 19, no. 1 (Fall 1998): 52–6.

Poirier-Bures, Simone. "A Few Words on the Writing Process." http: // www.english.vt.edu/~poirier/Writingprocess.html (20 July 2000).

Prentice, A., P. Bourne, G. Cuthbert Brant, B. Light, W. Mitchinson, N. Black. *Canadian Women, A History.* Toronto: Harcourt Brace and Jovanovich, 1988.

Quigley, Theresia. "Childhood in Limbo: A Study of Deborah Joy Corey's *Losing Eddie.*" *Children's Voices in Atlantic Literature and Culture.* Hilary Thompson, ed. Guelph: Canadian Children's Press, 1995: 79–84.

Rawlyk, George A. *Historical Essays on the Atlantic Provinces.* Toronto: McClelland and Stewart, 1967.

– "The Farmer – Labour Movement and the Failure of Socialism in Nova Scotia." *Essays on the Left: Essays in Honor of T.C. Douglas.* Laurier LaPierre, ed. Toronto: 1971. 31–41.

– *The Atlantic Provinces and the Problems of Confederation.* St. Johns: Breakwater, 1979.

Reichert, Richard. "*The Mountain and the Valley* Reconsidered." Masters Thesis, New Brunswick, 1971.

Reid, John G. *Six Crucial Decades: Times of Change in the History of the Maritimes.* Halifax: Nimbus Pub., 1987.

Ricou, L. "David Canaan and Buckler's Style in *The Mountain and the Valley.*" *Dalhousie Review*, vol. 57 (Winter 1977–78): 671–83.

Rimmon-Kenan, Shlomith. *Narrative Fiction: Contemporary Poetics.* London: Metheun, 1983.

Ritchie, Eliza. Review of *Rockbound*, by Frank Parker Day. *Dalhousie Review*, no. 9 (1929): 129.

Robb, Nancy. "David Adams Richards: Universal Truths from the Miramichi Roots." *Quill and Quire*, vol. 54, no. 4 (April 1988): 24–5.

Ruthven, K.K. *Feminist Literary Studies.* Cambridge: Cambridge University Press, 1984.

Sager, Eric W., Lewis R. Fisher, Stuart O. Pierson. *Atlantic Canada and Confederation: Essays in Canadian Political Economy.* Toronto: University of Toronto Press, 1983.

Said, Edward W. *The World, the Text, and the Critic.* Cambridge, Mass.: Harvard University Press, 1983.

Sarkar, E. "Ernest Buckler's *The Mountain and the Valley*: The Infinite Language of Human Relations." *Revue de l'Université d'Ottawa*, no. 44 (July-September 1979): 354–61.

Sartre, Jean Paul. "Existentialism is a Humanism." *Existentialism from Dostoevsky to Sartre.* Walter Kaufmann, ed. New York: New American Library, 1975: 345–69.

Scherf, Kathleen. "David Adams Richards: 'He must be a Social Realist.'" *Studies in Canadian Literature*, vol. 15, no. 1 (1990): 154–70.

– "David Adams Richards' *Blood Ties*: Essentially Women." *Room of One's Own*, vol. 14, no. 4 (December 1991): 23–39.

Seaman, A.T. "Fiction in Atlantic Canada." *Canadian Literature*, no. 68–69 (Spring-Summer 1976): 26–39.

– "Visions of Fulfilment in Ernest Buckler and Charles Bruce." *Essays on Canadian Writing*, no. 31 (1985): 158–74.

– "Heroes, Heroines and the Lost Kingdom in the Unpublished Novels of Frank Parker Day." *Myth and Milieu: Atlantic Literature and Culture 1918 – 1939.* Gwendolyn Davies, ed. Fredericton: Acadiensis Press, 1993: 136–46.

Simmons, Ernest Joseph. *Introduction to Tolstoy's Writings.* Chicago: University of Chicago Press, 1968.

Smart, Particia. *Writing in the Father's House: The Emergence of the Feminine in the Quebec Literary Tradition.* Toronto: University of Toronto Press, 1991.

Smyth, Donna. "Raddall's Desiring Machine: Narrative Strategies in the Historical Fiction." *Time and Place: The Life and Works of Thomas Head Raddall.* Alan Young, ed. Fredericton: Acadiensis Press, 1991: 65–7.

– "Contexts of Desire in the Kingdom of the Father." *Hugh MacLennan.* Frank Tierney, ed. Ottawa: University of Ottawa Press, 1994: 143–56.

Spettigue, D.O. "The Way it Was." Report in *The Canadian Novel in the Twentieth Century: Essays from Canadian Literature.* George Woodcock, ed. Toronto: McClelland and Stewart, 1975: 145–60.

Sorfleet, John R. "Thomas Raddall: I Was Always a Rebel Underneath." *Journal of Canadian Fiction*, no. 2 (Fall 1973): 45–64.

Staines, David. "Mapping the Terrain." *Mosaic*, vol. 11, no. 3 (1978): 137–51.

Statistics Canada. http://www.statcan.ca/english/Pgdb/People/Labour/labor07a.htm (14 October 1999).

Stern, J.P. *On Realism.* Boston: Routledge and Kegan Paul, 1973.

Stevens, David. "Writing Region Across the Border: The Two stories of Breece Pancake and Alistair MacLeod." *Studies in Short Fiction*, vol. 33, no. 2 (Spring 1996): 263–71.

Strong-Boag, Veronica. *The New Day Recalled: Lives of Girls and Women in English Canada, 1919–1939.* Markham: Penguin Books, 1988.

Sturgeon, Linda-Ann. "David Adams Richards: Loving Against the Odds." Masters Thesis, University of New Brunswick, 1987.

Summers, Merna. Afterword to *Blood Ties,* by David Adams Richards. Toronto: McClelland and Stewart, 1992.

Tallis, Raymond. *In Defence of Realism.* London: Edward Arnold, 1988.

Tallman, Warren. "Wolf in the Snow." *Contexts of Canadian Criticism.* Eli Mandel, ed. Chicago: University of Chicago Press, 1971.

Taylor, James O. "Art Imagery and Destiny in Alistair MacLeod's Fiction: 'Winter Dog' as Paradigm." *The Journal of Commonwealth Literature,* vol. 29, no. 2 (1994): 61–9.

Thomas, Clara. "New England Romanticism and Canadian Fiction." *Journal of Canadian Fiction,* vol. 2, no. 4 (Fall 1973): 80–6.

Thompson, Hilary. "Budge Wilson – a Profile of the Author and Her Work." *Canadian Children's Literature,* no. 97 (spring 2000): 18–25.

Toner, Patrick. *If I Could Turn and Meet Myself: The Life of Alden Nowlan.* Fredericton: Goose Lane Editions, 2000.

Toye, William. *The Oxford Companion to Canadian Literature.* Toronto: Oxford University Press, 1983.

Tremblay, Tony, "Road from the Stilt House." *Fiddlehead,* no. 180 (1994): 116–20.

– "Introduction: Richards Among His Readers." *Pottersfield Portfolio,* vol. 19, no. 1 (Fall 1998): 6–10.

– 1999a. "David Adams Richards: Canada's 'Independent' Intellectual." *The Hollins Critic,* vol. 36, no. 4 (October 1999): 1–14.

– 1999b. "'Even More Symmetry Here Than I Imagined': A Critical Reading of Recent Maritime Fictions." *Dalhousie Review,* vol. 79, no. 2 (Summer 1999): 269–77.

Van Herk, Aritha. "Scant Articulations of Time." *University of Toronto Quarterly,* vol. 68, no. 4 (Fall 1999): 925–38.

Van Rys, John. "Diminishing Voice in Buckler's *The Mountain and the Valley.*" *Studies in Canadian Literature,* vol. 20, no. 1 (1995): 65–79.

Vaughan, R.M. "An Instinct for Life." *Books in Canada,* vol. 22, no. 6 (September 1993): 15–18.

Vauthier, Simone. "Time and Space in Alistair MacLeod's 'The Road To Rankin's Point.'" *Critical Essays on Contemporary Maritime Canadian Literature.* Wolfgang Hochbruck and James O. Taylor, eds. Trier: WVT Wissenschaftlicher Verlag Trier, 1996: 157–78.

Veltmeyer, Henry. "The Capitalist Underdevelopment of Atlantic Canada." *Underdevelopment and Social Movements in Atlantic Canada.* Robert Brym and James Sacouman, eds. Toronto: New Hogtown Press, 1979: 17–35.

Wainwright, J.A. "Fernhill Revisited: Isolation and Death in *The Mountain and the Valley.*" *Studies in Canadian Literature,* vol. 7, no. 1 (1982): 63–89.

- "Days of Future Past: Time in the Fiction of Charles Bruce." *Studies in Canadian Literature*, vol. 8, no. 2 (1983): 238–47.
- *World Enough and Time: Charles Bruce, a Literary Biography.* Halifax: Formac Pub. Co. Ltd., 1988.
Walker, William Roland. "The Theme of the Artist in the Novels of Ernest Buckler." Masters Thesis, Windsor, 1972.
Weinzweig, Helen. "So What is Real?" *Quarry,* no. 34 (Spring 1985): 72–7.
Wellek, Rene. "The Concept of Realism in Literary Scholarship." *Concepts of Criticism.* Stephen G. Nichols, ed. New Haven: Yale University Press, 1963:
West, David Stanley. "Romance and Realism in the Contemporary Novels of Thomas H. Raddall." Masters Thesis, New Brunswick, 1977.
Westwater, A.M. " 'Teufelsdrockh is alive and doing well in Nova Scotia': Carlyean Strains in *The Mountain and the Valley.*" *Dalhousie Review,* no. 56 (Summer 1976): 291–8.
Wiens, E.J. "The Lumpenproletariat in *The Golden Dog and Roger Sudden.*" *Studies in Canadian Literature*, vol. 14, no. 2 (1989): 63–83.
Williams, David. *Confessional Fictions.* Toronto: University of Toronto Press, 1991.
- "From Clan to Nation: Orality and the Book in Alistair MacLeod's *No Great Mischief.*" *Alistair MacLeod: Essays on His Works.* Irene Guilford, ed. Toronto: Guernica Editions Inc., 2001: 43–71.
Williams, Raymond. "Realism and the Contemporary Novel." *The Long Revolution.* London: Chattos and Windus, 1961: 274–89.
Willmott, Glenn. "On Postcolonial Modernism: The Invisible City in *The Mountain and the Valley.*" *The American Review of Canadian Studies*, no. 25 (Summer-Autumn 1995): 301–21.
- "The Frontier beyond Empire: East of Everything in Thomas Raddall's *The Nymph and Lamp.*" *Canadian Literature*, no. 157 (Summer 1998): 56–78.
Wilson, S.J. *Women, the Family and the Economy.* Toronto: McGraw- Hill Ryerson ltd., 1986.
Woodcock, George. "A Nation's Odyssey: The Novels of Hugh MacLennan." *Canadian Literature*, no. 10 (1961): 7–8.
- *Hugh MacLennan.* Toronto: Copp Clark Pub. Co., 1969.
- Review of *Lives of Short Duration,* by David Adams Richards. *Books in Canada,* vol. 11, no. 3 (March 1982): 5.
- *Introducing Hugh MacLennan's Barometer Rising.* Toronto: ECW Press, 1989.
Wyile, Herb. "Taking the Real Home to Read." *Open Letter,* seventh series, no. 6 (Fall 1989): 5–15.
Wynn, Graeme. "The Maritimes: The Geography of Fragmentation and Underdevelopment." *A Geography of Canada Heartland and Hinterland.* L.D. McCann, ed. Scarborough: Prentice-Hall Canada Inc., 1982: 156–215.
Young, Alan. "The Pastoral Vision of Ernest Buckler in *The Mountain and the Valley.*" *The Dalhousie Review,* no. 53 (Summer 1973): 219–26.

- Introduction to *Ox Bells and Fireflies*, by Ernest Buckler. Toronto: McClelland and Stewart, 1974: xi–xvi.
- 1976a. *Ernest Buckler.* Toronto: McClelland and Stewart, 1976.
- 1976b. "The Genesis of Ernest Buckler's *The Mountain and the Valley.*" *Journal of Canadian Fiction*, no. 16 (1976): 89–96.
- Introduction to *The Cruelest Month*, by Ernest Buckler. Toronto: McClelland and Stewart, 1977: vii–xiii.
- *Thomas H. Raddall.* Boston: Twayne, 1983.
- "The Genesis and Composition of Thomas H. Raddall's *His Majesty's Yankees.*" *Essays in Canadian Writing*, no. 31 (Summer 1985): 142–57.
- ed. *Time and Place: The Life and Works of Thomas Head Raddall.* Fredericton: Acadiensis Press, 1991.

Zagratzki, Uwe. "Neil Gunn and Alistair MacLeod: Across the Sea in 'Scotland,'" *Critical Essays on Contemporary Maritime Canadian Literature.* Wolfgang Hochbruck and James O. Taylor, eds. Trier: WVT Wissenschaftlicher Verlag Trier, 1996.

Zizek, Slavoy. "How Did Marx Invent the Symptom?" *Mapping Ideology.* Slavoy Zidek, ed. London: Verso, 1994: 296–331.

Index